THE BATTERING SYNDROME

WHY MEN BEAT WOMEN
AND
THE PROFESSIONAL'S GUIDE TO INTERVENTION

THE BATTERING SYNDROME

WHY MEN BEAT WOMEN
AND
THE PROFESSIONAL'S GUIDE TO INTERVENTION

BY
MICHAEL GROETSCH

CPI Publishing
Brookfield, Wisconsin

Note:

Many of the illustrations given in this book derive from the author's personal interviews with more than 20,000 batterers and victims. Others come from written accounts in newspapers and magazines. Names of individuals and citations to source material have been omitted in most cases and certain facts have been altered to protect the privacy of victims and their families. Anecdotal material taken from published accounts is presented for purposes of illustration only, and the author does not vouch for its accuracy. The conclusions and advice expressed in this book are solely those of the author and do not necessarily reflect the views of the publisher.

ISBN 0-9651733-6-4

Printed in the United States of America

First Edition

To my wife, Barbara, and my sons
Joshua, Jeremey, Gene, and Justin,
who have brought me a sense of oneness.
To my parents, Ewald and Johnteen,
who gave me my values.
To Robin, wherever she may be.

Acknowledgments

I would like to express my deepest gratitude to all who assisted me in bringing this book to its final conclusion. Without their friendship, support, and technical assistance, *The Battering Syndrome* would not be a reality.

Foremost on my list is my wife, Barbara, and my sons, Joshua, Jeremey, Gene, and Justin. They have not only tolerated my obsession with the batterer, their unwavering belief and encouragement that this book would be published was a factor in its completion. In addition, Joshua's meticulous assistance in the completion of the final draft of the manuscript, even at the expense of his social life, will always be remembered.

I would also like to thank those friends and professionals who allowed me to share my wisdom with them in their relative area of expertise. Judge John Shea of New Orleans Municipal Court, a man of integrity and morals, should be recognized as a pioneer relative to the issue of spousal abuse. The policies and procedures that he developed and allowed me to implement in his court since 1976 have become a model for the rest of our nation's judiciary. While his early efforts to concentrate on crimes of spousal abuse were often met by resistance and opposition, the dissenters now address him with respect and praise.

I will always value the friendship and support provided to me by Dr. Ciro Juarez-Nunez. The insights that he has shared with me in my quest to understand the batterer have contributed heavily to my knowledge of a man that few understand.

Dr. Halina Margan, an adjunct professor at Tulane University School of Social Work, is also to be recognized for allowing me to share my insights of the batterer with her students over the last decade. While my concepts may clinically challenge the ideologies of some professionals in the field of social work, she has always afforded me the opportunity to present to her students philosophical perspectives that are so essential to academic growth.

Ms. June Foley is to be credited for the technical support, advice, and feedback that she so willingly gave while typing the first draft of *The Battering Syndrome*. At times when I questioned whether this project would be completed, her encouragement always motivated me to continue.

I also acknowledge the many professionals who so graciously provided me with technical assistance in the final draft of the manuscript. While Fredrick Preis, a labor specialist and attorney, assisted in the chapter directed to personnel managers and supervisors, Philip Foto, an assistant city attorney in New Orleans, shared his insights relative to the section that addresses prosecutors and judges.

Thanks are also in order for Joette Quarrella, M.Ed., who as a lifelong friend and professional educator, shared her wisdom concerning the chapter that focuses on the school system. Dr. Anthony Margavio, my sociology professor from the University of New Orleans in 1968, re-emerged in this project to re-educate me in sociological concepts that he had taught me so many years before.

William Rittenburg, a friend and an attorney in private practice, served as my legal advisor. I will always remember how available he made himself to me.

It is also important that I acknowledge the board of directors and staff of the Metropolitan Battered Woman's Program in Jefferson, Louisiana. They have served their community well and have undoubtedly saved an untold number of lives over their years of operation.

Finally, I will always be grateful to the staff of the Crisis Prevention Institute for bringing this book and its related video training programs to the public.

Table of Contents

Preface

It wasn't until one of my closest friends, a psychiatrist, asked me what triggered my passion for the subject of spousal abuse, that I gave it much thought. After all, as a student of sociology at the University of New Orleans in the early 1970's, and as an active participant in the social revolution that occurred during that period of American history, we were all trained to have a social conscience. We were all conditioned to react to social ills and social injustices in the same manner that firefighters are trained to respond to fires.

When I made an attempt to answer my friend's question, I found it interesting that I could not provide an immediate or specific response. I was neither a product of domestic violence nor had ever been directly victimized in such a way. At least I thought that was the case. Upon further exploration, however, I began recalling an incident almost thirty years earlier that nearly cost me my life. Call it repression if you must, but my friend's inquisitiveness sparked a traumatic memory which made me recognize that as a teenager, I had been a victim of domestic violence. In fact, I had almost been a victim of domestic homicide.

It is difficult to believe that I had forgotten the following event. Perhaps I consciously minimized its occurrence in an attempt to deal with the trauma. Perhaps I consciously denied its significance in an attempt to avoid emotional conflict. Now that I recognize the magnitude of this event, I also understand the roots of my passion that led to the writing of this book.

I met Robin in the summer of 1967. We were both freshmen at the University of New Orleans. She also worked mornings as a cashier in the University's cafeteria. The first time that she added up my purchase, I flirted with her. On the second day, I asked her name. On Friday of the same week, I asked her for a date and she accepted.

As I picked her up at her home, we agreed to see *The Graduate*, starring Dustin Hoffman. It was one of the many movies of the sixties era that stimulated conversation and a sense of conscience.

Following the movie, we drove to a quiet restaurant. She had a shrimp dinner while I ordered pasta. We sipped wine until the restaurant softly flashed its lights in a subtle reminder that it was time to close. Conversation about the movie had made us lose sight of time.

In our conversation that night, I could detect an aura of apprehension about Robin. While she appeared interested, she also held me at a distance. While she touched my hand affectionately, her hands seemed tense and were warm and clammy. Twice during the course of the evening as I raised my hands during spontaneous gestures, I noticed that her face and shoulders tightened as if she felt threatened. Robin's walnut-colored eyes projected a sense of innocence. They also projected a sense of distrust and sadness.

There was no doubt that we both had thoroughly enjoyed each other's company. As we left the restaurant to go home, however, neither of us could anticipate that we would not date again. In moments our enjoyable first outing would turn into a nightmarish ordeal.

From the moment that we drove out of the restaurant's parking lot, I could sense that I was being stalked by a man in a bright red Corvette. As I approached the highway leading to Robin's neighborhood, the driver of the other car put his bright lights on me and tailgated my car while racing his engine. He then sped up beside my vehicle and began yelling obscenities in a spate of unconnected dialogue. While I instinctively sensed who the assailant was, it was affirmed when Robin said that he was her ex-boyfriend. She warned me that he was violent and always carried a gun. I knew that we were in trouble.

As I drove into Robin's neighborhood, the other car pursued aggressively. I didn't make an attempt to lose him, fearing that such a response would be provocative. Instead, I tried to gather my thoughts of how to handle him once we arrived at Robin's home. I was only eighteen and had no experience with such men. I took a deep breath and pulled into her driveway. He pulled directly behind me and blocked my exit. I knew we were in danger.

Before either one of us could react, Robin was pulled from the passenger side of the car and punched in the face. As she fell to the ground, he began stomping and kicking her with his feet. I could hear a crushing sound as if he had broken her bones. As I tried to exit the opened passenger door to assist her, I was immediately met and forced back into the car by the assailant, who had a gun pointed toward my face. I quickly retreated behind the steering wheel. He pursued and held the gun to my right temple. He cocked the hammer and told me that he was going to kill me. I was convinced that he would.

Amidst all the screaming and noise, no one came to our aid. No police; no neighbors; no one. It was apparent that we were on our own. While my negotiations with the man lasted only minutes, it seemed like hours. He was sweating profusely and crying hysterically. Twice his tantrums caused him to tighten up and nearly pull the trigger. Robin negotiated with him from outside the car while I did the same from within. Although I assured him that she and I had never dated before, he called her a whore and claimed that we were sleeping together. Each time that I made the assertion that we had just met, he became more enraged, demanding a confession and curling his index finger around the trigger of the gun. Approximately fifteen minutes after the ordeal began, the assailant's overt threats began to transform into apologetic remarks and pleadings. He bargained that if I left and never looked back, he would let me go. He didn't have to bargain further. I assured him that if he let me go safely, I would not call the police nor would I date Robin again. It was at that point that his crying and sobbing stopped. He had control.

I never called the police. I don't know what happened to Robin. I do know that she withdrew from school. I was only eighteen years old. I didn't want to be a dead hero.

Michael Groetsch

Introduction

National crime statistics reveal that nearly 7 percent of all homicide victims in this country each year are women who are killed by their husbands or boyfriends.[1] These percentages indicate that approximately 1,500 women annually, almost four for each day of each year, are murdered by men who claim to love them. Such numbers suggest that during the decade of the 1980's, as many as 15,000 women were slain by their intimate partners. The fact that a woman is killed by her husband or boyfriend at least every six hours in this country is shocking. Perhaps more shocking is a 1990 FBI report that stated that 30 percent of all women murdered in the United States were killed by their male partners.[2] There is no way of measuring those who were tortured, mutilated, or injured by their mates during this same period. If so, such numbers would run well into the millions.

The magnitude of spousal abuse within the United States is incomprehensible. Murray A. Straus reports that nearly two million women in America are physically abused by their mates annually,[3] although many professionals indicate that the actual number may be five or ten million. Such a tremendous differential in statistical guesstimates suggests that an accurate estimate is perceptually evasive. These beatings generally occur behind closed doors, and it is probable that for every one case that is reported, ten to twenty go unnoticed. The unfortunate fact is that spousal abuse is still viewed by most as an act of private violence more acceptable than the beating of a stranger. It is this very perception that provides the batterer with a cloak of secrecy within which he hides. Although the home is supposed to be the ultimate refuge from violence and harm, criminal justice experts actually suggest that one is more likely to be mugged within the family unit than on the darkest, most crime-ridden street of urban America.

This assertion is supported by U.S. Department of Justice statistics, which reflect that nearly 15 percent of all homicides in this country involve family or intimate relationships.[4] Each year approximately 3,600 people kill another family member or person with whom they were romantically associated. Over a period of eleven years, the same period of time that we fought in Vietnam, it can be estimated that approximately 40,000 individuals died at the hands of a relative or intimate partner. This is nearly equal to the number of American military casualties that occurred over the decade that we were at war in Vietnam. Because police reports do not always clearly define the relationships between perpetrators and murder victims, the true number of domestic murders may actually surpass the number of soldiers who died in the war. It is a sad commentary to suggest that family members may have killed in the same numbers as did the enemy while we were in military combat.

In light of such dramatic statistics, it is difficult to believe that sociologists who published university textbooks only twenty-five years ago did not perceive spousal abuse as a significant social problem. It is extraordinary that the physical abuse of women by their partners, a social problem that has been with us for centuries, has only recently, as late as the 1970's, come to the forefront as an issue that demands societal response. Still, while it may seem fashionable for society to perceive and for advocates to boast that great strides have been made to curtail this pathetic aberration, the sad reality is to the contrary. While some may feel that significant change and progress have been made, research clearly illustrates that the vast majority of perpetrators are still not arrested for their actions. Furthermore, domestic abusers actually prosecuted and found guilty by the courts remain statistically insignificant.

Chapter I

The Batterer's Continuum

While it is critical for us to recognize and address the enormity of spousal abuse in today's society, it is also crucial that we become capable of identifying the different types of men who commit such violence. What is it that drives a man to commit grave atrocities and heinous acts of violence against the woman he supposedly loves? More important, how does a family member, friend, or professional distinguish a batterer who is unlikely to repeat the offense from one who is capable of making the next beating a lethal one? If individuals are to make wise and competent decisions in their attempts to assist and protect battered women, they must be provided with the insight necessary in making those decisions. To assist a battered woman without knowing the dynamics of the male who abuses her is analogous to a doctor who treats a patient for pain without knowing the reason for its occurrence.

Before we make an attempt to understand why a man would batter his spouse, we must first recognize that all abusers are not the same and cannot be explained by using a single generic profile. There are actually several types of batterers, each type presenting a unique set of behaviors, character traits, safety issues, and concerns of its own. Likewise, the level and degree of abuse employed is also significantly distinct in both pattern and volatility.

Perhaps one of the most grave errors made by those who try to assist the battered woman in escaping the violence that engulfs her is the assumption that all abusers should be addressed in the same manner. There is an unfortunate tendency among the family, friends, and even professionals who assist and treat her to believe that all women are battered for the same reasons. This assumption is not only false; it often leads to poor judgment and related decisions that result in attacks and murders that could have been prevented.

Men who batter their wives or girlfriends must be viewed as individual points on a continuum. This spectrum contains three basic degrees of reference, each degree connoting the danger that the male presents to his spouse in regards to continued abuse and the potential for that abuse to become injurious or lethal. The three primary points on this spectrum are referred to as points one, two, and three. Increment one is to be viewed as the least volatile, while increment three is to be viewed as the most volatile. Likewise, the males who are placed on this continuum can be similarly referred to as Category One, Category Two, and Category Three batterers. Category One is the least dangerous, while Category Three is considered the most dangerous. Category Two falls somewhere in between.

The general premise of this spectrum is that such individuals

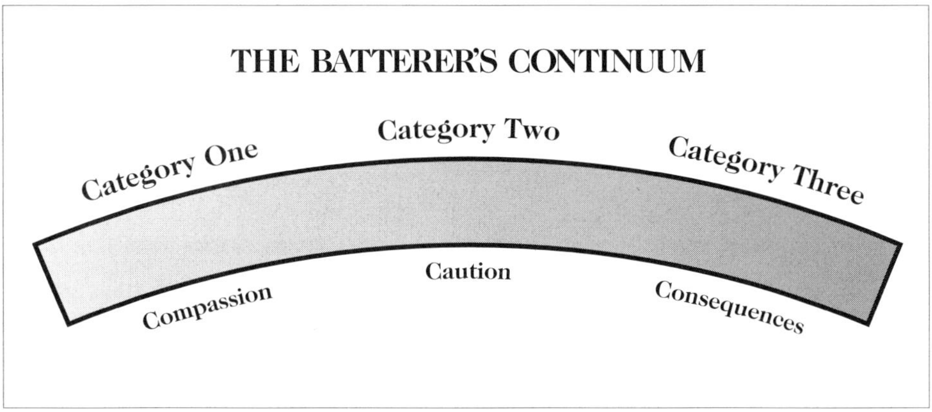

are distinctively different not only in the magnitude of abuse that they exhibit in a single episode of violence, but also in the ongoing nature of their aggression, which varies significantly from one type of abuser to another. It should be emphasized, however, that this continuum does not limit itself to only the three specific degrees of reference. While there are batterers who may fall anywhere between these three primary points, the spectrum simply presents the observer with starting points from which to measure the potential danger that a particular abuser presents to an individual victim.

The continuum concept presents a diagnostic thermometer by which the intensity of the male's violence can be appropriately assessed and the potential for the batterer to injure or kill his victim(s) can be adequately measured. This multi-dimensional approach also helps to distinguish batterers who are treatable from those who are beyond the scope of rehabilitation. Such an approach avoids the many contradictions, inconsistencies, and unanswered questions that linger whenever he is simplistically explained with a single generic profile. The batterer's violence, behaviors, and potential for treatment cannot and should not be addressed utilizing a single personality profile. Unfortunately, in most cases, this is currently the standard.

The following chart is a brief description of the Batterer's Continuum. As the chart explains, the left side of the spectrum reflects the least dangerous of the batterers, and psychopathology is not a factor of concern. The right side of the spectrum reflects the most dangerous of the abusers, and individual psychopathology is always present.

Again, it should be noted that each category on this continuum should be viewed as having several points of its own. In other words, Categories One, Two, and Three should be thought of as having several sub-categories as well. The spectrum should always be viewed as possessing infinite points across its inner plane. The three primary categories are simply starting points of reference.

A comprehensive and detailed description of all three groups on this continuum can be found in Chapters Two through Seven.

THE BATTERER'S CONTINUUM

Category One	Category Two	Category Three
Least Dangerous	**Moderately Dangerous**	**Very Dangerous**
1. Normal male; abnormal circumstances	1. Several character defects	1. Personality disorder
2. Situational, isolated abuse	2. Abuse is not situational, nor is it isolated; violence is sporadic	2. Ongoing, systematic chronic patterns of abuse
3. Etiology of aggression: 90% external 10% internal	3. Etiology of aggression: 50% external 50% internal	3. Etiology of aggression: 10% external 90% internal
4. No previous violent relationships with women	4. Some previous violent relationships with women	4. All previous relationships with women were violent
5. No premarital abuse	5. Some premarital abuse	5. Frequent premarital abuse
6. No use of weapons	6. Some use of weapons	6. Frequent use of weapons
7. Feels remorse	7. Feels limited remorse	7. Feels no remorse; does not have a conscience
8. Very treatable	8. Moderately treatable	8. Not treatable

*See the Profile Assessment Chart in the Appendix for a more detailed and comprehensive description of the Batterer's Continuum.

Chapter II

The Category One Abuser: Motivated to Change

The Category One batterer is the least dangerous of the three groups, particularly when the abuse is considered on an ongoing or lethal basis. The victim of Category One violence generally reports that the male has no previous pattern or history of beating her. She also states that his physical aggression has been isolated to one or two episodes or, at worst, that it has been confined to a series of occurrences over a brief and defined period of time. The Category One batterer has no history of premarital abuse, nor has he had other intimate relationships in which physical violence was an issue of concern.

In sharp contrast to the fluid aggression of the Category Three batterer, the Category One abuser presents with a higher degree of impulse control. Unlike Category Three violence, the Category One batterer reportedly does not use weapons, does not systematically torture his victims, and does not seek to mutilate or to disfigure his spouse's face or torso. He also does not have a pattern of beating his mate during periods of pregnancy. While many of his counterparts on the continuum frequently throw acid in their victims' faces, assault them with sharp knives, and threaten or shoot at them with loaded guns, the Category One abuser rarely has a history of this form of aggression. As a result of the Category One abuser's impulse control, his victim's injuries are generally less severe than are the injuries of the victims of the others, and the possibility that his attack will be disabling or lethal is greatly reduced.

The victim's injuries are also less severe because the Category One abuser does not consciously intend to harm or injure his victim. Unlike the often premeditated assaults of the Category Three batterer that are filled with blatant efforts to disfigure, cripple, and even murder his spouse, Category One attacks are spontaneous and without malice. While it is not suggested that the injuries to a victim of Category One violence cannot become disabling or fatal, the results of such attacks are generally not very serious.

For the most part, the aggression that a Category One abuser displays is directly correlated to the onset of a substance abuse problem, a chronic level of stress, anxiety, trauma, or depression that has been brought on by factors external to himself. His emotional condition and aggression relate closely to negative events that may be catastrophic and beyond his immediate control. His victim frequently reports that the abuse began shortly after the loss of a job or a significant financial setback. Losses such as the death of a loved one, or the separation from an intimate friend or partner, may also trigger isolated but violent outbursts. One such male was arrested after allegedly punching his wife in the face. His nine-year-old son was run over and killed by a car the week before. He was overcome by grief. In other words, the emotional conflicts that the Category One batterer feels are created by variables and events that are external to himself.

While this may seem to be a rather simplistic explanation to many incidences of isolated spousal abuse, it should be understood that a Category One batterer is generally a normal male who faces abnormal circumstances. It is known that individuals differ widely in their stress thresholds. It is perhaps a normal male with a shallow threshold and poor coping skills who is most likely to become a Category One batterer. To reiterate, the etiology of these attacks correlates closely with external variables, as opposed to ongoing psychopathological conflicts. When these external stresses are eliminated or reduced, the internal issues and subsequent physical abuse will, in most cases, cease. Relatively speaking, it is estimated that Category One attacks are 90 percent externally motivated.

Category One batterers rarely come to the attention of the police and the criminal justice system. It is estimated that less than 5 percent of all spousal abuse cases that appear before a court are of this nature. Most of these males feel a deep sense of remorse and guilt for their inappropriate and aggressive behavior and are quite responsive to the needs of their victims. While it is true that the Category One abuser may minimize and rationalize his violent behavior to himself and others, he generally does it to a lesser degree than his more disturbed counterparts. He also has a keen sense of responsibility for his actions and will frequently seek help for his problems before coming to the attention of the judiciary.

While studies strongly suggest that the arrest of a batterer is a significant deterrent to reducing domestic violence,[5] it is perhaps this male who reacts most to police and court intervention. It is his ability to feel remorse and to bond with others that distinguishes him from the Category Two and Three abusers. It is also his significant level of impulse control and the fear of consequences that further buffer him from contact with the court system. As a result, the Category One batterer seldom has a police record. In relation to the criminal justice system, he is the least likely to get arrested for his actions and the most likely to seek help for his emotional problems, when necessary.

In direct contrast to the low number of Category One batterers who make up a court docket, it is this type of batterer that probably accounts for the majority of a clinician's self-referred battering caseload. As indicated, he is genuinely remorseful, empathetic, and painfully aware that he has done wrong. He is motivated to change his negative behavior and will often seek out a therapist without being coerced.

Therapeutically, the Category One abuser presents with reasonably good insight and has the ability to get in touch with and express his feelings and emotions. He is clinically capable of loving, sharing, and developing relationships that are anchored in integrity, respect, and mutual concern. As a result, a Category One abuser who is motivated to change his behavior is an excellent candidate for psychotherapy and should be encouraged to enter such a process. Under ideal circumstances, the prognosis for his positive rehabilitation ranges from good to excellent.

Also clinically significant is that, within the aggression of the Category One batterer, there is an absence of individual psychopathology. This is particularly true when he is compared to any of the personality disorders profiled and described in the D.S.M. IV, a diagnostic manual published by the American Psychiatric Association.[6] His profile is not characteristic of a person who has a narcissistic, paranoid, or antisocial disorder. Nor can he be classified as being obsessive-compulsive, borderline, or histrionic. The Category One abuser also does not possess a multitude of character traits that signal these disorders. His profile is generally devoid of traits such as suspiciousness, pathological jealousy, hypervigilance, irrational outbursts, or temper tantrums. Nor does he display an aura of personal entitlement by relating to others in an egocentric, grandiose, and exploitive manner. He does not engage in self-mutilation and generally does not threaten or attempt suicide. While it is not intended to suggest that a Category One batterer does not possess or exhibit undesirable character traits, it is suggested that he does not possess them in a significant number to warrant concern. If he did, he would be more appropriately classified as a Category Two or Three abuser.

With the exception of the situational conflict that confronts him and the related aggression that results, the interpersonal skills and lifestyle of the Category One abuser are relatively normal. He is generally viewed as a good companion, husband, father, and provider who lives up to his parental obligations and societal expectations. He usually maintains a regular job and is viewed by others as non-threatening and non-abusive in his social and interpersonal relationships. He is an individual who has a history of complying with the laws, values, and mores of the community in which he lives. While the moral character of the Category One batterer is not necessarily beyond reproach, he should be viewed as a normal individual who, in the absence of his situational stress and related aggression, functions no differently from the average male. Perhaps many males, given the wrong set of external circumstances, are capable of Category One abuse.

Chapter III

The Category Three Abuser: The Serial Batterer

On the extreme opposite end of the continuum, and in striking contrast to the Category One batterer, lies the domain of the Category Three abuser. He is not only the primary issue of concern on the three point spectrum, he is potentially one of the most dangerous individuals in American society. What substantiates this claim is the volume of domestic violence reported by our nation's news media within a single afternoon. A brief review of our local and national newspapers provides us with an endless array of reports that validate the degree and volatility of this male's aggression. Such reports vividly detail incomprehensible and perverse acts of torture, mutilation, and murder committed by men against women whom they claim to love. In the most gruesome of the murders, mention is made that the male dismembered and decapitated his victim's lifeless corpse. These accounts generally profile a male who is ruthless, intensely cold, and without remorse. The frightening reality is that these crimes are committed and reported with such frequency that many of us become desensitized and do not recognize the graphic magnitude of their occurrence.

It would certainly be stretching the truth to state that the majority of Category Three aggressors inevitably murder or decapitate their victims. This is not so. What is factual, however, is that they all batter their intimates on a chronic, ongoing, and systematic basis. The Category Three assailant routinely beats his spouse, breaks her bones, and bruises her torso. Many victims state that they have difficulty recalling when one beating ends and the next begins.

These attacks are not limited to those who have known each other or have been married for extended periods of time. One victim reported that her husband intentionally broke her arm while on their honeymoon. Another reported how her husband gave her a black eye on their first date. Both men justified the attacks by saying that they had had too much to drink. Their victims reported that within two years of marriage they were being physically abused no fewer than five times monthly. While a woman may rationalize that the premarital abuse she experiences will cease after marriage, the strongest probability is that it will continue. In fact, the odds are that it will increase dramatically.

The Category Three abuser is also a Serial Batterer. He has an extensive history of abusing multiple victims over much of his lifetime. In fact, when reliable information is available, it is not uncommon to discover that all of his relationships with women are violent ones. During a court hearing involving spousal abuse, a victim testified she was aware that her husband had battered his first wife to death and had also been arrested for stabbing two of his former girlfriends. While she expressed concern for her personal safety, she also expressed concern for his victims that were yet to come. Any woman who contemplates intimate involvement with a male who has a history of violent relationships should consider his past in predicting the future. The probability of him beating her as he did his former lovers is certain. Serial Batterers are no more capable of changing their behaviors than are serial rapists and serial killers.

Whereas some Category Three assaults are spontaneous and without warning, many are premeditated and well planned. In an alarmingly high number of these attacks, the woman is permanently injured, disfigured, and disabled. While the majority of these batterers may never actually murder their victims, all have the potential to do so.

This male does not present a danger to his spouse alone. He is a virtual threat to anyone who he perceives is trespassing on his turf. He views his spouse as a personal possession to which he has unquestionable property rights. During periods of estrangement and discord, when the battered woman seeks refuge from his overwhelming domination and unpredictable rage, those who provide assistance become potential targets of his aggression. This applies to attorneys and personnel who assist her through the courts. It relates to social workers and professionals who treat her clinically and who serve as her advocate. Most vulnerable to his irrational and often gun-wielding attacks are close relatives and friends who frequently provide the victim and her children with refuge from further harm. One such male stormed into the New Orleans residence of his estranged girlfriend's home. As her family and friends sat frozen with fear on both sides of the dinner table, he shot five of them with blasts from a .22-caliber rifle. After the shooting was over, he had murdered his girlfriend, her mother and stepfather, her new boyfriend, and her four-year-old child.[7]

On one day 1990, the Associated Press reported that murder-suicide domestic killings left twelve members of three families dead within a single twenty-hour period. It noted that in Spanaway, Washington, one male smashed through a sliding glass door, shot and killed his ex-wife, their fourteen- and six-year-old daughters, and her new husband. In Belleville, Illinois, another man armed with a handgun killed his wife, daughter, and one-year-old grandson. He then shot at firefighters and committed suicide by staying in his burning home. In Buxton, North Dakota, a man shot himself to death only after killing his wife and eleven-year-old daughter. While these were certainly not the only domestic murders that occurred on that day, they were highlighted in a single report to illustrate the graphic nature of domestic violence.

The prevalence of second-party attacks by the Category Three assailant on the significant others of the battered spouse has never been fully documented. It is imperative, however, for relatives, friends, and associates of such a victim to recognize the perils that exist and to develop legal and appropriate strategies of defense. An appropriate defense should be anchored in hypervigilance, a strong safety plan, and an understanding of the behavioral and personality dynamics of the batterer. To assist in such a relationship with blind insight and without the use of a safety plan places one at great risk.

It is not suggested that professionals, relatives, and friends should abandon the battered woman. Without support systems, she and her children have absolutely no hope of escaping the web of violence in which they are trapped. It is also not suggested that all such batterers inevitably harm, injure, or kill those who intrude in his relationship with his spouse. To reiterate, however, the potential for someone to be caught within his wrath of violence is always present and proper precautions must be taken.

While most beatings of the Category Three batterer fall considerably short of murder, they frequently involve inconceivable and heinous acts of torture and mutilation. Over a relatively brief period of time, the New Orleans Municipal Court heard shocking testimony from numerous victims of abuse. One victim told of how her husband shoved the barrel of a loaded .38 revolver up her vagina, and threatened to discharge it if she refused to have sex with him. Similar testimony came from a woman who was rushed to a hospital after her boyfriend had taken the splintered end of a broken stick and forced it up her rectum. Another victim reported she was held down while her boyfriend pushed a hot curling iron to her face and torso. She suffered permanent scarring and disfiguration over about 25 percent of her body. A victim painfully testified that her husband attacked her with a set of nunchuks, partially severing her vocal cords. He completed his attack by scalping her forehead with a rust encrusted knife. One battered woman displayed grotesque scars on her arms, legs, neck, and face. She claimed that the scars were caused by her boyfriend, who viciously bit her during his attacks. In many of his assaults, he ripped flesh from her body with his teeth. These stories are endless, and so is the number of their victims.

The Category Three abuser's aggression is not limited to physical violence alone. He also exhibits a perpetual pattern of emotional and psychological abuse designed to further suppress his victim into an intensely submissive state. Through a pattern of psychological foreplay, he seeks to totally absorb her personal identity into his own. His intimidating and dominating behaviors are calculated attempts to control her thoughts, spoken words, and actions. In essence, the systematic psychological abuse of his victim allows him to absorb her until her identity evaporates.

The foreplay that he employs in his attempt to exploit her identity comes in the form of humiliation, shame, isolation, and fear. He depletes her sense of self-worth and self-esteem by dogmatically insisting that she is ugly, stupid, a poor mother and wife, and unworthy of family and friends. When he batters, many of the blows go to the face in a blatant attempt to destroy her attractiveness. When she expresses an opinion, he publicly orders her not to speak, suggesting that her ideas and thoughts are useless. When in social gatherings, he ridicules, scorns, and belittles her in the presence of others. When she tries to provide a second income for her family by getting a job, he insists and dictates that she is incapable of holding a job and must cease trying. When she performs household responsibilities, he addresses the results with negative scorn. Even in their sexual relationship, he attempts to make her feel guilty for not having sex when he demands it, and when she complies, performs perverted acts that further humiliate her into a shameful state.

In an effort to isolate his victim from the rest of the world, he not only refuses to allow her to work, but also prevents her from developing new relationships and demands that she disassociate herself from relationships she already has. He frequently refuses to allow her to speak or visit with friends, siblings, and parents, always suggesting they are "bad for her" and that it is in her best interest. In many instances, he takes the car keys in an attempt to prevent her from visiting with family and friends. When she violates his dictates, he verbally intimidates and physically batters her into submission.

In actuality, this batterer brainwashes his spouse in the same manner that a military captor brainwashes a prisoner of war. The Category Three batterer does not have a wife or girlfriend; he has a hostage. His methodical use of humiliation, shame, torture, and isolation is further reinforced by intimidation, fear, and the perpetual threat of being physically attacked, tortured, and dying a violent death. Fear can be so incapacitating that many battered women who contemplate pulling out of relationships find themselves too inhibited to do so, painfully aware of the potential consequences. One victim, who considered fleeing New Orleans in an effort to avoid further abuse, had difficulty deciding whether to tell her abuser the exact time she was leaving or to lie and slip out when he was not watching. She reasoned and concluded that the second alternative was the most risky. She stated, "When he finds out that I lied, he will hunt me down, find me, and kill me. But if I tell him the truth, while he may try to disrupt my departure, his rage will not be as intense and perhaps my life will be spared."

In his effort to dominate and control his spouse, the Category Three abuser's behavior is often well calculated and premeditated. He frequently threatens to kill her, the children, and even himself. He exhibits a portfolio of intimidating behavior with a primary objective of controlling through fear. Those who possess guns regularly remind their victims that they will use the weapons if necessary. In fact, these men frequently discharge guns within their households, sometimes coming dangerously close to where their mates are sitting or standing. One woman testified that her husband shot the phone off the wall with a .38-caliber pistol because she refused to hang up as demanded. Another stated that during her mate's rage, he held a loaded gun to her head and to the head of her four-year-old son. Other men are known to shred their mates' clothes with sharp knives and then threaten to do the same to the women's bodies. Threats of burning her house and setting her on fire with gasoline are reported with surprising regularity. There is perhaps no victim of such abuse who has not had her furniture destroyed, windows shattered, doors smashed in, or car vandalized by this male during his infantile tantrums.

These are the behaviors that she experiences when they are still together. After she leaves, he pursues her in the same manner that a predator pursues its prey. He follows and stalks her in the shadows of the night. During the course of his pursuit, he often attacks while suggesting that if she does not return, he will kill her. If she parks and leaves her car unattended, he slashes her tires, cuts the wires underneath the hood, throws acid on the paint job, and smashes in the windows with a hammer or brick. One victim who tried to elude her ex-husband discovered that he used a blowtorch to burn the interior of her new car. He left a note attached to the burned-out shell stating that she was next. Another caught her husband in the process of using a sledgehammer on her car. Although the police were summoned, they indicated that they could not arrest him because the title was in both their names. After they left, he beat her with the hammer for having called them.

If she continues to decline his efforts to reconcile, this batterer calls her on the phone over and over again, vacillating between hysterical pleadings and intimidation and threats of physical harm. He places notes under her door and sends mail stating that he loves her, but he violently retaliates if she does not return. He harasses her on her job and stalks her as she leaves. One male, while imprisoned for a previous attack on his girlfriend, allegedly had his sister and a couple of friends throw acid in her face as she left the office where she was employed. Immediately following the attack, he called from jail to claim responsibility for the attack and to say that he still loved her.[8]

As the battered spouse sleeps in the darkness of her bedroom, this male defuses the electrical box, severs the telephone wires, and breaks windows or doors to gain entry into her residence. He enters with life-threatening weapons, reflecting on what he will do if she does not submit. Even when she does not resist his demands, he destroys her property and beats her body with his fists. As intended, he always leaves an aftermath of violence behind him. During his exit, he may kidnap her children and threaten to keep or harm them if she does not agree to reconcile.

There is nothing more terrifying for a battered woman than an estranged husband who regularly crashes through windows or doors in the middle of the night. In many instances, he is also armed. The trauma that she and her children experience is beyond words. The terror that a victim feels as she lies in a state of sleepless hypervigilance is emotionally and physically paralyzing. She does not know when or how he will strike. What is certain is that he will.

Regardless of his individual techniques, the Category Three assailant systematically instills fear into the soul of his battered spouse. There is absolutely no one other than the woman herself who understands the magnitude of fear that engulfs her. The fear of knowing that if she betrays or defies him, he will injure, torture, or kill her. The fear of being stalked by a predator. The fear of not knowing when or how he will attack.

The Category Three batterer is vividly aware that when he destroys his mate's self-esteem and identity and successfully isolates her from financial and emotional support systems, she becomes putty in his hands. Putty that he transforms into an image that pleases him; a shape that he desires; a shape that he controls. Through acts of gross intimidation, terrorism, and abuse, the batterer does not merely attempt to alter, modify, or control his spouse's identity, he attempts to engulf it. Her identity does not become one with his, it becomes his. She becomes nothing more than an empty shell; an emotional vacuum. As an individual, she loses her ability to think and feel. Instead, he begins to think for her, to feel for her, and to act for her. Ultimately, he wants her to interact and relate to the outside world through him alone.

What is it, however, that causes a man to batter his wife's face, to bruise her torso, and to punch and kick her in the abdomen when she is pregnant? What drives him to callously beat her with a lead pipe while her children watch and cry in fear? What type of male would stick jagged objects up his mate's vagina in an attempt to mutilate her sexual organs? When she tries to escape his ruthless violence, why would he pursue her as an animal pursues prey? What is the profile of a man who stalks, batters, tortures, and mutilates a woman he claims to love?

Mass media perform a grave injustice when they report and suggest that men murder their wives as a result of financial problems, job stress, marital discord, or the many external factors that they generally focus on in an effort to explain such incomprehensible acts of violence. One newspaper reported that a male had killed his wife complaining that she was not spending enough quality time with him.[9] The media often justify a domestic homicide by categorizing it as a "crime of passion." Family, friends, professionals, and clinicians alike are frequently guilty of blaming such crimes on superficial and external factors that have no direct correlation to the true etiology of the batterer's aggression. An attack in which the assailant walked into a department store where his estranged wife worked and shot her at point-blank range with a small caliber handgun best exemplifies this issue. In responding to a question from the press regarding the incident, a clinician reportedly stated, "these men are choking on stress."

No one in American society will escape life without experiencing financial setbacks, job losses, or external stress that are both overwhelming and intense. Yet, even under the worst case scenario of external circumstances, the greatest percentage of American males will never physically abuse their mates, particularly in the manner that a Category Three batterer assaults his victim. This is not to suggest that external stress cannot trigger acts of anger and rage. Surely it can, as has been described in cases of Category One aggression. Most males, however, have both the socialization skills and impulse control necessary for controlling their rage. The chronic batterer, the Category Three, does not possess such an ability.

Although stimulated by it, the Category Three's aggression and violence is not caused by his external environment. It is not rooted in financial problems, a job loss, or in the recent death of a close friend. His violent acts are not brought on by a demotion at work, his wife's failure to have dinner ready when he demands it, her infidelity, or one of the many rationalizations that he commonly uses in an attempt to minimize what he has done.

Instead, his aggression surfaces as a result of an enormous degree of internal conflict and unresolved turmoil. While it has been suggested that the anger of the Category One abuser is 90 percent externally motivated, the opposite is true of the Category Three abuser. External factors are significant only in that they trigger what is already there. He is a cauldron of smoldering anger ready to explode. Anger that—unlike the anger of the Category One abuser—is based firmly within the dynamics of his individual psychopathology.

In specific psychiatric terms, the Category Three abuser is considered to have a personality disorder. Such a disorder would be best described as a psychological cancer that robs the individual of the social and interpersonal skills necessary for functioning within the acceptable framework of society. His behavior is generally inappropriate, inept, and repugnant to those who interact with him. He is without a conscience, sense of remorse, or an ability to bond with others. He is often visibly distressed, exhibits marked mood swings, and displays frequent signs of anxiety, anger, and related depression. While it is true that all individuals with personality disorders are not batterers, it is probable that nearly all Category Three batterers have personality disorders.

In the D.S.M. IV, numerous personality disorders are described in candid and vivid detail.[10] When these profiles are applied to the behavioral traits and patterns exhibited by the Category Three batterer, it becomes evident that at least six of the disorders are applicable to his psychological makeup. Without doubt, the Category Three batterer can be considered to have one or more—or even a combination—of several of the following disorders: 1) Narcissistic Personality Disorder, 2) Antisocial Personality Disorder, 3) Borderline Personality Disorder, 4) Histrionic Personality Disorder, 5) Paranoid Personality Disorder, 6) Obsessive-Compulsive Personality Disorder.

While there is an obvious and intense association between chronic spousal abuse and personality disorders, acts of domestic violence can occur for other reasons as well. Some attacks may be related to thyroid problems, hormonal dysfunctions, a psychotic break, brain tumors, or a single episode of drug usage. Even issues of nutritional deficiencies may at times play a significant factor in some assaults. For example, it is a medical fact that hypoglycemia (low blood sugar) can bring about noticeable mood swings when a regimented diet is not followed. When the physiological and psychological effects brought on by these factors in combination with a low stress threshold and limited impulse control are considered, the possibility that such an individual will become physically aggressive is very high. There is also a host of other mental illnesses listed in the D.S.M. IV that could result in unpredictable explosive violence.

While there are certainly many ways in which to explain chronic and ongoing physical attacks on women by their boyfriends or husbands, the association between personality disorders and such assaults is significant and explains the majority of attacks that occur in American society.

Chapter IV

Personality Disorders of the Category Three Abuser

The Narcissistic Batterer

One of the most common of the chronic battering profiles is that of the narcissist. In fact, narcissism is a predominant trait among most Category Three batterers, irrespective of the disorder that they possess. The individual exhibits a grandiose sense of worth and self-importance.[11] In the context of social interaction, he makes endless self-references and has an insatiable need for constant attention and admiration.[12] His relationship with his spouse is purely exploitive and parasitic, lacking any measure of integrity or respectability. He sees her importance only in relation to how she can meet his many needs, desires, and demands. He feels entitled simply because he exists. His interactions with his mate and significant others are always one-sided and non-reciprocal.[13] While she chronically neglects her own needs and the needs of her children in an attempt to satisfy his, he feels absolutely no responsibility to reciprocate. When his needs are not satisfied or fulfilled in the manner to which he feels entitled, he often goes on a rampage of spontaneous violence.

This male is actually involved in a love-hate relationship with himself. On the surface, he displays a high degree of self-confidence and is quite boisterous about his accomplishments, achievements, and personal aspirations.[14] Below the surface, however, his self-esteem is very fragile and vulnerable and is easily impacted by the remarks of others. Consequently, he often responds aggressively to the slightest criticism, even when it is presented in a constructive and non-threatening manner.[15]

In his family relationships, he is emotionally shallow and incapable of empathizing with a spouse who is in emotional distress or physical pain.[16] While he may occasionally appear to display concern for his spouse and children, it is generally an attempt to manipulate the relationship. Once he has accomplished his objective, however, his caring demeanor quickly transforms back into parasitic demands.

Within the narcissism of the Category Three batterer, there exists a disturbing analogy between his behavior and the normal narcissism that a child displays during the early years of its life. For example, it is not only expected, but perfectly acceptable for an infant to make overwhelming emotional and physical demands on its mother. It is also not anticipated that the infant will reciprocate that which the mother provides. While the parent nurtures, cuddles, caresses, and feeds the child on immediate demand, the child routinely disregards the mother's sleep and daily routine. The child, of course, does not intentionally inflict discomfort and stress upon its parent. The infant is merely trying to have its many dependent needs met as they arise. The mother enters into a relationship with her baby that is based on non-reciprocal and non-conditional love. She provides nurturing willingly and instinctively and is fully aware that the child does not yet love her; instead, the baby needs her.

As the infant grows into a young child of five or six, however, the child becomes perceptually aware that interpersonal relationships are more than non-reciprocal and self-centered demands. As it begins to recognize that throwing a tantrum or biting someone is not an acceptable means of extorting a response, such behaviors begin to dissipate and are replaced by more socially acceptable alternatives. As the child learns that jealousy and possessiveness are undesired traits in a relationship, it begins to replace them with personality traits that are. During this early socialization process, the childhood qualities of self-centeredness and self-interest begin to be replaced with those of giving, sharing, and mutual concern for others. The previously dependent infant and demanding child begins to transform into a mature, loving, and giving person. The child begins to break out of its narcissistic shell and enters into interpersonal relationships with integrity, where it feels that the well-being of others is as important as and equal to its own.

Of course, the case presented here is an ideal one. Many children, as a result of extreme emotional, physical, and environmental deprivation, never manage to fully emerge from their natural stage of narcissism. They remain psychologically fixated and begin to display chronic levels of narcissism beyond their early years and well into their adult lives.

The Category Three batterer diagnosed as having a narcissistic personality disorder displays many of the same behaviors as a narcissistic child. For instance, when he does not get his way, he goes into a childlike tantrum where objects are tossed and broken. During his infantile behavior, he breaks windows, furniture, doors, mirrors, and virtually anything in sight. His tantrums also include hysterical sobbing, threats, and obscenities, and often a tantrum results in his throwing his family, friends, and relatives out of his home. Such temper tantrums are as frequent and common to this batterer as the air he breathes.

Also like a young child, he often bites his victim when in the midst of emotional conflict. His bite, however, is far more powerful than that of a child. He tears flesh from his victim's limbs and torso, causing injury and serious scarring. The male who bites his victim is perhaps the more disturbed and dangerous of the Category Three batterers. Biting in itself symbolizes one of the most primitive and animalistic forms of aggressive behavior. While the actual number of women who are bitten by their batterers is unclear, an interviewer will find that it is reported with surprising regularity. A victim always seems surprised when asked if her spouse bites her, not because it has not occurred, but because the interviewer was aware that such a possibility existed.

The manner in which the Category Three batterer relates to his spouse is also very childlike. It is expected of a three-year-old to respond to its mother in a rather possessive or jealous manner, particularly when the child perceives that she is showing affection to another. We have all witnessed a scenario in which the mother picks up another infant while her own child verbally and physically protests until the mother places the other infant down. Such behavior is anticipated and acceptable during the narcissistic stage of a young child's life.

The Category Three abuser relates to his spouse in the same manner that the child relates to its mother. The victim frequently reports that the male attacked her because she gave "too much attention" to another person, particularly when the exchange was with a male. If she speaks to a male neighbor, he accuses her of having an illicit affair and demands that she cease the interaction. The same occurs whenever she speaks with men at social functions. No matter how superficial or limited the conversation, this batterer feels threatened and overwhelmed.

His possessiveness is not limited only to her association with the male gender. He is also intimidated by her relationships with distant relatives, friends, parents, and even her children. He is threatened by virtually anyone who he feels may take his place as the focus of her attention. As the child is possessive of the mother, so is the batterer of his spouse. His jealousy is beyond childlike; it is pathological.

The most pathetic act of narcissism that the Category Three male displays is the manner in which he perceives his unborn child. Instead of seeing the impending birth as an event that brings a greater sense of oneness and joy to his life, he generally views the newborn as competition for attention from the woman who "feeds him." He views the baby as someone who will inevitably relegate him to a secondary position in the relationship with his spouse. In fact, this male is so intimidated by this possibility that he not only beats the woman when she is pregnant, but he also makes obvious and blatant attempts to kill the unborn child.

Police officers and court personnel report that they see an alarmingly high number of women in various stages of pregnancy who have been kicked and punched in the abdomen by their assailants. One victim testified that she suffered a miscarriage after her husband beat her in the stomach with a large pipe. Another described how her husband struck her in the face with a baseball bat, knocking her down a steep staircase. As she attempted to get up from the floor, he began to stomp on her chest while she clutched her womb in an effort to protect her unborn child.

There is little doubt that many acts of battering that occur when a woman is pregnant, particularly when he targets the abdominal area, are probably conscious attempts by the Category Three batterer to kill the fetus that intimidates him. His motivation to kill the unborn child, however, is not based in jealousy alone. Such an act is his greatest measure of control. It is the ultimate means of inflicting pain on his victim. While her physical wounds may heal quickly, grief related to the death of her unborn child is perpetual.

This male is no more capable of loving his wife than is the infant of loving its mother. He feels that the primary reason for a woman's existence is that of convenience. To him, she is merely a caretaker that must attend to his personal needs, desires, and demands while disregarding her own. This batterer views the outside world only in terms of how it can meet and satisfy his needs. Like the narcissistic infant, this batterer is involved in a non-reciprocal relationship with his spouse. He is nothing more than a parasite that depletes her confidence, self-esteem, individuality, identity, and, in some cases, her life.

The Antisocial Batterer

The most flagrantly aggressive of the Category Three batterers is one who possesses an antisocial personality disorder. While some abusers are relatively discreet in the battering of their mates, the violence of the antisocial batterer is blatantly public. He beats his spouse in front of family, friends, strangers, and neighbors. He attacks and assaults her in restaurants, nightclubs, and in the midst of large social gatherings. One such male attacked and pounded his wife with both fists in the middle of a crowded courtroom. Another threatened his spouse inside a small church with a loaded revolver as the choir stopped singing and watched in disbelief.

Besides displaying a total lack of impulse control, the antisocial batterer is also oblivious and unconcerned about the consequences of his behavior.[17] As a result, he is the batterer who is most likely to come to the attention of the police and the criminal justice system. He often has an extensive criminal record consisting of both petty and major offenses, such as theft, robbery, drug offenses, and endless acts of personal violence. The antisocial batterer does not discriminate among the objects of his battery. He is known to get into physical encounters with his friends, neighbors, co-workers, and supervisors. Unlike some batterers, he does not isolate his physical aggression to his spouse alone. To the antisocial batterer, spousal abuse is merely a sideline.

As a result of his lack of impulse control and total disregard for the consequences of his behavior, the antisocial batterer is not only the most likely of the Category Three batterers to find himself incarcerated; he is also the most likely to pursue his wife upon release from jail. The majority of batterers who appear before a court respond to the overwhelming authority of the judiciary. The threat of imprisonment is generally enough to keep many batterers away from their estranged mates. Written restraining orders, for example, that require the male to make regular status appearances before the court, are generally very effective deterrents. Of course, this tool is productive only within a system that closely monitors its orders and executes penalties when they are violated. For most batterers, the fear of incarceration is a strong and effective method of reducing the incidence of spousal abuse.

The antisocial batterer who comes before a court, however, respects no one. He is neither impressed nor intimidated by a judge's verbal dictate or written order. He is not intimidated by the threat of incarceration. If he should go to jail for an attack on a woman, he immediately pursues her upon his release. One batterer was known to have served twelve separate jail sentences for abusing the same woman. On his last conviction, the judge noted that it appeared the defendant was serving a life sentence on an installment plan. In reality, a woman who tries to disassociate herself from the antisocial male, no matter how motivated she is to do so, often finds that he will pursue her at any cost or consequence.

Professionals should always advise a battered woman to establish a strong support system and to assert herself in becoming totally independent and free of the batterer's grasp. When it relates to a chronic antisocial batterer, however, advising the victim to be assertive can intensify an already dangerous situation. Therefore, it is imperative once the decision to take action is made that appropriate safety precautions are taken. In fact, suggesting that she consider arming herself should not be viewed as inappropriate or unprofessional. Of course, arming oneself against such an assailant should be considered only after extraordinary legal steps have been taken by the battered woman to curtail his violence. Prior to taking such measures, victims who decide to arm themselves against sociopathic batterers should also participate in certified firearms training programs that can instruct them in the proper use and storage of weapons.

While I recognize that taking a position relative to firearms is ideological quicksand, I also feel that not to take a position is to deny the imminent danger that sociopathic batterers present to their victims, particularly those who have received little or no protection from the justice system. If a perfect stranger continued savagely attacking you after serving several jail sentences for the same offense, would you not take measures to protect yourself? The fact is, upon their release from jail, most antisocial batterers, no matter what consequences are imposed, will pursue their victims with reckless obsession. With this type of batterer, the woman's life and safety may ultimately depend on how she takes the defensive.

The antisocial batterer's lack of impulse control and disregard for consequences extend beyond the injuries that he inflicts on his spouse. He is callously indifferent to the privileges and rights of all individuals.[18] He violates society's standards, mores, and values without hesitation or consideration of how his actions will impact or harm those around him.

In practically every aspect of the antisocial batterer's life, he is pathetically dysfunctional. In the area of parental obligations and expectations, he is chronically derelict in meeting the responsibilities that he has to his wife and kids. Like the narcissist, he always places himself first, callously disregarding the most basic needs of his children.[19] Even when he is aware that his family is in need of food and medicine, or that the rent and utilities are delinquent, he squanders his paycheck on gambling and booze. After exhausting his own funds, he demands the savings of his spouse or children in a desperate attempt to continue his drunken orgy. When she refuses his demands, he threatens her and the children with physical harm until she concedes.

In the area of domestic violence, the antisocial batterer is more than a spouse abuser. He is also frequently a child abuser.[20] Battered women attached to an antisocial abuser often articulate case histories that reflect a male that batters not only his spouse, neighbors, and friends, but his own children as well. Much of the child abuse comes as a spontaneous reaction to his rage during or following an incidence of spousal abuse.

The antisocial abuser often premeditates child abuse in an attempt to force his wife into submitting to his relentless demands. He knows that when all else fails, the best means of intimidation is by threatening, kidnapping, or physically abusing her kids. As in the beating of the woman, he is known to employ weapons such as knives, sticks, belts, and guns in his attack on a child. Women frequently report that their batterers held guns to the heads of their terrified children. The antisocial batterer is very aware that his victim's children can readily be used as pawns in his quest to manipulate.

It is worth noting that many individuals with personality disorders, even during periods of unbridled aggression, have enough impulse control to avoid beating their children. Some abusers seem to reason that there are a different set of societal standards when it comes to the battering of a woman and a child. They reason that, while they have the right to physically abuse their wives, they do not have the same privileges with their children.

As indicated, however, the antisocial abuser is not influenced or inhibited by the values of the community in which he lives. He has a chilling disregard for the standards of society and consequences imposed for violating those standards.[21] When he is reprimanded or punished for violating community sanctions, including those pertaining to family violence, he rationalizes his behavior and repeats the offense. If there is a direct correlation between the acts of spousal abuse and child abuse, it is more apparent within the context of the antisocial abuser.

To put the issue of child abuse into proper perspective, it should be noted that while Category One batterers rarely abuse or injure their children, the Category Three abuser, particularly the antisocial abuser, may be as much of a physical threat to a child as he is to his spouse.

In the area of employability, he is as blatantly impotent as in the care of his children. He has significant periods of unemployment and is a classic "job hopper."[22] He generally quits or gets fired as a result of unacceptable and inappropriate behavior. He rationalizes that his job losses are a result of external factors over which he has no control. A noteworthy case is a male who vented to his wife that he was fired for unsatisfactory work performance after his supervisor demanded that he perform a job function in which he had no training. He commented that his boss always had it in for him. He made no mention of his supervisors and several co-workers having to physically restrain him after he attacked another employee with a knife.

This male's unemployability has little to do with job market opportunities or his vocational suitability for a particular job. Even when market opportunities are in abundance in his area of expertise, he rarely finds himself employed. His occupational patterns persist and repeat themselves from one job to the other. Although terminated as a result of inappropriate behavior, absenteeism, tardiness, etc., he minimizes his responsibility for the job loss, always rationalizing and feeling unjustly persecuted by superiors.

In actuality, his transience in employment is for reasons compatible with the rest of his profile. He is emotionally inept and socially dysfunctional in interpersonal relationships. This certainly carries over and influences his ability to function within the context of occupational settings. Like every other aspect of his life, it is not external factors that impact his ability to maintain a particular job. Instead, it is his repugnant behavior, lack of impulse control, and lack of concern for others that frequently force him from the job market.

His unemployability also produces the secondary problem of his being continuously dependent on others for financial assistance and support. He demands and feels entitled to have his wife, parents, friends, and even his children come to his aid when he finds himself financially down and out. When they fail or refuse to assist his financial needs, he often responds in a hostile, aggressive, and violent manner in an attempt to intimidate the other party into meeting his dogmatic requests.

As is characteristic of anyone who spends his life lying, stealing, conning, manipulating, and using others in an effort to feed his own needs, the antisocial male has great difficulty in sustaining close personal relationships.[23] Instead, he devours his relationships both financially and emotionally until they have nothing left to give. He then develops new ones while never completely severing the old. Old relationships, particularly with his spouse, are often held in reserve in hopes of extracting whatever resources are still available.

The Borderline Batterer

The Category Three batterer who exhibits a borderline disorder is plagued with a severe identity disturbance.[24] He is always challenging and questioning who he is, what he is, and why he is. He is an individual who may consider himself a Republican on a Monday, a Democrat on a Tuesday, and neither by week's end. Likewise, he may advocate for abortion one month but will cross the street and join the pro-lifers the next. His views, beliefs, and related commitments rapidly fluctuate from one end of the spectrum to the other, without ever establishing a period of consistency or stability. His philosophical beliefs are extremely transient, and he finds himself on the prowl for an identity that he never obtains.

As a result of his chronic lack of identity, he frequently experiences intense moments of alienation in which he feels totally detached and isolated from both his primary and secondary associations. His sense of alienation is particularly intense during periods of estrangement from his spouse. During such periods of isolation, his sense of emotional distress is so profound that his condition is best described by what sociologists call a "state of anomie."[25] When detachment from others becomes intense and the feelings of alienation are overwhelming, suicide is seen as a means of escape.

The borderline profile may help to explain why some Category Three batterers commit suicide while the majority do not. Although the threat of suicide is a common behavior which the Category Three abuser uses to manipulate others into acceding to his demands, he seldom follows through with his threats. For example, histrionic batterers commonly threaten to commit suicide in an effort to solicit attention and to acquire control over their relationships.[26] Once they have achieved that control, their threats dissipate and evolve into more standard forms of intimidation and manipulation. The batterer who has a borderline personality disorder, however, is more capable of turning his threats into reality. This is particularly true when he cannot quickly re-attach himself to his spouse like a fetus. He is also the Category Three batterer perhaps most prone to commit murder-suicide.

As illustrated, marked and rapid mood swings are characteristic of this batterer. The shifts in mood, however, are not generally bipolar in their content. The male does not fluctuate from a manic stage (extreme high) to a depressed stage (extreme low) during the course of his mood swings. Instead, he goes from a relatively normal emotional state to one that is dysphoric.[27] Associated with these mood fluctuations is his identity disturbance, sense of rejection, lack of external stimulation, and an intense fear of being alone.[28]

Many battered women state that they can sense with some level of certainty when this male is about to explode. They note that he begins to appear withdrawn and displays high levels of irritability, arguing and complaining about issues of relative insignificance. They further describe him as appearing anxiety ridden and verbalizing a spat of unrelated and inconsistent gripes. While many acts of spousal abuse are spontaneous and unpredictable in their occurrence, it is perhaps the abuser with a borderline personality who exhibits a greater degree of warning prior to his physical rage.

Like other Category Three abusers with personality disorders, this batterer's interpersonal relationships are intensely unstable and filled with turmoil. His identity disturbance, fear of abandonment, and related mood swings create an atmosphere of interpersonal exchange that is argumentative, combative, hostile, and chaotic. While he is capable of communicating with others in a normal manner for brief periods, his mood swings make it impossible for him to sustain stable relationships over a significant period of time. As a result, he is likely to have a long history of frequent separations and multiple divorces, always rationalizing and blaming others for his interpersonal dilemmas.

While the borderline batterer tries to give the appearance of being in control of the relationship, he is actually dramatically dependent on his spouse for his emotional needs. This trait is most apparent when she threatens to leave him. When she attempts to terminate the relationship, he uses specific strategies that are designed to keep her within his control. He has a tremendous fear of being alone and will do anything he must to prevent it from happening.

In his effort to lure his spouse back into his control, he may agree to seek help for his problems and will make promises to change his behavior. Like all Category Three batterers, however, he will not follow through with such promises. Although he may make one or two appointments to see a therapist, as soon as he has his spouse back into his grasp, he finds fault with the therapist or uses some other rationalization to discontinue.

The most classic means of manipulating his spouse into staying in the relationship is through threats of suicide. He holds loaded revolvers to his head and threatens to kill himself if she leaves. He frequently slashes his wrists and overdoses on prescription drugs. While most of these attempts are intentionally superficial, some are severe or fatal. If this batterer successfully evokes a sense of responsibility or guilt from his victim and she opts to stay in the relationship, the cycle will inevitably repeat itself over and over again.

When he fails to manipulate her with threats of suicide, self-mutilation, or other manipulative acts, he resorts to personal violence. He begins to threaten her life and the lives of her children with guns, knives, bricks, gasoline, and fire. His beatings increase and intensify in an effort to validate his control. If she successfully leaves the relationship, he follows, pursues, intimidates, stalks, and torments her until she returns. As stated, there is nothing more frightening to him than the thought of being alone. His spouse is one of the few elements of an identity that he possesses. Her departure leaves him without a focus.

When incarcerated, the most painful experience of the borderline batterer is not necessarily the loss of his freedom. His greatest pain is perhaps the loss of control over his spouse. She is the one on whom he is most dependent. When he is removed from her, particularly when he does not have an opportunity to attach himself to another woman, his sense of isolation, alienation, and related dependency become overwhelmingly evident.

His identity disturbance, depression, and psychological turmoil are no more intense than his futile attempts to escape from them. Like the antisocial abuser, the borderline batterer indulges in a series of ongoing and self-destructive vices that are seen as an immediate release from the emptiness and boredom that engulfs him.[29] He is commonly known as a binge drinker who abuses alcohol to the point of oblivion while callously disregarding the impact that such abuse has on his life or on the lives of others. In the case of many with borderline personalities, substance abuse is an accurate and valid secondary diagnosis that adds fuel and combustion to an already aggressive and volatile profile. Alcohol abuse and chemical dependency not only provide him with what he sees as an acceptable excuse for his violence, they also serve as disinhibitors that allow his aggression to flow without restraint.

The Histrionic Batterer

Essential features of the histrionic batterer are his self-dramatizations and exaggerated expressions of emotion.[30] He responds to seemingly routine occurrences with nothing less than Oscar-winning performances. Issues that take place in his interpersonal relationships and external environments, even when they are obviously insignificant, frequently trigger Shakespearean responses. This Category Three is a sensational actor who intentionally plays out his moods and emotions in a dramatic and hysterical fashion. To a perfect stranger, his hysteria may appear to be genuine and spontaneous. To those who know him, however, it is repugnantly clear that his displays of unrestrained emotion are nothing more than rehearsed scripts.

For instance, experiences of rejection, failure, or grief, although minimal in their content, often result in childlike tantrums in which he falls to the floor, crying, sobbing, and pleading with those around him for personal reassurance and comfort. More specifically, if his dramatic response is a result of his perception that his spouse is preparing to leave him, his tantrums are thrown in the presence of family members in a calculated attempt to entice others into the script. During these antics, he throws, breaks, and destroys objects immediately accessible. Victims report that in the wake of his rampage, windows, mirrors, furniture, doors, car windshields, and other personal items are damaged beyond repair. Following his pathetic outburst, he may be seen curling up on the floor in a fetal position, begging his family and friends to rescue him from his fabricated trauma. He knows that if he is persuasive and is perceived as a helpless individual who has no control over his condition, they will come to his aid and rescue him from his "pain." In his efforts to seek attention and to extort the nurturance of others, the histrionic batterer portrays himself as a victim.[31]

Unfortunately, those around him, particularly family members, regularly play into his script. Instead of ignoring and allowing him to suffer the consequences for his inappropriate and often criminal behavior, they respond to his "condition" with overwhelming concern. As this batterer dramatically acts out his emotions, his parents, wife, and friends often make every effort to comfort him from his frivolous plight. In actuality, they take on what is comparable to supporting cast members. By feeding his juvenile demands, however, they simply provide food to an already well-developed disorder. The feeding of any disorder merely acts as a catalyst for its continuation. Although well-intentioned, a family member who plays an enabling role in response to this male's behavior merely perpetuates it.

A common scenario that exemplifies the interaction that transpires between the histrionic assailant, his family, and friends, is one in which the police are summoned following his attack on his wife. Upon the officers' arrival, this batterer frequently presents himself as a troubled individual who desperately needs help. In the course of acting out his role, he cries uncontrollably and appears emotionally traumatized. He has the uncanny ability to remove the focus of concern from those whom he has battered and injured and transfer it to himself. As his wife sits in the corner with a broken jaw and battered torso, it is common for family and police to shift their attention and empathize with her assailant. Through his sensational portrayal and dramatic behavior, the histrionic batterer is able to manipulate center stage and to emerge as a victim as well. In fact, his role is so well played that the battered woman is often pushed into the background and perceived only as a secondary victim.

When he senses that he has failed to acquire control over his surroundings through his regular routine, he resorts to other forms of dramatic behavior in an attempt to extort empathetic responses. If he recognizes that his original portrayal was unsuccessful, he turns to threats of suicide. In these threats, he superficially cuts his wrist or participates in other forms of self-mutilation. Threats of jumping from a bridge, overdosing on pills, or killing himself with a handgun are commonplace. Such dramatic acts of self-destruction by the histrionic batterer are his attempt to manipulate others into feeding his insatiable need for attention and reassurance.[32]

While it is not suggested that threats of suicide are always frivolous dramatizations, such behavior is the most successful tool of the histrionic batterer in extracting his childlike demands. It is his ultimate weapon in his emergence as a victim: a pathetically helpless man who is not responsible for his behavior and who desperately needs the assistance of others in excavating him from what he sees as an unjust existence.

One such batterer, after being addressed by a Municipal Court judge, acted as if he had been given the death penalty. As the judge admonished the defendant for having beaten his wife, the verbal reprimand was minimal at best. The judge simply issued a restraining order that prohibited the defendant from contacting or seeing his estranged wife. "It's over buddy," he said. "If you continue to pursue her, you know what the consequences are." As the defendant turned around to walk out of the courtroom, his body began to tremble and shake. While walking down the center aisle, he began to cry hysterically, his lips quivering and muttering that he could not go on without his wife. When his elderly mother opened the door for him, he appeared to have fainted, falling to the floor only after making certain that his fall was cushioned by outstretched arms and opened palms. As his sister ran to his aid, his mother cradled him in her arms, giving her personal reassurance that everything would be fine. The rest of the family began screaming for help. Even his wife, the victim, darted into the court's hallway, summoning the help of two police officers. When the police rushed to assist the man, he cried and insisted on being left alone. As he stood up and braced himself by placing his arms around the shoulders of his mother and sister and slowly descended the concrete stairs, he murmured how he would kill himself and get out of everybody's life. "No one cares anyway," he said, "no one."

When the histrionic batterer sees that his childlike behavior, tantrums, and threats of suicide are ineffective means of manipulation, he resorts to a more aggressive script in which he physically intimidates and threatens his family, friends, and strangers with blatant acts of harm and violence. When the rest of his script fails in its intent, his behavior frequently escalates into overt attacks.

To the histrionic batterer, the general payoff for repugnant behavior is twofold. First, like the narcissist, he is able to feed his relentless need for constant attention. A secondary payoff for his hysterical behavior is control. This man feels little control over his life other than the woman he dominates. He is keenly aware, however, that he can manipulate others through various behaviors designed to extort desired responses. Such behavior is an essential weapon in acquiring control over a world in which he feels grossly inadequate and enormously insecure.

The histrionic batterer in no way limits his acting to periods of perceived personal crisis. In routine interpersonal interaction, while appearing vain and bold, he often presents himself as an overwhelmingly flirtatious, friendly, charming, and vivacious individual. He frequently comes across as overzealous and inappropriately enthusiastic and extends himself to others beyond expectations.[33] He utilizes symbols such as job status, dress, personal style, and gestures in a seductive and flamboyant manner in his attempt to entice others.[34]

It becomes apparent, however, to those who regularly interact with him, that his personal demeanor is one of superficiality and shallowness.[35] Below the surface, he is an empty, cold, and insecure individual whose only purpose in pleasing others is in his desire to acquire, possess, and control. He views the rewards of social exchange only in terms of how others can feed and nurture his relentless desires. While he initially engulfs others and is quick to make friends, he invalidates their significance if he discovers that they cannot be exploited. He feels that when he extends himself to others, they owe him. It is when they do not return or repay their debt that he becomes hostile, arrogant, and violent.

The histrionic batterer also has a significant tendency to perceive his relationship with his partner as being more intimate than it may be.[36] He reads more into a relationship than may exist. Consequently, when she tries to withdraw, he stalks and attaches himself to her like a fungus. It is during her retreat that his dramatic dependency is blatantly evident. It is during her retreat that she is in the most danger.

The histrionic batterer is also tormented by intense boredom and has an enormous craving for stimulation.[37] Even when areas of his life are viewed by others with envy, he is generally bored to the point of despair. Consequently, besides the use of violence to stimulate his dull existence, as in other disorders, he gravitates toward inappropriate behaviors such as promiscuous sexual activities, uncontrolled gambling, and substance abuse. His indulgence in these multiple vices is an attempt to escape from a life that he finds intolerable.

The Paranoid Batterer

There is an endless stream of battered women each day who appear before a court, complaining that their husbands abused them after insisting that they were having an illicit affair. They describe a man who watches their every move and questions them in detail to explain their whereabouts for each moment of the day. Throughout the entire interrogation process, he will suggest, demand, and attempt to force his spouse to acknowledge that she has been unfaithful. He also threatens to kill her and the "secret" lover when he finds out. These women report that they are reluctant to speak to other men for fear that their interaction may be misinterpreted and result in violent retaliation.

This Category Three abuser is pathologically jealous and is obsessed with the issue of infidelity.[38] In an almost ritualistic manner, he perceives that she is having an affair, questions family and friends about it, follows and monitors phone calls, and with a total lack of validation, aggressively confronts her, demanding a confession. When she does not confess, and it becomes apparent that he has no foundation on which to substantiate his claim, he quickly shuns the obvious and returns to his initial perception of infidelity. Whenever family members or friends attempt to invalidate his suspicions, he discredits their input and believes that they have entered into a conspiracy with his spouse.

To the batterer with a paranoid personality disorder, the need to substantiate his claims is not of primary importance. Even when his spouse has unequivocal proof that his allegations are incorrect, he disregards the facts, while searching for "hidden" evidence.[39] In the search, he inevitably proves to himself that his initial suspicions were true. It is then, if not before, that he goes into a violent tirade in which he beats and batters his victim until she is bruised, broken, and sometimes dead.

Perhaps one of the most misleading perceptions of the news media and the criminal justice system is that the murder of one's wife is a "crime of passion." Media accounts often report that this batterer kills his spouse after claiming that she was having an adulterous affair. A defense attorney often tries to justify such a murder by arguing that the male's actions occurred because his client found out that she was having an extramarital relationship. "After all," one lawyer said, "we can all understand how a man can lose his cool over an issue of infidelity."

The phrase "crime of passion" tends to legitimize such a homicide. It certainly minimizes the male's actions and responsibility for the murder. Criminal law dictates that if a murder is found to have been committed in a spontaneous manner, it is often reduced to manslaughter. While the words "crime of passion" may suggest some level of spontaneity, many such murders are committed by men who have stalked, contemplated, and even planned their act well before its occurrence. These acts are not committed by normal individuals who spontaneously explode with unbridled passion. They are often committed by men who are paranoid and have other disorders, and who premeditate their actions long before they carry them out. They are perpetrated by men whose pathological jealousy and associated character traits drive them to commit some of the most grotesque and unthinkable crimes imaginable. All in the name of love. All in the name of passion.

This male's suspicious nature is not limited to his spouse. He is chronically hypervigilant, always scanning his environment for hidden agendas.[40] For example, if his boss orders a job study because of cost overruns, he perceives that the study is focused primarily on him and feels intimidated and threatened. When he passes a group of co-workers who are conversing, he may feel that they are talking about his poor work performance. When his family sits down to have a cup of coffee, he discreetly focuses on their conversation in an attempt to validate his suspicions that they are encouraging his spouse to leave him.

In practically everything he sees, he perceives a hidden meaning and views the outside world as one that is hostile.[41] In interpersonal relationships, he is somewhat reclusive and feels that others are conspiring or trying to take advantage of him. He generally trusts no one, and, when it appears that he does trust some people, he will analyze their actions for potential clues to their "true intentions." No matter how much his friends and family try to convince him that his perceptions are wrong, he intensely and narrowly searches for validation of his suspicions, with absolutely no appreciation of the total context of the situation.[42] He then disregards the facts that do not support his original claims and extracts those pieces of his investigation that do. In his jaded hypervigilance, even with the weakest of evidence, he is always able to prove to himself that his original allegations were warranted and correct. Through his paranoid demeanor, the validity of a situation is not important to his final conclusion. In his distorted perception, his initial definition of a situation always overrides his need for factual substantiation. The outcome of his inquiry always relates to the way in which it was originally defined.[43]

An interview that took place between a paranoid batterer and a New Orleans parole officer clearly illustrates this male's suspicious and hypervigilant nature. Although it was his sixth criminal offense for beating his wife, from the moment that he stepped into the courtroom he began suggesting that the officer had a sexual interest in his spouse. Through his warped perception, he was able to totally discount the parole officer's role as a court officer and legal advocate for his battered spouse.

On his third trip to court for screening and a pretrial hearing, the defendant began verbally accusing the parole officer of having a romantic interest in his spouse. Although she had been hospitalized as a result of the latest beating, he had difficulty believing that someone would be interested in his wife without sexual intent. While he was assured that the court took a great amount of time and interest in all cases of domestic violence, he remained unimpressed and continued to challenge the officer regarding his "true intentions." His wife explained that she had previously tried to get others to assist in her plight, but that her husband always viewed their intrusions with jealous rage.

Because of the paranoid batterer's fear that his environment and the people with whom he interacts are hostile and out to exploit him, he is generally tense, rigid, and on his guard. He frequently misreads the intentions of others and continuously prepares to counterattack those who present a perceived threat.[44] When confronted with his incorrect perception, he is quick to rationalize the facts in an attempt to absolve himself of blame for his actions and misguided opinions. When the confrontation concerns the beating of his spouse, he rationalizes, denies, minimizes, and externalizes his behavior. He always tries to justify his aggressive behavior by proclaiming that he was provoked by some external occurrence.

Within his guarded hypervigilance, the paranoid personality is also an intensely cold and emotionally shallow individual who has great difficulty in any expression of warm and gentle feelings.[45] Even within his primary family, the paranoid batterer is on his guard and perpetually poised to take the defensive. In intimate relationships, he does not have the ability to love. While his dramatic jealousy may give an outward appearance of caring for his victim, he is actually a pathological predator who stalks and beats his spouse with a total absence of blame, remorse, or concern.

The Obsessive-Compulsive Batterer

The battered woman often describes her attacker as someone who is obsessed with the issues of structure, order, and trivial detail.[46] She describes a man whose routine compliance to rules and procedures is so rigid and mechanical that in the field of psychiatry he is often referred to as the "human machine." This is an individual whose animated and conventional existence makes his every move a predictable one.

This Category Three batterer feels enormously insecure, whereas a sense of structure and order brings temporary relief and momentary control. An illustration of this trait is his excessive habit of making work lists.[47] When he completes fifteen of the twenty items on his weekly list of things to do, he derives a sense of order and control over his environment. While his recognition that he accomplished 75 percent of all that he set out to do may give him a sense of accomplishment, his preoccupation with insignificant detail inevitably leaves his most important objectives incomplete.[48]

His apprehension and indecisiveness in addressing his primary issues of concern are rooted in a deep fear of failure and rejection. If he can exhaust all his time on repetitive and simple details, he doesn't have to take the true risks of attacking the more difficult and sophisticated tasks. He can rationalize that he did his best, and that the important objectives were not completed because of a lack of time. His obsession with insignificant details is actually an attempt to avoid a sense of failure. He recognizes that if he addresses the most simple and trivial items first, he not only feels in control, but also can avoid addressing the complete agenda, thus avoiding the possibility of failure and related emotions.

Many of his co-workers, however, view his compulsive work habits as those of someone who is organized, efficient, reliable, and effective. After all, if he spends ten hours a day pursuing insignificant issues, he always looks busy, feels busy, and is busy. When he fails to reach his major goals, he simply justifies it by saying that he had too much to do. In reality, his preoccupation with the completion of insignificant detail often results in his being a grossly inefficient and non-productive individual.[49]

It is ironic that in his intense quest and desire to be a perfectionist and to avoid shame, it is his imperfection with prioritizing that ultimately leaves him with a sense of guilt, failure, worthlessness, and frustration. These emotions smolder within a cauldron of psychological turmoil. This turmoil will inevitably be transformed into unrestrained violence and the abuse of his spouse.

The Category Three abuser's rigid obsession with rules and order transcends his normal work schedule. While he may accrue considerable vacation time, he seldom takes it. He often postpones or cancels his vacation and gives the appearance of being the company martyr. He rationalizes his resistance to the use of his leave time by claiming that he cannot afford to take time off.[50] Below the surface, however, is the innate fear that if he leaves his work station for any period of time, he may lose control or others may discover his inadequacies. He also feels that leaving his work site would place the structure and order that he has created in questionable hands. Even at the expense of his leisure time, it is a risk he is unwilling to take.

When someone with an obsessive-compulsive personality does make an attempt to participate in leisure or play, his continued preoccupation with rules, regulations, insignificant details, and performance void any pleasurable benefits that may be derived from such activities.[51] To him, playtime, particularly that of sports, is nothing more than an extension of the workplace. He cannot differentiate between playtime, leisure time, and work. His rigid demeanor and adherence to rules makes even the most pleasurable of activities extremely stressful and tense. To the obsessive-compulsive individual, playtime is not recreational in its content. It is simply a time through which to prove his self-worth or abilities to others. In fact, losing is considered a matter of great significance. It becomes a challenge to his ego and self-concept. When his esteem is adversely affected, he often responds with aggression and rage.

A good example of this rigid compliance to rules and the inability to enjoy a sport for its recreational content can be seen in the story of a man who participated in a weekly bowling league. While other team members bowled simply to have fun, he was never able to relax or enjoy himself. From the first frame of each game, he would become intensely engrossed in a need to win. When his team won, he was euphoric, but when they lost, he became passive-aggressive and would not speak to anyone for the remainder of the night. Every ball that he threw was thrown with vengeance. Even his bowling style was rigid and tense.

On one particular night, as the team entered its final frame, his wife noticed that the computer had made a mistake. It had given them the win. If corrected, they would lose by three pins. All the players knew that he had noticed the error, and it was suggested that he would ignore it in an attempt to take the win. The team believed that his compulsion to win would supersede his ability to be honest. His wife felt that he would acknowledge the error and concede. "After all," she explained, "rules are rules, and his rigid compliance to them would cause him to acknowledge the error and concede to failure." A couple of moments later, looking disgusted and stressed, he corrected the mistake and took the loss. While his teammates were surprised at his response, his wife smiled and reiterated that his compliance to rules was absolute, even at the expense of losing. He looked devastated and did not speak for the rest of the night.

Another illustration of someone with an obsessive-compulsive personality is the balding middle-aged man who attended Little League baseball games. The man was obnoxiously dogmatic and rigid. He would routinely and aggressively challenge every call that the umpire made. When his son would swing at the ball and miss, he would stand up and scream at the boy, yelling that he was holding his bat incorrectly. When his son hit the ball but got called out before making it to the base, he violently scolded the child for not running fast enough. On one occasion, when his son was playing right field and missed a pop fly and allowed a run to score, the man screamed at the boy, left the ball park, and drove away in his car. Other parents tried to comfort the child as he left the field and cried. Two games later, the guy was permanently ejected from the park after arguing and physically threatening a coach over a rule dispute.

Although the leisure time and workplace of the person with an obsessive-compulsive personality may be grossly and adversely affected by his rigid and mechanical behavior, he often parlays his organizational skills into becoming highly educated. Of the six personality disorders discussed, those who are obsessive-compulsive are most likely to become educated. It is not that they are more intelligent than others; they simply possess greater abilities to follow the structures laid down by academic institutions. While the personal lives of those who are antisocial, narcissistic, and histrionic are often in constant chaos, the lifestyle of the obsessive-compulsive person is highly organized and rigidly focused. As a result, he is the most likely of the batterers to graduate from a university. A diploma propels him into professions of status, credibility, and virtual non-detection.

A primary danger of the obsessive-compulsive personality is his ability to enter, acquire, and maintain professional positions of relative power and control. His deep-seated insecurity and sense of inadequacy often prompt him to pursue careers in the military, law enforcement, political, or legal professions. Once he enters such professions, he uses his professional status as a means of eluding detection or responsibility for the abuse of his wife. If he should be exposed, these positions provide him with a buffer from standard consequences.

How many police officers would arrest a fellow officer for the abuse of his spouse? How many prosecutors would prosecute another lawyer? How many judges would incarcerate a fellow judge? When a Category Three batterer enters one of these professions, as many who are obsessive-compulsive do, he immediately establishes credibility and power that enable him to avoid the traditional consequences levied on less powerful men.

It is his ability to enter the mainstream strata of society that makes this man elusively dangerous. Professional positions or the appearance of professionalism establishes immediate credibility through the use of symbols. It is his clever use of these symbols that enhance his chances of avoiding responsibility for his behavior. An individual's mode of dress, the car he drives, the neighborhood in which he lives, the job he holds, and even his body language relay unspoken messages to those around him.

A perspective in sociology called symbolic interactionism helps to clarify this process. Sociologists argue that all forms of exchange, both verbal and nonverbal, involve interpretation of symbols. The symbols, whether actions, words, objects, or dress, define reality for the participants. Accordingly, the police are more likely to be suspicious of a poorly dressed black male driving an older car than a well-dressed white male driving a new Mercedes. The symbols communicate and define the reality of the event for police.

The manner in which symbols work is simple. How we react or respond to others is often based solely on our perception of who they are. Such perceptions are generally based on our psychic and visual inspection of the other person's inventory of personal qualities and characteristics. For example, if a district attorney defines a defendant who has been charged with spousal abuse as someone who does not look like a wife beater, the odds are that the D.A. will not prosecute. On the other hand, if the same prosecutor defines an individual who has been charged with the same offense as someone who looks like an abuser, the odds are greater that the accused will be prosecuted for his crime. Given the same facts and the same evidence, the defendant with the least number of positive symbols is always at a greater disadvantage than his more affluent-looking counterpart. This is why a seasoned defense attorney tells his client to appear before a judge or jury in coat and tie, cleanshaven, and, when speaking on his own behalf, to select his words carefully and non-defensively. The attorney knows that if his client utilizes symbols which project maturity and professionalism, the facts presented by a prosecutor often become blurred.

A recently televised movie based on a true story illustrates how symbols can dramatically impact the decision of a court and its affiliated systems. The victim featured in the movie had appeared before a court on many occasions, pleading for protection from a husband she described as dangerously brutal. While enough evidence existed to support her claims of physical abuse, he always presented himself in a dignified, articulate, and professional manner. Subsequently, he was always released with virtually no action taken. Following an incident in which the physical abuse was undeniably severe, the judge finally ordered him held in a local hospital for a psychiatric evaluation.

During the psychiatric interview, however, the defendant, again appearing articulate and professional, began to discuss his hobbies and interests with the examining psychiatrist. The doctor, realizing that both he and the defendant shared many of the same interests, had great difficulty in ignoring symbols and concentrating on the facts. After the brief interview, the doctor saw no reason why the defendant shouldn't be allowed a pass to leave the hospital temporarily. Upon his release, he immediately entered his wife's residence and murdered her with a large knife. By the time he was finished, he had stabbed his victim thirty to forty times.

To the average individual, domestic violence directed at a spouse is incomprehensible. To a judge, prosecutor, or other court employee, the depth and magnitude of what is heard each day is difficult to fully grasp. Victims relate how they are knocked down stairs in late stages of pregnancy and how jagged objects are rammed up their vaginas. They testify how loaded guns are held to their heads and to the heads of their children. They describe how severed lips, severed nipples, and finger nails are ripped from their bodies by the assailant. Crime photographs of the lifeless corpses of women and children are viewed with regularity. Still, it is difficult for law enforcement personnel to comprehend the magnitude of what they see. Perhaps this unwelcome wisdom is reserved only for those who suffer it. The fact remains, however, that such abuse becomes even more incomprehensible when the batterer not only looks like us, but sounds and acts like us as well.

I do not mean to imply that most individuals who are obsessive-compulsive reach positions of professional status and control. This is definitely not the case. Many find themselves unemployed or fill low status positions in the workplace. They may live on society's edge and can be found among the population of the homeless or in the crowded conditions of our nation's prisons. I suggest, however, that of all the Category Three batterers discussed, the one who is obsessive-compulsive is the most likely to gravitate to professions whereby his use of power, control, and symbols buffer him from the consequences of beating his wife.

Women who are married to an obsessive-compulsive mate describe their personal relationship with this male as similar to that of a military recruit and a drill sergeant. In his intimate and family relationships, as in all interpersonal interaction, he is described as controlling, demanding, overbearing, formal, and critical. His relationship with his spouse and family is anything but democratic. Instead, it is a dictatorship; one in which he has total external control. It is his way and his way alone. There is no room for compromise or negotiation. When his wife attempts to question or challenge him, he beats her. He doesn't have a spouse; he has a terrorized victim.

This military-style demeanor extends into every aspect of his marriage. He tells his spouse when to eat and when to sleep; when to wake up and when to clean house. He tells her what to cook and what not to cook. He tells her whether she can go to work or stay home. Even his sex life with her is formalized and scheduled. One woman complained that the total lack of sexual spontaneity with her husband was perhaps as painful as the physical abuse that he inflicted on her. She described how he would set aside one hour every second week on the same night to have sexual relations with her. Any attempt to interest him in sex prior to their scheduled time was fruitless. She noted that even when they had sexual relations, it was mechanical and totally devoid of intimacy or feeling. She intentionally avoided using the phrase "making love," explaining that sex had nothing to do with love. "Like everything else," she said, "it was simply something on his list of things to do."

It is not that some who are obsessive-compulsive do not occasionally feel the desire to express their innermost feelings. Many complain, however, that as they try, they become stilted and emotionally blocked. An obsessive-compulsive batterer related that certain music would stimulate his senses and emotions to a point where he felt emotionally fluid and spontaneous. However, when it came to outwardly expressing the same emotion that he felt to his wife, he became formal, rigid, and stiff. In reality, he was incapable of expressing any significant level of affection or intimacy towards family or friends.[52] One woman described this male perfectly as she told of her husband's inability to express warm emotion. "When others would cry, his eyes would always remain clear and dry. When others would hug, he always stood at a distance. When others would tell him 'I love you,' he responded by saying 'me, too.'"

The Multiple Diagnoses and Mixed Personality Disorder Batterer

A high percentage of Category Three batterers cannot be clearly diagnosed as fitting into only one of the six personality profiles described. Instead, many abusers possess several of these disorders simultaneously. Although they may possess most, if not all, of the character traits of a single disorder, investigation often reveals that they possess all the traits prevalent in a second or third disorder as well. For example, a Category Three batterer is capable of being diagnosed jointly as an antisocial, borderline, and narcissistic batterer. Any individual who is found to have two or more such profiles simultaneously is considered by the D.S.M. III (earlier version of D.S.M. IV) to have multiple diagnoses.[53] It is such a male who ultimately becomes the most chronic and dangerous of the men who physically abuse women. If a single disorder presents a significant danger to his victim, those males who possess multiple disorders are potentially the most lethal of all batterers.

Similarly, the Category Three abuser frequently has a mixed personality disorder. This disorder is determined when an individual possesses a multitude of character defects; however, the defects are not neatly grouped in any one of the diagnostic categories in sufficient numbers to constitute a specific disorder.[54] Instead, the defects are scattered across the boundaries of several of the personality disorders illustrated in the D.S.M. IV. It is a hodgepodge effect. While a certain disorder may be diagnosed when an individual displays five or six specific character defects, a mixed disorder is determined when there is a combined total of five or six traits from several different specific categories. In other words, if an individual presents with a couple of defective traits from the antisocial category, one or two from the borderline, and a couple of others from the obsessive-compulsive category, the total sum of all these will result in the batterer being categorized as having a mixed personality disorder.

While this may seem quite confusing, just remember that psychiatrists diagnose a personality disorder in the same way that medical doctors diagnose a physical illness. For example, if you went for a visit to your family practitioner complaining that you were feeling physically ill, he would ask you to describe your symptoms. If, in response, you told him that you had fever, a headache, diarrhea, muscle and joint pain, and had been vomiting, he may diagnose you with a particular strain of the flu. In other words, the total sum of several symptoms of a specific profile will result in the determination of a specific physical diagnosis. If your symptoms had been different, he may have diagnosed you as having an illness or disease of a different nature.

A psychiatrist essentially performs the same procedure. When a patient complains of significant emotional or psychosocial problems, he is asked by the doctor to describe the symptoms or problematic areas. If the patient describes a pattern of several dysfunctions and behaviors such as drug abuse, trouble with the law, frequent fights, unemployability, deceitfulness, promiscuity, disregard for others, and an inability to maintain personal relationships, he may be diagnosed as having an antisocial disorder.[55] Likewise, if he describes to the doctor emotional discomfort relating to his rigidity, inability to show affection, inability to enjoy leisure time, and the fact that he is a workaholic who gets sidetracked by trivial details, he may be more appropriately labeled as having an obsessive-compulsive personality.[56]

In essence, the psychiatrist uses the same tools and methods in determining her patient's illness as does the internist. She develops a profile from the patient's combined symptoms to establish the type of illness that the patient possesses. In the area of personality disorders, if the patient has several well-defined character traits that fall within the boundaries of a single category, he will be diagnosed as having a single specific disorder. If the patient has several well-defined traits that fall within the boundaries of one disorder and, upon further investigation, numerous additional traits that fall within the boundaries of a second, it may be determined that he has multiple disorders. And finally, if the patient has only one or two traits from several of the disorders described in the D.S.M. IV, he may be diagnosed with a mixed personality disorder.

CHAPTER V

Characteristics of the Category Three Abuser

It is the multiple diagnoses and the mixed personality disorders described in the D.S.M. III that help explain the great number of common traits shared by most Category Three batterers, irrespective of their primary disorders. While there are six personality disorders of the Category Three abuser, all of which involve unique traits and behaviors of their own, there are also a large number of common traits that are prevalent in almost all chronic batterers. Although the various disorders may aid you in focusing on an abuser's specific profile, there are a host of characteristics that are common to all. This chapter is a discussion of common traits and behaviors that are shared by the majority of these males. In addition to many common psychological traits, there are a host of behavioral patterns and actions that are universally shared by the Category Three abuser.

The repetitive nature of a victim's testimony leads one to sense that the chronic batterer's behaviors and actions are often premeditated. In case after case, testimony relates how the defendant broke the woman's windshield and slashed the tires on her car. The victim describes how he entered her home through the bedroom window, beat her, destroyed her furniture, and left through the front door. Claims of telephone harassment, pulling of weapons, threats of murder-suicide, biting, childlike tantrums, and stalking are repeated so frequently that an experienced prosecutor becomes capable of foreseeing a victim's testimony prior to its disclosure. While the ruthlessness of the behaviors of the Category Three abuser is striking, so is the repetitiveness of their occurrence.

Since this male's patterns are directly related to the disorder that he possesses, one can predict with accuracy the continuation of his actions. A victim's safety is based on the support and protection that the police and court systems are willing to provide. He beat her before the police arrived and will batter her after they leave. He pursued her before the court intervened and will stalk her afterwards. This is unless the courts are willing to threaten him with incarceration if he persists in terrorizing his victim and are also willing to immediately imprison him when it continues. Judicial support is an essential element of controlling this male's behavior while his victim is attempting to terminate her involvement with him. Otherwise, his behavioral and psychological patterns are so methodical and absolute that she has no hope of escaping his relentless control.

The severity and scope of the traits that are listed in this section correlate closely to the degree of the male's diagnosis. The farther the male is to the right of the Batterer's Continuum, the greater is the probability that his actions will continue. While the judicial system may find itself successful in forcing the chronic batterer into leaving his current victim alone, it is only a matter of time until he finds another. Although the advocates of treatment for the batterer may use this issue to further their cause, the fact remains that the Category Three batterer is not treatable and must be held accountable for his ruthless crimes.

Any woman who is planning to enter into such a relationship, or who may have already entered, should be advised to study these characteristics with vigilance. Many of the traits described within the profile of the Category Three abuser emerge very early in a relationship. In many instances they become apparent on the first date. These traits should act as red flags, as warning signals. They should alert a woman against the dangers that may lurk deep in the shadows of the relationship. A woman should never rationalize that this batterer will modify his behavior or that things will improve once she is married. The possibility that a Category Three abuser will change is almost non-existent.

While many of the characteristics described in this section may also be part of the six profiles previously discussed, the liberty of listing them again is taken to illustrate the elusiveness of the profile boundaries. When a woman recognizes that her intimate partner possesses multiple traits of the Category Three batterer, it is imperative that she acknowledge the enormous risk factors. To ignore such characteristics and warning signs places her in great danger.

Psychological-Emotional Commonalities

Denial/Minimizations

The depth of the Category Three batterer's denial system is extreme. His denial is of such magnitude that he instinctively convinces himself and others that he is not responsible for his victim's injuries. It is difficult to understand how a man, after being arrested several times for savagely beating his wife, can disavow personal blame for his actions. But he does.

However, the majority of all chronic batterers who possess lengthy criminal records for domestic violence fully deny responsibility for their behavior. A multiple offender, who had been booked six times in four months for attacking his wife, denied the assaults by claiming that his spouse always overreacted during verbal altercations. When noted that each time his wife appeared in court she had cuts, abrasions, and bruises to her face and body, he countered by saying that she was clumsy and frequently fell. Another defendant, who had more than twelve domestic arrests in as many months, claimed that he frequently had trouble with his neighbors who called the police and reported a domestic disturbance as a means of retaliation. When it was argued that his wife was taken to a hospital emergency room after the last incident, he suggested that she was injured by one of the neighbors during a scuffle.

While much of the denial is an obvious attempt to avoid the consequences of violent behavior, it is amazing how capable the Category Three abuser is of shunning responsibility for his behavior and of blaming others, including his victim, for her injuries. It is difficult to grasp how a man can shatter his wife's face and torso with his fist while threatening her with a loaded gun, and then deny that it ever took place.

Tied closely to his denial is his uncanny ability to minimize the obvious. While his victim's injuries may be severe or disabling, he inevitably reduces the attack to a minor occurrence. After one defendant was shown that his wife had suffered a serious spinal injury and a broken shoulder in the assault, he insisted that he hit her only once. He noted that she sustained the injuries after slipping and falling over a coffee table. When challenged by prosecutors with evidence that he had also held a knife to her throat, he responded by saying that it was only a small pocketknife. Another defendant who beat his victim unconscious with a metal pipe, leaving fifteen to twenty large linear-shaped bruises across most of her arms, legs, and back, insisted that he had struck her only twice. One batterer, after being arrested for pulling and discharging a loaded revolver into the bed where his wife slept, asserted that it was just "a small broken gun" that accidentally fired when he dropped it.

There is not a chronic batterer who does not deny or grossly minimize his responsibility for the injuries that he inflicts on his victim. If confronted by limited evidence, he firmly denies. When confronted with absolute evidence, he simply minimizes.

Rationalization/Externalization

Without hesitation, this male always externalizes the reasons why he batters his spouse. He cunningly convinces himself and others that he was provoked by his spouse or circumstances beyond his control.

His ability to externalize his aggressive behavior is also reinforced by those around him who quickly search for superficial reasons to explain his violent rage. As stated earlier, the news media are perhaps one of the greatest offenders of this issue. While the batterer rationalizes that his attack was caused by his children's misbehavior, his wife's unjust refusal to follow his dictates, her alleged infidelity, or financial problems, the press reports such claims as fact. While he blames his violence on job stress, personal grief, self-defense, and so on, such excuses are reinforced by those around him. These enabling responses not only tend to justify his violence, they also perpetuate it.

Even when the attacks of a Category Three batterer are nearly fatal, he attempts to justify his actions by blaming others. "She made me do it by running around on me." Following the validation that she has not been unfaithful to him, he may further assert, "She was thinking about doing it. Any man who would let his wife mess around on him is a fool."

Lack of Remorse/Empathy

It is frightening to witness the lack of remorse that the chronic batterer often displays following the beating of his spouse. His absolute detachment and chilling lack of empathy following a beating, particularly when he has murdered his victim, are shocking. His absence of remorse is not only real, it is intense.

While the Category Three batterer's inability to feel remorse may be difficult to understand, it is symptomatic of his personality disorder and his inability to bond. If he cannot bond with his spouse, he cannot sense her pain.

Inability to Love/Inability to Bond

Research reflects that most men who chronically abuse intimate partners were raised in domestic war zones. As infants and young children, they were reared in hostile environments, in which emotional and physical violence were the norm. Instead of feeling safe, they felt threatened. Instead of feeling secure, they felt distressed. Instead of love, they experienced rejection. Instead of learning trust, they learned apprehension and vigilance.

Domestic war zones are incubators for future violence. Early childhood experiences riddled with emotional deprivation are breeding grounds for instability. We cannot expect young boys who are raised in dysfunctional homes where they are abused or where they watch their mother being abused to grow up to bond with others. If you cannot trust daddy, whom can you trust? The fact is, if you destroy the bonding stage of a child's life, you destroy the child. You also destroy his ability to bond as an adult. Instead, he becomes a predator; a stalker; a batterer who is without a conscience.

In his attempt to love, the chronic batterer finds himself emotionally impotent. He is incapable of respecting or responding to the needs of his mate. In fact, he is incapable of loving at all. What some may perceive as love is simply a pathological dependency on his mate. The batterer controls and possesses his intimate partner; he dominates and absorbs his spouse; her only relevance lies in how she can pacify and quench his many needs. This is not love. In the art of loving, the batterer is hopelessly derelict.

The inability of a chronic batterer to bond was clearly exhibited by a young man of twenty who sat in his counselor's office and wept like a child. He revealed that he had struck his wife with a wooden leg from a broken chair. He described how he had struck her several times as she lay on the bedroom floor bleeding profusely from her forehead. She begged him to stop, but he kept beating her. After she lost consciousness, he hesitantly rushed her to a nearby hospital. It was discovered that the blows to her head had caused organic brain damage. The doctor told him that his nineteen-year-old wife, mother of two young sons, would suffer permanent paralysis and confinement to a wheelchair.

As the man continued to weep, the therapist discussed the batterer's feelings concerning the hideous act that he had committed. After two hours of dialogue, it became obvious that his tears were not of remorse. He was not weeping because of the pain and suffering that he had inflicted on his wife. He did not feel any degree of guilt or grief concerning the devastating results of his terrible act. He cried because he thought that his wife would leave him, that he would lose his possession. His two-hour conversation with his counselor was totally devoid of concern about his wife's welfare and well-being.

In his book *The Art of Loving*, Erich Fromm describes love as a relationship in which each partner equally respects the other in an atmosphere of sharing and mutual concern. He further asserts that love involves partners who look out for one another's well-being. Love is a relationship with integrity and respect.[57] It is an emotional bond whereby neither party intentionally exploits or brings harm to the other.

It goes without saying that the batterer does not fit this description. Instead of respecting his mate, he ridicules and scorns her. Instead of sharing, he dominates; instead of protecting her from harm, he viciously strikes and bruises her body. It is not a relationship with integrity; it is one of indignity and pain.

Fromm also suggests that the ability to love has become a lost art for many people in today's society. What many may perceive as love is simply a relationship built upon a foundation of domination and submission.[58] A relationship devoid of equity and integrity. A one-sided and nonreciprocal relationship in which one partner controls the other.

Fromm further claims that the most powerful emotional need of an individual is to feel a sense of interpersonal fusion,[59] a need to feel one and whole with someone else. We generally attempt to fulfill this desire by developing a truly loving relationship with another. This need is best fulfilled in a family unit where love and integrity exist and where the man, woman, and child are all capable of mutually loving, sharing, and respecting each other. The sense of oneness that can be achieved through such a process is perhaps the most important psychological need of a human being. When that need is met, one usually achieves stability in other areas of life. When it is not, an individual's life generally appears to be in distress and turmoil.[60]

Unfortunately, many relationships tend to acquire a false sense of oneness through self-destructive means. The Category Three batterer best exemplifies this pattern. During the course of his relationship, he will come to completely dominate his mate. He rarely seeks to develop a relationship with an independent woman. Instead, he generally seeks those who exhibit dependent or submissive traits. The batterer will usually create a relationship with a woman he can absorb and control. If his mate attempts to become independent from him, he intimidates her back into dependency. If she tries to acquire her own identity, he destroys it by verbally and physically attacking her ego, self-esteem, and self-image. He absorbs her to the point of having her relate to the outside world only through him.

Fromm suggests that in such a relationship, both partners are seeking a sense of oneness. He dominates, she submits; it becomes a process of pseudo-symbiosis. The batterer absorbs the woman like a sponge absorbs water. Through such a disturbingly destructive relationship, both partners acquire a false sense of oneness, which fades as quickly as water evaporates.

Emotional Intensity

If asked to list a primary trait of the Category Three abuser that attracts his partner to him, it would be the emotional intensity that he projects to those around him. While he may be a social parasite and misfit, he is often anything but dull. He frequently lives on society's edge, always trying desperately to belong. In doing so, the Category Three batterer can be very stimulating within the context of interpersonal relationships.

It is this trait that perhaps best explains the great attraction and admiration that I had for one of my uncles when I was a small boy. I can still recall my outings with him in vivid detail. I remember riding in his car at high rates of speed and jumping from bridges with him into deep areas of a lake. I recall walking with him across a train trestle and clinging dangerously to its side as the train passed. This uncle shared his food and beer with me. He also shared his craziness. It was exciting to be with him. He was intense. In fact, he was less like an uncle and more like a playmate.

In retrospect, however, I now realize that his traits and behaviors reflected a personality disorder. I have since learned that he frequently assaulted my aunt during the days when battered women stayed in the closet. He was also a man who lived on society's edge. In a predawn fog, he was killed when his speeding car struck a large tree. It is believed that he was under the influence of alcohol at the time of the accident. While my uncle's explosions of intensity brought him periodic pockets of life, it eventually brought him the finality of death.

The fact that relatively normal and well-adjusted women frequently find themselves involved with batterers who have personality disorders must be explained. Isn't it possible that the male's intensity triggers their response? There are certainly many other variables that create chemistry between men and women in these relationships. The batterer's emotional intensity, particularly early in the relationship, however, is a significant trait that cannot be denied. A badly battered newlywed summed it up perfectly when she said, "He was the most exciting man that I ever met. He was so much fun until he shot me. My friends told me that he was dangerous and would hurt me, but I guess I was blinded by his stimulating qualities."

Feelings of Inadequacy, Low Self-Esteem, Depression, Mood Swings

The Category Three abuser has extremely low self-esteem and feels intensely inadequate. On the surface, he may project the appearance of being self-confident and grandiose. If you scratch below the surface, however, you find a man with a terrible self-image and a significant sense of inferiority.

While the identity disturbance of the borderline personality helps explain why severe mood swings are exhibited by some of these males, a deep sense of inadequacy, prevalent in almost all Category Three batterers, may further explain the spontaneous mood swings exhibited by others with a borderline personality.

After all, while many of these males get depressed because they do not know who they are, others who possess some level of identity simply do not like what they see. The Category Three batterer generally possesses significant dislike for himself. His poor self-image is frequently transformed into feelings of insecurity, depression, and anger. These feelings often result in acts of aggression and violence.

It is perhaps these simple dynamics that explain the spontaneous rage that many Category Three abusers exhibit. As previously discussed, most of the male's explosive behavior is related to internal emotional conflicts. Much of this turmoil is in direct correlation to the low opinion that he has of himself. External triggering agents such as stress, failure, and criticism act as catalysts in releasing his anger and transferring it into aggression. Hence, a low self-image has the distinct ability to come out sideways in the form of rage and violence, particularly that of spousal abuse.

A woman described how her husband's transformation from a relatively normal mood into rage always seemed associated with times in which he had been personally criticized or challenged. She noted how he would take criticism, even when it was constructive, and internalize it to the point of becoming quiet, withdrawn, and sullen. As his depressed state deepened, he would explode into violent rage, beating not only her, but the kids as well. His sensitivity to criticism became so overwhelming that following a reprimand from his boss, she and her kids fled their home moments before he took a gun, placed it into his mouth, and pulled the trigger. Following his suicide, she cried and confided that she realized his death was the only way out for him. "His sense of inadequacy was so severe," she said, "that his life had to be more painful than his death. It is something that he confronted every hour of each day. Now he is at peace and so are we."

Dependency, Possessiveness, Jealousy

Although this male generally does not exhibit the number of character traits necessary to constitute a dependent personality disorder, his dependency on his mate is pathetically severe. His attachment to his spouse is similar to that of a young child to its mother. While the child looks to the mother to have its emotional and physical needs met on demand, so this batterer looks upon his wife.

He is an individual who never let go of his umbilical cord. He has carried it over his shoulder since birth, always seeking to attach it to an unsuspecting victim. After it is attached, the woman finds it almost impossible to sever. If she does, he forcibly reattaches it to her again and again, sapping her fragile identity. Should she be successful in permanently removing it from her torso, or should he find that she has nothing left to feed on, he quickly drapes the cord over his shoulder and seeks another victim to exploit. When the timing is right, he pulls the cord from his shoulder and implants it into the belly of his new prey.

While the woman's dependency on the batterer may appear to be overwhelmingly intense, there may be nothing more intense than the dependency that he has for his victim. This dependency is deeply rooted in his personality disorder. The batterer is obsessed with the physical presence of his spouse, and when she is absent, he experiences intense feelings of uncertainty and isolation. During periods of estrangement, his dependency often results in blatant acts of stalking and physical violence. It is his pathological dependency that warrants his victim to acquire a strong support system before she flees. If she does not, the intense emotional ties that the batterer has for his partner will inevitably force her back into submission, or they may even result in injury or death. The learned helplessness of the battered woman, coupled with the chronic dependency of her abuser, is a very dangerous combination.

The Category Three abuser also displays pathological levels of possessiveness and jealousy. He possesses his spouse in the same manner that he lays legal claims to his car, his home, and other personal property. He sees her as a possession that no one has the right to take away. In his attempt to maintain control, he tries desperately to isolate her from family, friends, and even distant acquaintances. If he keeps her isolated from potential support systems, he avoids the impact and influence of those who can help her escape.

If the victim of a Category Three abuser tries to escape his control, he pursues her in an effort to retrieve what he perceives as his. An example of this trait is a defendant who was facing a jail term for the relentless stalking of his former wife. When reprimanded by the judge and the prosecutor, he dogmatically replied, "This is my wife and no one, absolutely no one, has the right to keep me away from her." During the time that he was awaiting sentencing, he was re-arrested after kidnaping her at gunpoint in an attempt at forced reconciliation. During his arraignment on new felony charges, he reasserted his position that she belonged to him and that the court had no right to interfere. Although he was sentenced to a lengthy jail sentence in both cases, as he was being ushered away in shackles by two deputies he arrogantly reminded the court that she was his. Two years later, he pursued her immediately upon his release. He was later charged with her murder.

The chronic batterer's jealousy should never be confused with that of a normal male or a Category One abuser. Instead, it is a pathological trait that serves as a trigger to many of the savage beatings that he inflicts on his victim. In many instances his jealous rage is a prerequisite to murder. It is most unfortunate that many women view this male's jealous nature as flattering evidence that he cares. In actuality, it is only a measure of his psychopathology.

In an effort to inhibit his rage, he needs to be continuously reassured that he is not losing his spouse to someone else. When she is away from him, even for insignificant periods of time, he interrogates her as to her whereabouts. If he calls her on the phone and she does not answer, he demands a detailed explanation of her absence. If her phone is busy, he demands to know to whom she was speaking. He inquires not only of her current social activities and personal relationships, he interrogates her about her past. He intimidates and pressures her into discussing her former boyfriends, their dating habits, and even past sexual intimacies with men. When she is coaxed into sharing her most intimate secrets, although he promised not to get angry, he beats her while in a jealous rage.

The Category Three abuser is jealous of everyone. He demands more than her disassociation with men. He also resents her relationships with parents and family members. He is particularly defensive of personal friendships that she may develop with girlfriends. He knows that such friends may influence his spouse's decision to leave him. To reiterate, the jealousy is not a normal reaction to potential loss. Instead, it is the pathological reaction of a malignant disorder.

Emotional Dominance

The profile of the chronic batterer is one of relentless domination. His intimidating and dogmatic demeanor assures him a position of leverage and control. It is utilized to guarantee him the primary role in a relationship filled with gross inequities.

The Category Three abuser is intolerant of disagreement and firmly believes that any resistance or misbehavior should result in severe consequences.[61] In discussions with his spouse, there is absolutely no room for negotiation or compromise. It is his way and his way alone. When he speaks, he expects her to listen. He does not want her opinion and will rarely ask for it. He expects his spouse to follow his orders and dictates without apprehension or hesitation. She learns early in the relationship that any challenge to his authority provokes a physically aggressive and violent response. To challenge his demands without first developing adequate support systems places her in a position of potential danger.

Within his dogmatic demeanor, he is a rigid traditionalist. He is a sexist who firmly believes that the distribution of power within an intimate relationship should heavily favor the male. While this trait may also be shared by many American males, researchers have found that batterers are significantly more conservative in their views.[62] He sees himself as a dominant patriarch, as the infallible ruler of a totalitarian relationship. He views any challenge to his position as intrusive and unacceptable, and he perceives a woman's right to co-exist relative to how she can serve his needs. All chronic batterers feel that a woman's place in a relationship is relegated to that of a caretaker. As far as the abuser is concerned, a woman is to cater to his emotional and physical needs. She is to take care of his sexual and physical desires. When he demands sex, she is to provide it. When he wants to be fed, she is to feed him. When he is down and out, she is to assist him financially. When he is in need of a place to stay, she is to provide shelter. When he needs emotional support, she is to support him. When he is incarcerated for his misdeeds, she is to rescue him. She is his servant; she is his slave. When she does not provide those things that he demands, he beats her in violent retaliation.

Unfortunately, this male's sexist views are often reinforced by the woman's enabling responses. The battered woman frequently tries to improve her relationship or to minimize her beatings by ignoring, justifying, and rationalizing her assailant's shortcomings. She spends much of her time trying to justify his beatings, insulating him from consequences. When he goes on a drunk, she doctors him to sobriety. When he misses work as a result of a hangover, she calls his boss with fabricated excuses. When he has no money, she borrows and gives it to him. When he is arrested for his beatings, she often drops the charges because she doesn't want to hurt him. When she fails to accommodate him, she experiences a profound sense of guilt and fear. He is keenly aware of her instinctive guilt and knows how to push her buttons. He knows when to use intimidation or self-pity. He knows when to use affection or fear. He is a shrewd navigator of premeditated strategies that are designed to extract what he desires.

The dominance of the Category Three abuser extends into all primary aspects of his partner's life. He controls her emotionally, sexually, socially, occupationally, and financially. A victim frequently reports that when she considers physical and emotional abuse as one, it is apparent that the attacks by her assailant are perpetual. Prior to, during, following, and between his physical attacks, he assaults her ego, identity, and self-esteem to the extent that his verbal attacks are as painful as the physical. His emotional assaults range from subtle sarcasm to overt verbal intimidation of harm and death.

A disturbing number of battered women also report that they are forced into sexual relations with their husbands immediately after being severely beaten. This act should not be misconstrued as an act of contrition or remorse. Instead, it is nothing less than rape. It is sexual violence. It is a further attempt to humiliate and dominate her. A victim stated that she knew never to resist her husband's sexual attacks. "Resistance," she said, "would only provoke more beatings. When he forced me into having sex, he would call me a 'bitch' or a 'whore' and always remind me that I was no good. I almost believed him."

His dominance of her social activities and related associations are also well calculated. If he can limit her interaction with others and restrict her physical movements, he knows that her ability to develop support systems will be significantly limited. He knows that the fewer resources she has, the fewer chances there are of escaping his control. A woman testified that her batterer made it a point never to buy a second family car. While he could well afford another vehicle, he did not want her to have such mobility. He also kept both sets of car keys in his pocket, even when he slept. When she requested use of the car, he always interrogated her as to where she was going, why, and how long she would be gone. She found it less intimidating to take the bus.

Finally, the batterer's dominance over his mate's occupation or career is well-known to his victim. Exceptions to the rule of occupational control by the batterer generally occur when the woman's job is paramount to the immediate financial needs of the abuser. Otherwise, his restriction of her working outside the home is a calculated attempt to isolate and control. The Category Three abuser is very aware that a woman without resources is a woman without alternatives.

No Insight, No Motivation, Non-Therapeutic

His lack of insight into his anger and related aggression makes the Category Three abuser a clinical nightmare. His inability to understand why he batters his spouse leaves him not only unmotivated to change, but non-therapeutic as well.

This batterer has tremendous difficulty in understanding or verbally articulating his feelings of inner turmoil. He is incapable of comprehending the many emotions that generate his sense of rage. He is unable to distinguish among guilt, hurt, inadequacy, and grief. He cannot separate feelings of anxiety, stress, failure, and rejection. Instead of focusing on each emotion for its own roots, he simply confuses and groups them together into the single emotion of anger. He does not see that each has distinct etiologies and qualities of its own. Unlike those who are capable of understanding their emotional conflicts and are able to address them in healthy and productive ways, the batterer's conflicts always come out aggressively in destructive and damaging acts.

His lack of insight into his internal conflicts not only inhibits him from appropriately addressing feelings of rage, it also prevents him from assuming responsibility for his actions. He always justifies his violence citing provocation. If he does not understand his aggression, it is easier to blame someone or something else. It is easier to externalize his violence. It is more palatable to blame his assaults on his wife's infidelity than to leave such assaults unexplained.

An informal study with a group of males that had pled guilty to the beating of their wives illustrates the dramatic lack of insight chronic batterers have into the roots of their aggression.[63] In a sample of forty abusers, each one was asked to give a single explanation of the reason for their beatings. While all the men rationalized and minimized their violence, thirty-nine specifically cited external reasons for their rage. The other one simply stated, "I was too drunk to remember." It is worth noting that not one of the forty interviewed cited an emotional or internal reason for his abuse. There was not a single defendant who possessed insight into the actual origin of his violence.

The Category Three abuser is not only devoid of insight, he also has no motivation to change. For an individual to want to modify dysfunctional behavior, he must first recognize and acknowledge that he has a problem. Instead of admitting that he is responsible for his rage, the batterer spends his entire life blaming others.

As a result of his lack of insight and related denial, the chronic batterer is rarely motivated to seek help for his violent behavior. While he may shed tears or display what appears to be remorse, a closer review always suggests that the tears are nothing more than premeditated manipulation. He tries to manipulate a spouse who is preparing to flee the relationship. He tries to influence a court system that is prepared to incarcerate him. When his wife returns and the court dictates are lifted, however, the inevitable occurs. He quickly withdraws from therapy and resumes his abuse.

While there is a strong movement to provide treatment for domestic abusers, it must be recognized that the Category Three abuser is beyond clinical intervention. As stated before, almost all chronic abusers have personality disorders. Many are considered to have multiple disorders. Closely allied with the disorder is the problem of substance abuse. It is well known within the mental health field that the prognosis for such individuals is very poor. The prognosis for a chronic batterer who has multiple disorders with a dual diagnosis of alcoholism must therefore be less than very poor. These factors, along with a total lack of motivation and insight, present an impossible case scenario for even the most trained therapist.

The promotion of counseling for these males, particularly when they face and try to avoid prosecution for their crimes, is one of the most abused and misused defense strategies practiced by attorneys who represent the batterers' interests. Not only are these males beyond treatment, but such advocacy also gives false hope to the victim and often leads to reconciliation and the continuation of the cycle of family violence. The termination of the relationship, not therapeutic intervention for the male, should be the primary focus. The life of a woman or her child may depend on it.

Perhaps the only optimistic observation that can be made regarding the behavior of the Category Three batterer is that he will eventually burn himself out. Like all those with personality disorders, he seems to mellow in his elder years. This usually occurs in his fifties, sometimes in his sixties. He doesn't become nice, however; he simply becomes less mean. This mellowing tends to occur in the last chapter of his life. This is generally the last chapter of his victim's life. Can she really afford to wait? Should she?

Alcohol and Substance Use or Abuse

There is a significant correlation between the use of alcohol or mind-altering drugs and the beating of one's spouse. A victim will frequently ask the court to assist the batterer in acquiring help for his drinking or drug problem. The woman is often convinced that the issues of chemical abuse and physical abuse are directly related. She is further convinced that if you eliminate the first problem, the second will automatically cease. In fact, in a sample of forty victims who were asked by a New Orleans probation officer whether they felt alcohol or drug use by their partners played a causative role in their beatings, thirty-two responded in the affirmative.[64] Ninety percent of the thirty-two also suggested that the elimination of the substance abuse problem would eliminate the physical violence.

While the association between substance and spousal abuse may be very high, alcohol and drug usage should not be misconstrued as an etiology of spousal attack. Straus notes that "at an individual level, some of the psychological attributes believed to predispose individuals to substance abuse (low self-esteem, low frustration tolerance, power needs) are similar to those believed to predispose individuals to spousal violence."[65] The fact is, substance abuse is only one of several symptoms that make up the personality disorder of the Category Three batterer. Focusing on alcohol as being the culprit in the abuse of one's spouse is like focusing on a single issue of inadequacy, jealousy, insecurity, dependency, lack of an identity, etc., as being the cause. Single traits are not the cause of such abuse. Instead, it is the cumulative effect of all symptoms that inevitably leads to an abusive male. The male does not beat his wife systematically because he is a drunk. He beats her because he has a personality disorder. To reiterate, alcohol abuse is merely a symptom of his disorder.

While it is probable that the majority of men who beat women are substance abusers, it is also just as probable that the majority of substance abusers are not batterers. In other words, alcoholics are not generally wife beaters, but wife beaters are almost always prone to substance abuse. The probability is that even in the presence of heavy drinking, spousal abuse will not occur without the existence of numerous symptoms that make up a disorder. The single issue of substance abuse, in the absence of other factors described, should not be blamed for the violence that a male inflicts on his spouse.

There is, however, a strong association between alcohol or drug usage and the potential for spousal abuse to be injurious or even fatal to its victims. While alcohol use alone is not the cause of Category Three violence, it may definitely intensify it. It is plausible to suggest that while a Category Three abuser always presents a significant danger to his victim, he is more dangerous when under the influence. If blood samples were taken of individuals charged with spousal murders, it is suggested that a disproportionate number would test positive for alcohol or drug usage.

Why is it that alcohol and drug usage further reduces the limited amount of impulse control of the Category Three abuser? Perhaps the most popular theory is that of disinhibition. Most would agree that alcohol acts as a depressant affecting the part of our brain that controls inhibition. As alcohol physiologically affects this level of functioning, our inhibitions are released and our aggressions sometimes flow. Without any level of impulse control, it is reasonable to conclude that the Category Three abuser would then act out his rage without restraint. The amount of rage that would surface may relate to the specific disorder that he possesses and the type of substance that he ingested. For example, if he has a multiple disorder and ingests both alcohol and diet pills, the possibility is that his aggression could be catastrophic.

Although it cannot be denied that there is a relationship between spousal abuse and the physiological effects of substances, such as the numbing of the inhibitions and impulse control of the batterer, this association should not be perceived as one that is singular. Straus factors in other variables as to why batterers abuse more often when they are drinking. His research suggests that aggression while consuming alcohol is a learned behavior. People learn that their behavior while under the influence will be attributed to the effects of the alcohol and not to the individual's personality characteristics. He suggests that we learn that it is acceptable to become physically aggressive when drinking and that it is also acceptable to disavow our responsibility once violence has occurred.[66] He also notes that people learn to react differently while drinking according to the context in which it takes place.[67] For example, an individual consuming the same amount of alcohol at a church wedding as in a bar would react differently because of the context in which it was consumed. At the wedding, he would be expected to "control himself," while in the bar he would be allowed to "let loose." Likewise, a batterer who is under the influence and attacks his wife at home probably would not consider doing so in the dining area of a crowded restaurant. The fact remains, he is often able to show restraint when it is appropriate for him to do so.

Straus argues that men "learn a script for violence by observing that individuals are excused and forgiven for violent behavior which occurs while drinking."[68] He can rationalize that it was the alcohol that made him violent. The fact is that many chronic batterers get intoxicated so they can justify their violence. As an eloquent speaker once stated, "The batterer doesn't beat his wife because he drinks, he drinks in order to beat his wife."

The deviance disavowal theory gets major support from defendants who appear regularly before the court for terrorizing and brutalizing their mates. In many cases, it is a defendant's only defense. While externalizing their actions, they often blame the beatings on the alcohol, asserting that they had too much to drink. Unfortunately, the family and victim of the defendant often buy into the disavowal defense of the attacker. After all, the personality dynamics of the abuser are incomprehensible to most. If, however, the attacks can be explained and attributed to the issue of substance abuse, it becomes understandable and somewhat more acceptable.

Defense attorneys who represent a batterer generally find it very easy to rationalize his violence on the basis that the defendant has an alcohol or drug problem. Such lawyers inevitably exploit the issue of alcohol and drug abuse in defense of their clients.

They use this ploy as the ultimate smoke screen, as a way of justifying what the batterer has done. "After all," they always argue, "he is not responsible for his actions because he is an alcoholic." They then assert that it is incumbent upon the court to offer him a chance to rehabilitate himself in lieu of punishment. "If you put him in jail, he will only come out worse."

Forget that the defendant broke the victim's legs and arms. Forget that he stabbed her with a steak knife several times after sexually assaulting her. Disregard that he mutilated and murdered his victim. The defense always focuses on the same issue: substance abuse. "It is not my client's fault that he did what he did. It is his drinking that made him do it." The defense attorney is cunning in utilizing the disavowal defense to convince a judge or a jury that something other than the defendant is responsible for an incomprehensible and gruesome attack. Juries and judges are asked by the batterer's attorney to virtually disregard the fact that a defendant has an extensive history of physical violence against the same victim. They are asked to ignore his history of beating her when she was eight months pregnant, or that she was hospitalized several times following previous assaults. They are asked to ignore the fact that he was sober during many of the past attacks. They are urged to focus only on the assertion that he has a drinking problem. This is the disavowal concept in its finest hour.

Straus's argument—that the disinhibition effect of alcohol consumption is not in itself a causative factor of spousal abuse—gets heavy support from the fact that most men in our society consume alcohol, yet only a small percentage actually batter. Those of us who have learned that personal violence under any circumstance is unacceptable, and who have not been taught to disavow responsibility for our actions, help validate the contention that alcohol in itself is not a causative factor of spousal abuse. If the physiological release of our inhibitions were a primary cause of spousal attacks, then all of us would be prone to becoming wife beaters. All of us would be potential murderers. The fact remains, the majority of us who indulge do not react violently or aggressively toward our mates. It is also relevant to note that most spousal assaults probably occur in the absence of alcohol usage. An excellent example of this assertion is a woman who was interviewed following a trial in which her husband was found guilty of beating her. She stated that although her husband had been sober for over a year and attended three A.A. meetings weekly, he would come home and physically beat her following each meeting. In essence, the man beats his wife, not the alcohol, and even in the absence of alcohol, the Category Three abuser will continue to attack her.

If anything should be disavowed by the courts, it is the smoke screen of alcoholism as a valid defense or justification for the brutal beating of a woman. The single trait of alcoholism or substance abuse does not cause a man to beat his spouse. It is the combination of traits that constitute his personality disorder that does. Through his life, he has learned to be ruthless. He has also learned that there are no consequences for his violent behavior. He will continue to disavow his behavior until someone stops him.

Manipulation

This male is a professional manipulator. His daily existence relies heavily on how he is able to manipulate others. It is a matter of survival, a matter of control. When his spouse finally decides that she's had enough of his abuse, he knows how to lure her back into the relationship. When she is on the verge of leaving him, he cries, pleads, begs, and threatens suicide. Threats of suicide are his ultimate means of manipulation. He convinces his victim that should he kill himself, his blood will be on her hands. She will be the one to blame for his final act of self-destruction.

The Category Three batterer has the uncanny ability to make his victim feel pity, guilt, and shame. When he fails to evoke such emotions, however, he turns to the use of terror and intimidation. He harasses her by phone, sends threatening notes, and stalks her. He is very aware of when to use pity and when to use fear in his attempts to extort a desired response.

If she leaves him, he promises "to get help" for his problems if she reconciles. He promises that he will change. After she returns, however, he quickly reneges on his promises and resumes his violence.

Exploitation and Entitlement

The Category Three batterer is a parasite that feeds off others, particularly his spouse and family. He bleeds them for all that they have and does so without a sense of reciprocation.

During his frequent periods of unemployment, he exploits his spouse for financial assistance and support. Much of the money she gives goes toward vices such as gambling, cigarettes, alcohol, and so on. He relies on her to take care of family necessities such as food, rent, and utilities. When separated from his wife, he solicits the aid of parents and relatives for housing and financial needs. He bounces from one relative to another, using their home and food without a thought of repayment.

This male also bleeds his spouse and family emotionally. He absorbs them into his infantile games and keeps them in a constant state of turmoil. His family's daily existence becomes preoccupied with feeding his insatiable needs and demands. Family members live on the edge of an emotional cliff, choosing to pacify him rather than to risk a greater crisis. The batterer's demanding and volatile nature, and his family's enabling responses, leave them filled with anxiety and distress.

His exploitation even extends into having others pay for his crimes. When arrested for beating his spouse, he calls from jail and demands that she pay his bail. It is not unusual for the victim herself, the one who was assaulted, to hire an attorney to represent the interest of the defendant. If she refuses, he turns to his parents, relatives, or close friends for assistance. He knows that if he shops around, he will be able to manipulate a friend or family member into giving him the assistance that he needs.

The chronic batterer goes through life with a sense of entitlement. His egocentric nature demands unconditional love. He feels that those around him, particularly his spouse and immediate family, should meet his every desire. He continuously extracts the emotional support, financial assistance, and the attention of others without reciprocation. He feels that he is entitled to his demands regardless of the ruthlessness of his behavior. His sense of entitlement is boundless.

Behavioral Commonalities

Ongoing, Chronic, Systematic Abuse

The Category Three abuser has a systematic pattern of ongoing and chronic abuse of his spouse. He possesses the Battering Male Syndrome. His victim has difficulty relating how often she has been attacked, suggesting that it has been constant or "too frequent to remember." She reports that she has been perpetually abused throughout her relationship with the batterer.

An individual act of violence is often followed by what is commonly known as the "honeymoon phase." Immediately after a beating, the abuser often displays fabricated remorse, superficial concern, and various behaviors that seek reconciliation. It is during this period that he brings her flowers, assures her that she is loved, and promises that he will never hurt her again. Once he is convinced that his victim has been lured back into the relationship, however, he resumes his chronic and systematic patterns of abuse, immediately followed by attempts to reconcile and the onset of the "honeymoon phase."

Premarital Abuse

The batterer has a history of beating his spouse early in the relationship. Many women find themselves being assaulted during the courtship phase of the relationship. Others report that they are physically attacked on their honeymoon. Early signs of aggression may be somewhat subtle, such as slapping, pushing, grabbing, and extreme jealousy. After he recognizes that he has secured the relationship, however, his subtle aggression turns into blatant violence.

Premarital abuse is a primary indicator of future violence. There is little doubt that a victim can predict her future with the batterer by simply reflecting on the past. If he beats her early in the relationship, his abuse will only get worse. The most overt warning sign of future violence is premarital aggression.

Multiple Abusive Relationships

The Category Three abuser is a Serial Batterer. His current victim is not the first and will definitely not be his last. He has abused multiple victims over many years of relationships.

His victim often relates that she is aware that he beat his former wives or girlfriends. His criminal record frequently reveals that other women have charged him in the past for physical abuse. It is not unusual for a single victim to charge him with domestic violence several times during the same year. All of his future intimate relationships with women will be violent ones.

Injuries to His Victims

He frequently injures his victim to the degree that she requires medical attention or hospitalization. The most common injuries are bruises to the face, blackened and swollen eyes, broken noses and cheekbones, swollen lips, and broken teeth. While many of the injuries are centered around the facial area, she also suffers severe bruising and bone fractures of her torso and extremities, internal injuries, puncture and gunshot wounds, and so on. Many of the injuries that he inflicts are permanently disabling.

Use of Weapons

He employs weapons such as knives, guns, clubs, etc., in his attacks on his victim. He continuously reminds his spouse that he has a weapon and will use it if necessary. He frequently holds a gun to her head and to the heads of her children. In many instances he discharges the gun during his rage. In some assaults, the gunshot serves as a warning to his victim. In many, he actually shoots her. The Category Three abuser's primary weapon of choice is a handgun.

Tortures and Mutilates His Victim

He mutilates and tortures his victim in the same manner that a military captor abuses a prisoner of war. He burns her with cigarettes and beats her with clubs. He holds hot irons to her face and torso and cuts her with sharp objects. He throws acid in her face and holds loaded guns up her vagina. In cases where he has murdered his victim, he has been known to mutilate her torso by the decapitation and dismembering of her body parts.

Potentially Homicidal

While it can be argued that the majority of chronic batterers never kill their partners, it is also true that most chronic drunk drivers never cause auto fatalities. When addressing the issue of homicide, however, instead of absolutes, we are dealing in probabilities. Just as the multiple offender drunk driver is capable of killing on the highway, the multiple offender Serial Batterer is capable of killing in the home.

Given the wrong set of triggers and circumstances, the chronic batterer is capable of murdering his spouse. While some of these killings are spontaneous, many are premeditated and well planned. Although the percentage of Category Three individuals who murder their victims is relatively low, the actual number who kill each year is very high. The fact remains, while he may never kill his spouse, the potential is always present.

Potential to Harm or Kill Others

The Category Three assailant is capable of committing mass murder. He is a potential threat to anyone who gets in his way, particularly when someone is intruding in the relationship with his spouse. He frequently injures or kills his spouse's parents, children, friends, roommates, and new boyfriends. Many of these attacks occur when the male perceives that they are assisting or influencing his wife's decision to leave him. There is perhaps no time in which he is more dangerous than during periods of estrangement.

Beats His Pregnant Spouse

There are a significant number of women who claim that they are battered by this male while pregnant. Many of his blows are to the stomach region of the victim. She reports that she is not only punched in her stomach, but knocked down and kicked as well. These beatings are intended to injure both the woman and her unborn child. Many of the beatings are probably a blatant attempt to kill the fetus and to eliminate the threat that he feels over the impending birth.

Use of Intimidation and Terrorism

He uses intimidation and terrorism in an effort to immobilize his victim. The behaviors may range from passive phone call threats to overt stalking and physical assaults with loaded weapons. These actions are designed to maintain control when the couple is together and to force her back into the relationship after she has left. Like his physical attacks, the terrorism is systematic, chronic, and ongoing. It often traumatizes his victim to the point that she experiences a sense of helplessness.

Isolates Her from Others

He makes every possible attempt to isolate her from family,

friends, and support systems. He recognizes that if he is able to keep her from developing close personal relationships and support systems, she is less likely to leave him. In his attempts, he refuses to allow her to work, visit friends, use the car, or participate in activities that give her exposure to others.

Interferes with Job Opportunities

The chronic batterer is very threatened by his spouse's attempt to find employment. He is aware that a job will empower her. It will create financial independence and contacts that may enhance her ability to leave him. If she seeks employment, he threatens to harm her if she continues. If she has employment, he harasses her in an attempt to get her fired. His primary means of harassment include making ongoing, threatening, and intimidating phone calls, sending obscene letters, and stalking her on or near the job site. His harassment and threats escalate dramatically during periods of estrangement. He knows that if she loses her job, he regains control.

Stalks His Victim

Stalking his victim is one of the most intense forms of intimidation. It is an act of passive violence. It is violence from a distance. Stalking is a covert method of maintaining control.

He visibly sits across from her residence, doing nothing more than watching her. He follows on foot and pursues her with his car. He rides past her home over and over again. He hides and watches from the shadows of the night. He conceals himself behind shrubbery and buildings. He intentionally lets her know that he is watching. Without speaking a word, he conveys how easy it would be to kill her. When she is seen with friends, particularly boyfriends, his stalking often turns into physical and violent confrontation.

Damages Her Car and Personal Property

His relentless destruction of her car is symbolic of his desire to destroy her. Most of the damage is done after she tries to flee the relationship. It is both a measure of revenge and an attempt to immobilize her.

He slashes her tires and throws bricks through her windshield.

He opens her hood and destroys the engine and wiring beneath. He cuts her seats and interior with a knife and sets the car on fire. Damage to a vehicle is one of the most commonly reported acts of vandalism committed by this male. It is also one of the most difficult to substantiate.

Besides the destruction of her car, he destroys her household property. Victims report that during and after a beating, he breaks furniture, kicks in the television, and pulls phone cords from the wall. He rips and burns his victim's clothes and smashes windows and mirrors with heavy objects. The Category Three assailant not only systematically batters his spouse's face and torso, he perpetually damages and destroys her personal property and belongings.

Keeps Her Under Surveillance

The Category Three batterer watches his victim's every move. If her phone is busy when he calls, he demands to know to whom she was speaking and why. If she is not at home when he arrives, he wants to know where she's been and with whom. He monitors her mail, discussions with others, social activities, and virtually everything that she does. He manages her movements in the same manner that a warden manages inmates.

Kidnaps Her Children

In an effort to coerce her back into the relationship, he frequently kidnaps her children as a means of leverage and control. Traumatized children often find themselves a focus of his narcissistic rage. He forcibly enters the residence of his estranged spouse, grabs the children, and forces them into his car. He then speeds away. He calls his spouse and uses the terrorized children as a bargaining chip. He is very aware that the children are his best means of leverage in negotiating his estranged partner's return.

Bites His Victim

He is often known to savagely bite his victim. Biting is a primitive act of aggression that is indicative of the Category Three abuser's level of psychopathology. During the peak of his childlike tantrums, he uses his teeth as a weapon, piercing and tearing the flesh from her limbs and torso. A victim frequently appears in court displaying scars and injuries that occurred as a result of the batterer's bite. To some victims, biting is so routine that they accept it as a relatively normal act of aggression.

Phone and Mail Harassment

The intimidation and harassment peak during periods of estrangement. He calls her on the phone incessantly, alternating between hysterical pleadings and threats of suicide. When neither works, he threatens her with violence and death. Many batterers make thirty to fifty harassing calls a day. One victim logged as many as 300 calls during the course of a week. Although she had her phone number changed, the calls resumed.

Another method of harassment is through the mail. He also places notes on her car windshield and attaches them to the door of her residence. Like the phone calls, his messages range from emotional pleadings to threats of violent retaliation.

Unemployability

Most chronic batterers, depending on their disorders, are not capable of holding a job for extended periods of time. Many of these men hold several different jobs during the course of a single year. Others find themselves unemployed for months at a time. After the loss of a job, the batterer always rationalizes that he was unjustly fired or that he quit because the job did not meet his standards. Between his periods of unemployment, he becomes increasingly dependent on others, particularly his parents, family, and spouse for financial support.

Criminal Record

Many batterers have lengthy histories of committing petty and major crimes. The length of the criminal record is often related to the type of disorder the batterer possesses. A review of his record frequently reveals arrests for behavior related to his aggression. His most common arrests are for criminal trespassing, criminal damage, assault, threats, disturbing the peace, concealed weapons, and simple and aggravated battery.

Childlike Tantrums

Childlike tantrums are one of the most common behaviors exhibited by the Category Three batterer. Emotions such as rejection, failure, grief, stress, and insecurity are all expressed with infantile rage. These tantrums range from verbal assaults to destruction of personal property and threats of suicide. During the peak of his rage, he may bite his victim, destroy her household furniture, and curl up in the corner of a room while crying hysterically. Such childlike tantrums are prevalent among all chronic batterers, regardless of their specific disorders.

Devalues His Spouse

In an attempt to deal with his deep sense of inadequacy and to exert his dominance, this male systematically devalues his spouse. Between the systematic beatings, he assassinates her character and her self-esteem. He assaults her ego publicly and in the privacy of the bedroom. He continuously reminds her that she is stupid, ugly, and worthless. In his emotional abuse, he devalues her to a level of personal insignificance. He also attempts to convince her that she is unworthy of love and is incapable of caring for herself.

CHAPTER VI

Recognizing the Battering Male Syndrome

Over the last decade and particularly the last few years, sociologists, psychologists, defense attorneys, and members of the judiciary have accepted and promoted the Battered Women's Syndrome as a viable defense for a woman who has violently retaliated against her abuser. U.S. Department of Justice statistics reveal that for the year 1993, nearly 591 women killed their intimate partners.[69] However, unlike the men who kill their partners out of pathological rage, many of the women who kill do so only after suffering years of incomprehensible physical and emotional abuse.

Defense attorneys, using the Battered Women's Syndrome, assert that many killings are justified because a woman sees no way out of her plight except through violent means. Expert witnesses who understand the dynamics of the syndrome argue that such women believe that any attempt to leave the batterer's grasp will result in violent assault or death. Such a perception is widely reinforced by the incredible number of women who are stalked and killed each year after making assertive attempts to flee the relationship.

Lenore Walker insightfully discusses the dynamics of the Battered Women's Syndrome in her essay entitled "Battered Women and Learned Helplessness." She ingeniously compares the helplessness that a battered woman experiences to the same helplessness experienced by animals that were the subject of research on the same issue. In her paper, she describes a study performed by Seligman in 1974 involving newborn rats, who immediately after their birth were physically restrained by the researcher. "The rats were held in the experimenter's hand until all voluntary escape movements ceased. They then were released. This procedure was repeated several more times. The rats were then placed in a vat of water. Within thirty minutes, the rats subjected to the learned helplessness treatment drowned. Many did not even attempt to swim and sank to the bottom of the vat immediately. Untreated rats could swim up to sixty hours before drowning."[70]

She also discusses a series of projects conducted by researchers Seligman, Maier, and Overmier in which dogs were placed in cages and administered electrical shocks at random intervals. "The dogs learned quickly that no matter what response they made, they could not control the shock. The learning of the unpredictability and non-contingent nature of the aversive stimulus was of prime importance. At first the dogs attempted to escape through various voluntary movements. When nothing they did stopped the shocks, the dogs ceased any further voluntary activity. When the experimenter attempted to change this procedure and teach the dogs that they could escape by crossing to the other side of the cage, the dogs still would not respond. In fact, even when the door was left open and the dogs were shown the way out, they remained passive, refused to leave and did not avoid the shock. It took repeated dragging of the dogs to the exit to teach them how to voluntarily respond again. The earlier in life the dogs received such treatment, the longer it took to overcome the effects of this so-called learned helplessness."[71]

While it may not be palatable to compare the behavior of a battered woman to that of an entrapped animal, her plight and existence are strikingly similar to the experiences and responses generated by the researchers. Like the research animals, when she tries to evade her abuser's domination, he utilizes strategies that make it almost impossible for her to do so.

Unless her escape is carefully planned and she is well protected, a victim of Category Three violence will rarely elude her abuser's grasp without provoking his violent retaliation. In many cases, the retaliation turns deadly. While there are several reasons why she may choose to remain with the batterer, her primary motivation for staying is that she doesn't want to die.

When the chronic batterer's level of control and magnitude of violence is considered, it becomes apparent why his victim does not terminate her relationship without some degree of hesitation. If you consider the ruthlessness of his attacks and the extent of his control, it becomes less difficult to comprehend why she often chooses to stay in such a volatile and physically dangerous relationship. While many professionals still continue to question and place blame on the battered woman for electing to remain with her assailant, given things as they are, one should question her ability to leave. Even when she is able to muster the courage to flee, she generally finds that needed resources are very limited and that the criminal justice system is callously indifferent to her safety needs.

A victim who begins to challenge her batterer's domination and control must be prepared to address the consequences of her decision. If she decides to terminate her relationship with the abuser, she must be prepared to seek services and protection from those individuals and agencies that can assist her. Unfortunately, most of her requests will be met with apathy and indifference.

The fact is, in most cases of chronic violence, instead of the system controlling the behavior of the batterer, the batterer controls the behavior of his victim. The cyclical scenario of the victim's relationship with her abuser and the criminal justice system is all too well known.

The battered woman perceives her assailant as overwhelmingly powerful. He is a man who controls her emotionally, physically, sexually, and financially. If she tries to think on her own, he beats her. If she tries to become independent of him, he tortures her. If she tries to elude his control, he finds her and rapes her. The batterer frequently threatens her with weapons. He holds knives to the throats of her children and loaded guns to her head and torso. If she is successful in physically leaving him, he stalks her from a distance, always threatening to kill her and her children if she does not return.

As she turns to the criminal justice system for help and protection, it shuns her. The police refuse to arrest him; but if they do, prosecutors refuse to prosecute him; but if they do, judges refuse to incarcerate him; but if they do, jailers refuse to keep him, proclaiming the issue of overcrowding or the use of "good time laws."

She then begins to search for safety in battered women's shelters that either do not exist or, if they do, are frequently filled to capacity. The economic toll of her newly found independence becomes apparent with devastating reality. She has taken her children with her, if she has any, but she has no means of feeding or clothing them. She is threatened with eviction with no means of paying her rent. Her children become ill, but she has no financial resources with which to take them to a doctor or by which to buy them medicine that may make them well.

It is at that moment, it is at that time, that the batterer triumphantly reemerges and regains control of the relationship. He shrewdly brings her money, gifts, and promises of getting help for his problems. He assures her that he will change and that it will never happen again. It is then that the battered woman begins to feel that the alternative of returning to her abuser is more appealing and pragmatic than where she has been. She not only needs him; she fears him as well. Each time she returns to him, however, her syndrome becomes more incapacitating, more powerful, and more blinding. In light of these incredible obstacles, it is amazing that we expect the battered woman to make rational decisions within the context of irrational circumstances. We expect her to make reasonable choices under unreasonable conditions.

There is no victim of Category Three violence who leaves her abuser without facing imminent danger. The battered woman, even if motivated to leave, is in no position to simply walk away from the abuse, no matter how serious it may be. She is intensely frightened that she cannot survive alone, and that even if she tried, he will murder her in the process.[72]

The learned helplessness that a chronically battered woman displays is not only similar to that of the research animals, but the earlier it develops in life, the more prominent it becomes later. Perhaps this is why research reflects that the majority of battered women are raised in early childhood environments where family instability and violence are dominant factors.

It is interesting that while the Battered Women's Syndrome has been widely accepted, the concept of the Battering Male Syndrome has yet to be recognized. If he is so ruthless and his numbers so very significant, then why in the past has he been so virtually ignored? If we accept that chronically abused battered women are strikingly similar in their traits, behaviors, and responses to abuse, it is without question that so are the men who beat them. The fact is, males who chronically beat their intimate partners have glaringly similar profiles, as illustrated by the Batterer's Continuum.

In light of the similarities of the psychological, emotional, and behavioral characteristics of the Category Three batterer, it is very surprising that the concept of the Battering Male Syndrome has not been embraced by the social science and academic communities. Its usage among professional groups who confront such violence has enormous potential. District attorneys, for example, who frequently prosecute cases involving spousal abuse, could use this syndrome, in addition to the Batterer's Continuum, to help differentiate between various types of batterers. With such concepts and the assistance of expert testimony, they could clearly define in the minds of a jury those batterers who are lethal and untreatable from those who are treatable and present no future danger to their victim. The Battering Male Syndrome would offer a jury insight into a dangerous predator whose potential to offend again, injure, and kill has been grossly minimized.

The Battering Male Syndrome also offers clinicians the ability to distinguish between batterers who are salvageable from those beyond the scope of rehabilitation. In conjunction with the Batterer's Continuum, it would offer therapists a multi-dimensional approach for diagnostic, assessment, and treatment purposes. While many mental health counselors will argue that any individual is capable of change, such an argument is not widely accepted by those professionals knowledgeable of personality disorders. Whereas such idealistic ideologies may be accepted by some, they are refuted by the majority. Most clinicians in the field of psychiatry would argue that chronic batterers who have personality disorders rarely change, presenting an ongoing and significant danger to the lives of their victims.

Why is it that we have so readily accepted the victim's syndrome, yet have virtually ignored the suggestion that the chronic batterer has a syndrome as well? Is it possible that the Battering Male Syndrome has been disregarded as a result of our culture's chauvinistic and sexist view of such crimes? The fact is, if we accept the male's syndrome, we place full blame on the batterer for his criminal rage. We would be forced to view his violence within the context of his psychopathology. We would have to challenge and reassess our desire to mediate and treat his violence and would have to take consequential measures that may not be fashionable or politically correct.

It is without doubt that the Battered Women's Syndrome emerged as a result of advocates who asserted that the victim's behavioral and emotional responses to chronic abuse were a result of learned helplessness and an attempt to survive. It was also accepted as a means of providing her with a defense when she chose a lethal response to her batterer's aggression. It is very probable, however, that her syndrome was accepted by society as a means of suggesting that she is mentally ill. It implies that she is unstable and somewhat responsible for her own circumstances. While it explained to many the emotional paralysis that kept her in the relationship, it also reinforced the perception of those who sought to blame her for staying in a relationship that she should otherwise flee. For every ten times that one is asked the question, "Why does she stay?" only once will you hear the more appropriate question, "Why does he beat her?"

It is incumbent on all professions who interface with the Category Three batterer to promote and recognize the concept of his syndrome. It is the responsibility of clinicians and members of the criminal justice system to accept the chronic batterer within the context of his psychopathology and to respond with methods and consequences not generally utilized. Until the Battering Male Syndrome is recognized, many responses to the battered woman's plight will continue to be inappropriate and ineffective.

CHAPTER VII

The Category Two Abuser: Proceed with Caution

While the Category One abuser has been described here as a normal male whose rage is rooted in unusually stressful circumstances, the Category Three batterer has been profiled as an individual who possesses a chronic personality disorder and does not have a conscience. The Category One abuser has also been described as a man without a history of violence against his intimate partners, who rarely uses weapons in his attacks, and presents little if any ongoing danger to his victim. The Category Three batterer, on the other hand, has been defined as an individual with an extensive history of ongoing violence against his partners. He is a ruthlessly dangerous predator who frequently uses weapons in his assaults. Many of his attacks are premeditated, and he should always be considered potentially homicidal.

In an effort to clearly explain the behaviors and character traits of the Category Two abuser, it was imperative to first profile the two extremes of the Batterer's Continuum. Without addressing the continuum in this manner, it would be very difficult to explain a marginal batterer, whose violent attacks are neither isolated nor ongoing in their occurrence. Instead, this male beats his victim sporadically, sometimes going several months at a time without committing another assault. At times, however, his hiatus between beatings is only a few days. While his violence may not be as systematic and chronic as that of the Category Three batterer, unless it is addressed, its continuation is almost certain.

The Category Two batterer occupies the central position on the continuum and should be viewed as a mixture of the extreme points on the spectrum. The Category Two batterer possesses a limited level of impulse control, thus only occasionally injuring or using weapons in his assaults on his victim. While he can be dangerous and is capable of killing his spouse, he is less likely than the chronic batterer to commit murder. Additionally, his tendency to terrorize, to stalk, or to employ the many acts of intimidation that are so characteristic of the batterer on the extreme right of the continuum is not as intense and systematic. This assailant is involved in less premarital abuse and has experienced fewer violent relationships with women than has the Category Three assailant. He is also less likely than the Category Three abuser to have a criminal record for domestic violence or petty crime. If arrested, he is more responsive to "stay away orders" than is the chronic batterer. In relative terms, he can be best described as a modified version of the Category Three abuser. Perhaps the best way to distinguish between the Category Two and the Category Three batterer is to measure the level of violence that occurs in an individual attack and the degree to which his violence is sustained.

Because of his marginal level of psychosocial functioning, the Category Two abuser should not be perceived as having a personality disorder. He does not possess enough character defects to constitute such a syndrome. If psychopathology is diagnosed only when an individual possesses defects in significant numbers, then the Category Two abuser can best be described as a battering male whose total number of character flaws fall short of the necessary sum. In other words, if it takes five or six specific defects to be labeled with such a diagnosis, the Category Two batterer may be seen as a male who possesses a minimal number of dysfunctional personality traits. While he may not have enough character defects to be labeled as having a disorder, he possesses too many negative traits to be considered a Category One abuser. He is also a male whose emotions and related aggression are easily triggered by external stimuli. If a Category One abuser's violence is brought on primarily by external stress and a Category Three abuser's aggression is caused primarily by internal character flaws and conflicts, then it can be said that the Category Two abuser's violence is triggered equally by both internal and external issues.

Like the Category Three batterer, the use and abuse of alcohol and mind-altering drugs among this group is significantly high. As with the chronic abuser, the Category Two abuser uses chemicals in an effort to mask his many psychosocial dysfunctions and shortcomings. The use of alcohol and substances provide him with a momentary escape from a self-perception that he disdains. It provides him with a false sense of confidence. It is under the influence, however, that he becomes the most volatile, the most unpredictable, the most dangerous. Like the Category Three abuser, this man totally disavows his violent behavior once it has occurred, blaming it on the alcohol and other provocative external issues. He frequently drinks himself into oblivion, ruthlessly beats his spouse, and dismisses the entire incident on the pretense that he had been drinking and lost control.

Alcohol and drug usage by this male also serves to merge his boundary into that of the Category Three batterer. This is because the character defects that he possesses begin to be exacerbated when he is under the influence. His deep sense of insecurity and inadequacy begins to seep out of his emotional pores until he is transformed into violent rage. His personality flaws lay just below the surface, and when he is drinking, it becomes very difficult to distinguish between his behavior and its related violence and that of the male who inhabits the most serious segment of the continuum.

Next to domestic estrangement, there is nothing that blurs the boundaries of the Category Two and the Category Three abusers more than intoxication. The fact is, an estranged and inebriated Category Two batterer may look, act, and be as much of a threat to his victim as the Category Three batterer. While he may not have as many defects as a male with a full personality disorder, the defects that do exist are quickly exposed and lubricated when he is drunk.

Whereas the Category Two batterer should be perceived as a serious threat to the life of his victim, he is not without hope. He should not be written off as being incapable of change. In some instances, this may not be the case. This batterer often possesses some degree of remorse, insight, and motivation that are prerequisites to change. He also has a marginal ability to bond with his spouse and children. He is less disturbed than the chronic abuser. His modified profile brings with it a modified prognosis. It is not suggested that the prognosis for a Category Two abuser is good. Given the right circumstances, however, there is a chance that he may alter his behavior, since psychopathology is not a primary element of concern.

Critical to any attempt at modifying this male's behavior is the use of leverage. Since his level of motivation to change is minimal at best, it is crucial to increase it through external pressure and control. The two best sources of coercion are the threats that his spouse is going to leave him and that the judiciary is going to put him in jail.

The best advice that can be shared with a victim who contemplates staying in a relationship with a Category Two abuser is to offer her assailant a single alternative. He either seeks psychiatric help or she will terminate the relationship. It is also critical that when she states her position, she follows through with her ultimatum. If he does not enter professional counseling, it is not a question of whether she should leave him; she must. If not, he detects her vulnerability and perceives all future assertions of leaving as idle threats. A situation in which this batterer promises to stop his violence, but refuses to enter treatment, is something that his victim must not tolerate. To refuse therapeutic intervention is to remove any hope of change. It will not happen. She must leave or forever be the target of his rage.

If this abuser is arrested for his attack, the judiciary can also play an integral role in pressuring him into a clinical setting that he would otherwise ignore. A judge can produce significant levels of external motivation by dictating mandatory counseling in lieu of incarceration. Monitoring the abuser's progress, however, is paramount to the success of such a process. Like the spouse who is prepared to leave if he does not enter treatment, the court must be ready to prosecute and incarcerate the batterer if he violates its orders. If the Category Two batterer perceives a lack of follow-through or vulnerability by his spouse or the judiciary, he generally reneges on his promises to his partner, ignores the court's orders, and ultimately re-offends.

External leverage with the Category Two abuser can enhance internal motivation. A spouse's insistence that she will terminate the relationship and a court that promises to prosecute him if he does not seek help are essential means of external motivation. The probability that the Category Two abuser will enter a clinical setting without the use of external pressure is remote. While coercion may not be the best way to initiate motivation, it does serve to intensify that which may exist.

A Category Two batterer who is serious about changing his behavior must become involved in a clinical setting and develop a strong support system if positive results are to be recognized. A batterer who regularly attends therapy but is without a support system (A.A., Batterer's Anonymous, etc.), or who has a support system but does not participate in therapy, will experience minimal change. One without the other will reap few benefits. It is imperative for the Category Two abuser to involve himself with both modalities if he is to have a chance of a successful rehabilitation. The argument for such dual treatment of Category Two batterers is twofold and is based within the limitations of each modality.

First, whereas group and individual therapy are essential in his effort to address deeply rooted emotional and psychological problems, it is very limited in the amount of time that a therapist actually meets with the batterer. The average time that a counselor spends with a client for weekly outpatient therapy is probably less than two hours. While psychotherapy may increase a client's insight into his inner dynamics, he has limited time to explore what he learns. Although counseling performed by a qualified professional is central to this batterer's rehabilitation, time limitations create many voids during the remainder of his week. If a Category Two batterer is to keep his anger under control, he must develop a strong safety net. To minimize his need to participate in regular support meetings is to ignore the magnitude of his emotional problems and related character defects.

The reality of most support groups, on the other hand, is that they are not designed for nor capable of addressing many of the batterer's psychological problems that exist below the surface. Such groups are excellent at allowing the male to vent his feelings and emotions and at discovering productive alternatives to physical violence, but most members are neither trained nor qualified to address the psychiatric roots of his aggression. While groups such as Alcoholics Anonymous, Batterers Anonymous, etc., offer productive means of addressing addictions, establishing identities, developing impulse control, and reducing the abuser's sense of social isolation, they should never be seen as a substitute for individual and group therapy.

A very common remark made by participants of Alcoholics Anonymous is that another member has been on a dry drunk. Such a term applies to a recovering alcoholic who has remained sober, yet has many behaviors that are far worse than those of his intoxicated state. A batterer who is on a "dry drunk" is actually someone who has managed to stop drinking, but has never dealt with the deeper problems that are related to his feelings of inadequacy, insecurity, lack of an identity, and so on. There is a strong probability that A.A. has a significant number of Category Two batterers who have stopped drinking, but who have never stopped abusing their partners. The fact is, unless a sober batterer jointly addresses his deeper psychological issues through professional counseling, the potential that his physical aggression will continue is very high.

It is also imperative for a chemically addicted Category Two batterer who enters the treatment process to recognize that his substance abuse and violence are two different areas of concern. He must never be permitted to rationalize that his drinking has led to his violence. That is not the case. The majority of substance abusers in our society never physically attack their mates. Drinking is not necessarily a prerequisite to physical violence. This batterer must recognize the distinction between his substance abuse and his violence, and should not blame one on the other. Instead, he must address each one as a separate area of rehabilitation. More important, he needs to address his problem of chemical abuse first. Unless he treats and ceases his use of mind-altering substances, he will never acquire the stability that is necessary in addressing his psychological problems and related violence.

Likewise, it is critical for professional clinicians to recognize the distinction between the batterer's violence and his chemical addiction. Too often, particularly for those who specialize in the field of substance abuse, therapists view the two problems as one. Consequently, they focus on and utilize the many modalities that comprise the treatment process of chemically addictive personalities. While many of these techniques may be beneficial in terms of the batterer's sobriety, the process often fails miserably at addressing the dynamics and symptoms that generate his aggression. To further complicate matters, many clinicians are not trained nor qualified in the treatment of personality disorders or the character traits that cause a man to violently attack his spouse.

It is most unfortunate that many uninformed therapists view the treatment of a battering male in such simplistic terms. They feel that to treat the substance abuse is to treat the violence. The result of such an erroneous professional perception can have devastating effects, since it gives false hope to the victim and continues to place her in significant jeopardy.

Two primary issues emerge when discussing the treatment concerns of the Category Two batterer. How does one distinguish between remorse and motivation which are real and those which are fabricated? More important, when the boundaries of the Category Two and Category Three batterers are blurred, how does one differentiate between them for the purpose of rehabilitation?

There is no absolute way to measure remorse or the willingness to change among batterers. While tears and related body language can and often do represent manipulation rather than empathy, there are actually two ways that those associated with the batterer can test the validity of his emotions. Both methods involve the use of time to determine his true intentions.

First, if his victim is considering staying in the relationship, she should physically separate from the male until he is six to twelve months into treatment. She should also deny all requests to return to him prematurely. Second, if the batterer has been charged with a criminal offense that does not require incarceration, his case should be reset at thirty-day intervals for a period of not less than one year. The defendant should also be ordered to produce evidence of his involvement with a treatment facility at each hearing. If he is an A.A. member or a member of another support group, he should be required to bring in his sponsor. If his spouse is still in a relationship with him, she should be asked to appear to validate his claims of treatment.

When these recommendations are closely followed, time becomes the victim's closest ally. A Category Two batterer who is faking remorse or a Category Three who is attempting to hide his personality disorder will not be able to endure the clinical process over a period of time. The probability is that an unmotivated Category Two abuser will drop out of treatment within the first few weeks, while the Category Three abuser will drop out almost immediately. In many cases, these men would prefer to risk incarceration, or the loss of the relationship with their spouse, than the reality of facing themselves in ongoing therapy. While they may initially enter treatment in an effort to manipulate their partners back into relationships or to avoid criminal prosecution, if not sincere, they cannot endure therapy. If these suggestions are followed, in most cases the batterer will burn out quicker than will his spouse or the judiciary. The test of time is perhaps one of the best measures of determining the Category Two abuser's level of motivation and intent to change his behavior.

While much of this chapter has concerned itself with the treatment of the Category Two batterer, it is written with both apprehension and concern. There is little evidence that the treatment of this batterer is successful. In fact, many therapists suggest that his prognosis is very dismal. This chapter is not an attempt to convince a victim of Category Two abuse to stay in the relationship with her abuser; it is only an effort to remain objective within a profession filled with opposing philosophies and theories on how to address such a batterer and his victim. For a complete overview of treatment modalities, recommendations, and suggestions for all three categories of batterers, refer to Chapter XI, which is directed at professional therapists and social workers.

After all concerns are addressed, it is the victim, regardless of the degree of her abuse, who must determine her course of action. Her decision should be made, however, only after utilizing the Batterer's Continuum as a diagnostic thermometer. She must approach her individual circumstances without illusion. The Category Two assailant often possesses many of the traits of the Category Three batterer. He lacks motivation to change and is potentially homicidal as well. A victim of Category Two violence must proceed with utmost caution.

Chapter VIII

How to Intervene Safely with Batterers

It is most unfortunate that professionals generally address the safety and needs of all battered women in a similar manner. Many professionals hold the perception that all spousal abuse is one and the same. Many fail to distinguish between the man who presents an ongoing physical threat to his victim and the one who is non-lethal.

You may be among those who do not recognize that the batterer falls on a continuum. As a professional, you may believe that all batterers are treatable, irrespective of their psychopathology. If so, you have entered into a passively collusive relationship with batterers.

Generic intervention, whereby all batterers and victims are lumped together, is a very dangerous process. Such a practice often results in a woman who is suffering Category Three abuse being given the same advice and assistance as the victim attacked by a Category One batterer. Well-intentioned professionals frequently and inappropriately recommend marriage counseling to victims of chronic violence in an attempt to reconcile and preserve the family unit. They often do not realize that the spouse and children of a Category Three batterer are in significant physical danger. They may not understand that the man who occupies the right side of the Batterer's Continuum has a personality disorder, defies rehabilitative change, and presents a perpetual threat to the lives of his family members.

Prescriptive Suggestions to All Professionals

In an effort to provide you with a prescription that serves as a safety guide, the subsequent chapters of this book address several different professional groups. The suggestions in this chapter, however, are generically applicable to any professional or individual, regardless of affiliation to the chronic batterer or his victim.

While most of the suggestions are specifically related to the

Category Three batterer, you should make modifications for other points on the continuum. The general rule is that the closer the batterer falls to the left side of the spectrum (Category One), the more these recommendations can be relaxed and, in some cases, eliminated.

Recapping the Batterer's Continuum

Recognize the Batterer's Continuum and the three forms of battering that it encompasses (See Chapter I). All batterers are not the same and cannot be explained through the use of a single generic profile. The manner in which we address the behavior of a domestic abuser and the needs of his victim should be relative to the category in which he falls.

As a professional, you must realize that in the absence of the continuum, all batterers do appear to be one and the same. By using the continuum, however, you will be capable of making informed and reasonable judgments. Always consider addressing the Category One abuser with compassion, the Category Two batterer with caution, and the Category Three assailant with consequences.

While the continuum may not explain every case of spousal abuse, it is diagnostically applicable to almost all men who physically attack intimate partners. Although some men may batter as a result of a psychosis, brain tumor, chemical imbalance, or other psychological or physiological abnormality, most batter relative to the three profiles associated with the Batterer's Continuum.

The Category One batterer falls on the left side of the continuum. He is a relatively normal male who experiences abnormal stress and external circumstances beyond his control. His abuse is isolated, and if properly addressed, is unlikely to repeat itself. This man does not present an ongoing threat to his victim. He generally feels remorse for what he has done, and if motivated, is very treatable. Generally speaking, the victim of Category One violence does not need a safety plan.

The Category Three abuser falls on the opposite side of the continuum. His violence is rooted in psychopathology, and his abuse is ongoing, systematic, and chronic. In psychiatric terms, the Category Three batterer is classified as having a personality disorder. This personality disorder is like a malignant psychological cancer. He does not possess a conscience. He is beyond the scope of rehabilitation. A victim of Category Three violence always requires a safety plan.

The Category Two batterer is a modified version of the Category Three. His beatings are neither isolated nor are they ongoing and chronic. Instead, his attacks are sporadic and inconsistent. It is possible for him to go for months without assaulting his victim. Within the context of stress, rejection, or substance abuse, however, his behaviors are often difficult to distinguish from that of the Category Three and can be very dangerous. Under ideal circumstances, the Category Two is marginally treatable. A victim of Category Two violence should always have a safety plan available.

Manipulation by Category Three Batterers

Always be aware that the personal agenda of the Category Three batterer is to manipulate you into giving him what he wants and is designed to coerce you into conceding to his demands. He is keenly aware of what buttons to push and strategically does so at opportune moments. For the Category Three assailant the use of manipulation has been a lifelong means of survival. Always base your responses to this batterer on facts, not perception. The various forms of manipulation that he employs are as follows:

Treatment Ploy

The chronic batterer will frequently agree to treatment in an effort to manipulate those around him. He will enter treatment as a ploy to lure his spouse back into a relationship or as an attempt to convince the judiciary to dismiss criminal charges that have been filed against him. After achieving such objectives, however, he will immediately withdraw from treatment and will resume beating his spouse.

Suicidal Gestures

The chronic batterer may use threats of suicide as a way to manipulate and control those around him. While suicide is always a possibility, in most instances he will not actually harm or kill himself. Instead, he is using such behavior in an effort to entice his spouse back into a relationship or in extorting from others a desired response.

Fabricated Remorse

Beware of remorse displayed by a Category Three batterer. The chronic batterer cannot and does not feel remorse. He is incapable of loving or bonding with others. His seemingly empathetic response following a beating is nothing more than a cunning attempt to manipulate and reestablish control over his victim.

Charming Demeanor

Do not allow yourself to be manipulated by the Category Three abuser's superficial charm or cunning behavior. His shallow charm will frequently make it appear that he is not as ruthless and dangerous as he is. Look beyond the surface and recognize the facts for what they are.

Use of Children

Recognize the batterer's manipulative use of his victim's children as bargaining chips and leverage in his relationship with her. He strategically withholds child support payments in an attempt to force her to return. He frequently uses threats to harm, kidnap, or acquire legal custody of the children as a means of control.

Use of Symbols

Never allow yourself to be swayed by symbols. Do not let affluence, professional status, power, or physical attractiveness to influence your perception of what the batterer has done or is capable of doing to his victim. Do not allow such symbols to minimize the obvious.

Denial

Do not "buy into" the Category Three batterer's extraordinary denial system. Never suggest or agree that something or someone other than himself is responsible for his violence. Never reinforce his attempts to minimize, externalize, or rationalize his violent behavior. Your reinforcement of such traits enhances their presence.

Provocation

Never accept the argument that the chronic batterer was provoked into his act of violence by superficial issues and external circumstances. With the exception of self-defense, there is no justification for violently attacking another individual. The argument of provocation is merely a smoke screen in his efforts to displace blame.

Victimization

Never "buy into" the Category Three batterer's portrayal of being a victim. While the batterer may have been victimized as a child, he is now a dangerous predator and must be held accountable for his violence. Never allow him to justify his crimes by making it appear that you condone or accept his reasoning for doing what he has done to his victim. Never reinforce his personal sense of victimization by shifting your concern from the woman's needs to that of the batterer. The Category Three batterer caresses the opportunity of appearing victimized.

Emotional Intensity

The emotional intensity of the Category Three assaulter is designed to draw you into his chaotic existence. The chronic batterer stages and feeds off a crisis and will perpetually attempt to lure you into his orchestrated turmoil. The more that you "buy into" his "games," the more you become his focus.

Use of Terrorism

His primary means of manipulating others into conceding to his desires and demands is that of fear. When all ploys fail in his attempt to control, he utilizes terror in his extortion efforts and exploitation of others.

Six Myths of Category Three Violence

Crime of Passion

Men do not kill their intimate partners because of passion. While the cliché "crime of passion" is a popular one for explaining domestic homicide, it is just another way of minimizing and justifying the batterer's violence. We all feel the emotion of passion at various points in our lives. It is felt at work, sporting events, and in interpersonal relationships. Yet few of us are capable of murder. To suggest that passion is a direct causative factor of homicide is to suggest that we are all potential murderers.

Stress

Stress is not a direct causative factor of Category Three violence. While no man will escape life without experiencing significant levels of stress, only a small percentage actually batter. If stress was an etiology of such battering, we would all be prone to commit domestic violence.

Culture

Our culture does not directly cause men to beat their intimate partners. The claim that men batter because society teaches and allows them to do so is actually a gross generalization. While American males grow up in a male-dominated culture that condones the control of women, only a small percentage actually batter their mates. Although our culture contributes to and reinforces the problem, it should not be perceived as a direct causative factor of why men batter women.

Alcohol and Substance Abuse

Alcohol and substance abuse are not direct causes of Category Three violence. The batterer's abuse of substances is merely a symptom of his personality disorder. Whereas drinking may be a means by which the chronic batterer can disavow his behavior, it in no way has a direct causative relationship to his aggression. Whereas alcoholics do not generally batter, batterers are very often alcoholics.

Mental Illness

The Category Three batterer should not be perceived as mentally ill. He is rarely psychotic or out of touch with reality. His personality disorder does not qualify him for the legal posture of being "innocent by reason of insanity." The fact is that he frequently premeditates his violence. He beats his victim with the full intent of harming her. He knows and understands right from wrong. He knows exactly what he is doing and doesn't care.

Treatability

As a result of his significant psychopathology, the Category Three batterer is not clinically treatable. The chronic batterer is without a conscience and is incapable of bonding with others. He lacks remorse, disavows responsibility for his actions, and has a dramatic absence of insight into his behavior. Most significant is the fact that the Category Three batterer has no internal motivation to change his behavior.

Addressing the Category Three Batterer

• **Do not allow the Category Three batterer to disavow his violent behavior by blaming it on "triggers" such as passion, stress, culture, or alcohol use.** While these triggers have the capacity of evoking ongoing and chronic violence from a male with a personality disorder, they do not generally have the ability to provoke a normal male into acts of systematic and chronic violence. To condone such rationalizations is to feed the disorder. Making him responsible for the consequences of his actions is the only means by which to modify his behavior.

• **Recognize that the Category Three batterer's traits of jealousy, dependency, and possessiveness are pathological in their content and are symptomatic of the batterer's personality disorder.** Such traits are not a measure of how much he cares for his victim. They are a measure of his psychopathology. Never "buy into" these characteristics. Doing so only reinforces such behaviors.

• **Never concede to the Category Three batterer's feelings of entitlement or his extorted demands.** Feeding his personality disorder increases his focus on you in meeting his ongoing and endless needs.

• **Address the issue of spousal abuse with intolerance.** Do not accept the excuses and rationalizations that men use for beating their wives and girlfriends. Avoid making chauvinistic or sympathetic remarks concerning such matters. Attitudes that appear to tolerate or condone such violence serve to perpetuate its existence.

• **When confronting the violent behavior of a chronic batterer, address him in an authoritative manner.** If you appear indecisive, weak, or vulnerable to his demands, denial, sense of entitlement, or position in the relationship, he will try to manipulate the situation even further. Assertively address his behavior and let him know that you will do whatever is necessary to stop the violence.

• **Never advocate for the treatment of the Category Three abuser.** Treatment of the chronic batterer gives the victim a false sense of security and sets her up for another beating. Instead, advocate for the safety and protection of his victim and her children.

It is important to recognize that as a victim's advocate, you must not simultaneously promote the agenda of the chronic batterer. When you promote his treatment, you actually place his victim in grave danger. While it may be politically correct to focus on the rehabilitation of the Category Three batterer, recognize that when you do so, you are entering into a relationship of passive collusion with the perpetrator.

Beware of programs that advocate and provide treatment to the Category Three batterer. Many do not comprehend the dynamics, severity, and lethality of his personality disorder. Many are not qualified to provide such services.

Keep in mind that defense attorneys who approach you on behalf of the Category Three batterer are generally acting only in the interest of their clients and will frequently ignore and sacrifice the safety of the victims in pursuing their clients' agendas. The primary objective of such an attorney is to have the batterer's criminal charges dismissed, regardless of the magnitude of his violence. The argument that he deserves treatment and that punitive consequences or incarceration will "only make him worse" are classic ploys designed to avoid criminal sanctions. Although such arguments may be valid for the Category One abuser, they are dangerously invalid for Category Three assailants.

• **Finally, always remember how very dangerous the Category Three batterer is.** He is a predator, stalker, and Serial Batterer. Never rationalize, minimize, or justify what he does or what he is capable of doing. He is one of the most dangerous men in our society. Not only are the victim and her children in significant danger, but anyone who is seen as interfering in his relationship with his spouse may be in danger, as well. Do not underestimate your personal vulnerability. Maintain utmost vigilance. The Category Three abuser is capable of homicide, and in some cases, of mass murder.

Addressing the Category Three Victim

• **Believe most of what the battered woman tells you.** The battered woman will describe incomprehensible stories of physical abuse, mutilation, torture, and kidnapping. She will tell you details that you may find difficult to believe. She will describe how she was burned with cigarettes and hot irons, stuck with safety pins, and chained to a bedpost so that she could not leave home.

Since the Category Three batterer is capable of doing almost anything to his victim, you should enter the situation with an open mind. Her statements are probably most accurate immediately following a beating and while she is in crisis. As time passes, she begins to rationalize the magnitude and may even justify what he has done. Believe the victim when she describes what he has done to her. If anything, the beating and circumstances surrounding an assault were probably much worse than she states. Her minimization of the attack is often as profound as that of the abuser.

• **Educate yourself on the concept of the Battered Women's Syndrome.** While it may be difficult to understand why a woman would stay in a relationship with a man who ruthlessly beats her, the answers lie within the context and complexity of this syndrome.

There are strong similarities between the behavioral responses of a chronically battered woman and those of prisoners of war. In extreme cases, she has been through no less. She has been systematically degraded, humiliated, tortured, mutilated, threatened with death, and robbed of an identity. Consequently, the battered woman may appear to be very protective of her abuser. She may recant earlier statements and even claim responsibility for what has happened. Her denial is often the result of being terrified of her batterer. She does not want to die.

• **Do not suggest that the victim of Category Three violence should try to keep the family together for the sake of the children.** The single most destructive factor in the emotional development of a child is a violent home. We cannot expect children who are reared in cesspools of violence to grow up as well-adjusted and loving adults. Such a setting is an incubator for future batterers and victims. Raising children in domestic war zones often does irreversible damage to their abilities to bond or to have healthy relationships as adults. If you destroy the bonding stage of a child's life, you destroy the child.

Similarly, marriage counseling should never be suggested; the violence of the Category Three abuser has no direct relationship to marital issues. Any attempt directed toward reconciliation merely subjects the battered woman to additional danger and violence.

• **Advocate for and support the battered woman's efforts to terminate her relationship with a Category Three abuser.** He beat her in the past and will certainly beat her in the future. There is no way of modifying or stopping his violence as long as she remains in the relationship.

Direct the victim to programs that will enable her to become financially, emotionally, and psychologically independent from her abuser. Do not allow her to become dependent on you in meeting her needs. Assist her in establishing an identity of her own.

• **Never address the victim in a judgmental or critical manner.** Challenge the violent behavior of the batterer and why he beats her, not the submissive behavior of the victim and why she stays. Do not imply to the victim of Category Three violence that it is the quality of her relationship with the batterer that provokes him to beat her. The battered woman should never be blamed for the violence of her assailant.

Although it may be difficult for you to fully comprehend her circumstances, a negative approach is counterproductive. While assisting the battered woman, project tolerance, acceptance, and support.

Don't assume that you know how she feels. No one other than another battered woman can comprehend the danger that she is in. Such a perception minimizes her danger, with the result that you may not adequately respond to her safety needs.

• **Recognize that your body language and voice tone convey unspoken messages to those with whom you interact.** Don't allow such factors to project indifference or a lack of concern for the victim. She is already intimidated by what has happened. Recognize that your presence may be intimidating as well. The manner in which you speak or address her is very important. Don't allow your attitude to reinforce her fears. Don't replace the batterer's hostile presence with your own. A professional who possesses a hostile attitude can be as threatening to the victim as her batterer. Don't victimize her a second time.

• **Never suggest to the victim that she drop the criminal or civil charges filed against a Category Three batterer.** She is generally very reluctant to pursue the charges against her assailant.

The slightest suggestion by a friend, family member, counselor, or court worker that she consider dropping the issue often results in its immediate occurrence. While such recommendations are usually made in attempts to "get the two back together" or in response to her fear of retaliation, it is never in the best interest of the victim to do so. Pursuing the charges, setting boundaries, and terminating the relationship are.

• **When assisting the battered woman relative to her abuse, never address her in view of the batterer.** There is nothing more intimidating to the victim than to discuss the violence while he is present. His presence will dramatically inhibit her responses to you.

• **If you provide assistance to a battered woman, beware of the written documentation and information that you place into her file.** Information that she gives or tells you in private is not necessarily confidential. In most cases it is subject to the subpoena process. Attorneys representing the interest of the batterer will frequently try to subpoena such records in an effort to assassinate and discredit the character of the victim.

• **Advise the battered woman to keep all written and physical information that substantiates her allegations of abuse.** She should keep all letters, notes, tapes, photographs, medical records, legal records, etc., relative to her batterer's behavior and violence. Such evidence will validate her claims of abuse when it becomes necessary to do so.

Advise a victim to take and keep all photographs that document the physical abuse that she suffered at the hands of her abuser. Since bruises are most pronounced several days after an attack, suggest that she take photographs at intervals of one, three, and five days.

• **Periodically contact the victim to see if she is safe and to let her know that you are available if she needs you.** Never allow the Category Three assailant to isolate his victim from family members, friends, and outside resources. He knows that if he can isolate her from those who offer alternatives to his domination and control, she is less capable of leaving him.

• **Recognize and accept that the chronically abused woman has a right to defend herself.** While a woman may take extraordinary measures in protecting herself from her abuser, the batterer often continues to remain a significant threat. In circumstances where her life is in imminent danger, she should be allowed the right to protect herself. In matters of Category Three abuse, any defensive aggression committed by a battered woman on her assailant should be reviewed within the context of the Battered Women's Syndrome.

• **Assist the battered woman in the development and implementation of a safety plan.** The safety of the battered woman and her children should be the paramount issue of concern in your interaction with a victim of Category Three violence. While protocol, formality, and paperwork can always take a back seat, the issues of protection and safety cannot. They are volatile and urgent matters, particularly during periods of estrangement.

Terminating her relationship with the batterer without first implementing a safety plan places the victim's life in imminent danger. Such a plan does not guarantee a Category Three victim a safe passage out of an abusive relationship; however, the greater the safety net, the more secure the victim's retreat.

If it appears that a victim is in significant and immediate danger, suggest that she leave her primary residence and seek safe shelter until boundaries can be set and a safety plan enacted. This is of particular importance during the termination phase of her relationship with the batterer.

• **A proper assessment of an individual victim's needs should always include a close and impartial review of her batterer's lethality and his potential to be rehabilitated.** Tools that will assist you in such an assessment can be found in the Appendix.

The Appendix includes two profile charts. The first is designed to assist you in determining the type of batterer that you are addressing. The second chart assists you in determining his ability to change or modify his behaviors and to respond successfully to a treatment program. Also included are a detailed questionnaire that will aid you in measuring the batterer's lethality and a comprehensive safety plan that a victim can utilize in her attempt to respond to his danger.

A proper assessment of the victim's needs and her batterer's violence should always include the profile charts, Lethality Questionnaire, and the safety plan in the Appendix. The planning strategy relative to the treatment and safety of the victim must never be based on perception and guesswork alone.

Chapter IX

The Criminal Justice System and the Batterer

It is incumbent on the criminal justice system to recognize and address the extreme danger that the chronic spouse abuser presents to both his victim and society. Research statistics and experts provide us with a profile of a man who is chillingly cold, incomprehensibly ruthless, and in many cases capable of mass murder. In terms of numbers, he is more dangerous than a serial killer or a serial rapist because he is in such abundance. The magnitude of the batterer's violence can best be illustrated by the following facts:

- A woman is murdered by her intimate partner an average of every six hours of each day in the United States.
- Domestic disturbance calls are among the most dangerous types of calls for police officers, resulting in approximately 10 percent of all police officers killed in the line of duty.[73]
- There are an estimated 1.8 million to 3.6 million American women physically battered by their intimate partners each year in the United States.[74]
- Over 1 million women each year seek medical help for injuries caused by battering.[75]
- The American Medical Association in 1991 declared domestic violence one of the nation's top five public health problems.[76]
- Statistics cited by the National Center for State Courts and the National Sheriffs Association clearly show that cases dealing with domestic relations are potentially the most dangerous matters to appear before any judge; such cases are more dangerous than those involving terrorists or drug dealers.[77]

While the above numbers and facts are stunning, the justice system continues to minimize the batterer's significant potential for violence. More the rule than the exception, police often refuse to arrest, prosecutors often refuse to prosecute, and judges often refuse to incarcerate the batterer for his attacks. Although spousal abuse has become one of our society's most serious and potentially lethal social problems, with few exceptions it continues to receive cursory and cosmetic response from the criminal justice system.

General Recommendations

The criminal justice system should recognize spousal abuse as one of the most serious crimes it confronts. Instead of being assigned low priority, as has been done in the past, domestic violence should be given priority response. Members of the justice system should respond to each case of spousal abuse as if it were a potential homicide until the lethality of an individual assailant can be determined.

The justice system has traditionally handled spousal abuse cases with less interest and emphasis than those of strangers who have been assaulted by unrelated assailants. When addressing the safety of a battered woman, don't employ such a double standard. A victim of spousal abuse is in no less danger or need than one who has been assaulted by a perfect stranger. The reality is that the battered woman is at greater risk because there is little doubt that her abuser will continue to pursue her. Conversely, strangers who assault unrelated parties seldom present an ongoing threat to their victims. The justice system must not tolerate double standards regarding crimes of violence. Spousal abuse must be addressed with the focus that it demands since there is such a high probability of repeat violence, injury, or death.

• **The criminal justice system should develop and project intolerance toward the behaviors and actions of the batterer.** Professionals should never joke or minimize what the batterer has done or deny the continued threat that he presents to his victim. Let the batterer and his attorney know that you consider the offense a serious one, and that you will do whatever is necessary to prevent its reoccurrence.

• **The criminal justice system should not treat spousal abuse as if it is an act of private violence.** Like all acts of violence, it should be prosecuted as a misdemeanor or felony offense within a court of criminal jurisdiction. If a civil court is to be utilized, it should be used only as an adjunct to the criminal proceedings, not as an alternative to it. It is not uncommon for members of the justice system to suggest that felonious domestic assaults involving weapons and injuries be sent to a civil jurisdiction for mediation and disposal. Would the same professionals consider referring felonious assaults involving strangers to anything but a court that has criminal authority?

• **All agencies of the criminal justice system should develop specialized units that concentrate their efforts on cases of spousal abuse.** Police departments, district attorney's offices, probation departments, and victim assistance programs should not only implement domestic violence programs, but also closely network with one another so that the arrest, prosecution, and follow-up of the batterer is performed with a greater level of continuity and efficiency. The networking of specialized units would provide the victim with a greater degree of safety and protection.

The staffs that comprise these units should receive comprehensive and ongoing training on the subject of domestic violence. It is only through a complete understanding of the abuser and his victim that members of the justice system can become capable of making reasonable judgments and sound decisions. Training should include clear and realistic methods of dealing with each batterer relative to his profile and position on the continuum.

It is also recommended that all domestic violence units develop and implement formal policies relative to the processing of spousal abuse cases. Without specific rules and procedures, decision-making often becomes too discretionary and inconsistent from one professional to the next, allowing bias, prejudice, and sexism to enter the decision-making process often leading to tragic results.

Once policy and procedures are implemented, they should be closely monitored for compliance. The violation of policies should be addressed with various forms of disciplinary action. This is particularly important since policy violations that result in the serious injury or death of a victim can lead to significant liability for the agency and personnel involved.

• **The criminal justice system should create a pro-victim, pro-arrest, pro-prosecution policy regarding spousal abuse cases.** The arrest and prosecution of the batterer have been shown to be strong deterrents to recidivism. In most cases, the only methods that the chronic batterer responds to are those that are punitive in nature. Without consequences or threat of penalties, the Category Three abuser seldom withdraws from the relentless pursuit of his victim.

Take the decision to arrest, prosecute, and incarcerate the batterer out of the hands of the battered woman. She will frequently ask that he not be arrested or prosecuted for his crimes. If incarcerated, she will often request that he receive an early release. Recognize that the thought process of the battered woman may appear illogical. She has probably been held hostage by her abuser for many years. She may still have feelings for him. She also fears him and doesn't want to die. By wanting to drop the charges, she is trying to convey the message that she is not responsible for his arrest. She is trying to soften her position so that he will not retaliate when he is released from jail.

Police departments can reduce the victim's exposure to retaliation by adopting pro-arrest and mandatory arrest policies. Additionally, if investigatory and evidence-gathering procedures are efficiently and comprehensively performed, district attorneys may find it possible to prosecute the batterer even in the absence of the victim's testimony.

• **The term Battering Male Syndrome should apply to all men who possess a personality disorder and who beat their intimate partners on an ongoing, systematic, and chronic basis.** Such a syndrome would help in spotlighting batterers who should be handled by police officers, prosecutors, probation officers, judges, and jailers with great vigilance and concern. It seems only appropriate that if attorneys are to use the Battered Women's Syndrome in the defense of a woman who has slain her assailant, criminal justice personnel should utilize the Battering Male Syndrome in convincing a judge and jury of the significance and magnitude of the man's violence.

Likewise, the term Serial Batterer should apply to all assailants who have a lengthy history of multiple victims. If we accept the terms serial rapist and serial killer to define men who rape and murder multiple victims over extended periods of time, then why not accept a term that describes men who physically batter multiple intimate partners over extended periods of time as well?

•**Jailers and judges should develop a policy whereby "good time" or an early release is not considered for domestic abusers, even in instances where the victim appears and makes such a re-**

quest. While incarcerated, the batterer will frequently call his victim in a coercive attempt to have him released. Such a policy removes her from being placed in such a position.

To take the decision out of the victim's hands of whether to arrest, prosecute, or incarcerate the batterer releases her from an unnecessary burden. It provides her with the ability to convince the abuser that she is not responsible for his incarceration.

• **All criminal justice agencies should create a "hands off" policy relative to staff members who try to intercede on behalf of a batterer who is also a peer or acquaintance.**

It is not unusual for police officers and court officials to "speak up" for a peer who has been arrested for domestic violence. Such activities result in significant danger for the victim and reasonable liability for the individual agency that the "lobbyist" represents.

• **Do not allow one victim's refusal to cooperate to affect the attitude and assistance that you show and provide another.** Many battered women, particularly if provided with adequate support and protection during the processing of their cases, will seize the opportunity to use the justice system to its fullest. Handle each case of spousal abuse as if it is your first, and don't allow those who drop charges to affect the sensitivity that you show others.

It is well known that in many criminal justice agencies, there is an unspoken policy not to address cases of spousal abuse because of the perception that "it is a family matter and she will drop the case anyway." Don't allow this perception to result in professional indifference. Your attitude is contagious. The more resistance you show the battered woman, the more resistance you can expect in return. On the other hand, the more support you display to her, the more you can anticipate her cooperation.

Even if you have great difficulty in accepting the victim's wavering responses, give the case your complete support for the sake of her children. If the high withdrawal rate in spousal abuse cases causes you to experience burn-out, remember the children who are caught up in the relationship as motivation to pursue the charges. If the victim cannot be assertive, it is up to you to take control.

• **All areas of the criminal and civil justice systems should work together in the issuance and follow-up of peace bonds, restraining orders, orders of protection, and conditional releases of**

batterers. Police officers, probation officers, prosecutors, and judges all play a significant role in the preparation and monitoring of these orders and should recognize their effectiveness when these orders are properly addressed.

The batterer is very cunning and becomes acutely aware of when written dictates carry no real consequences. If left unmonitored, he quickly recognizes that he can violate them without fear of revocation or incarceration. Their initial intent and credibility becomes destroyed whenever they are perceived as meaningless documents.

Victims frequently complain that the justice system virtually ignores such orders once they have been issued. Such inaction communicates to the battered woman that written and verbal restraints are fraudulent ploys to accelerate the conclusion of her case. She also becomes faced with an agitated and dangerous assailant who sees that she is getting little or no support from the justice system. If an order is issued, monitor it. If an order is violated, prosecute it. If the defendant is found guilty of the violation, don't hesitate to incarcerate him.

• **All members of the justice system should work together in legally removing all guns from the possession of the chronic batterer.** Police can begin this process by legally confiscating guns from the assailant during the investigation of a domestic disturbance. Prosecutors, probation officers, and victim assistance programs should advocate for their confiscation during the arraignment and trial process. Once weapons have been legally confiscated, judges should order and arrange for them to be destroyed.

The batterer will inevitably insist that his weapons be returned to him. Guns are one of his primary means of maintaining control over his victim and over those who interfere in his relationship with her. Whenever possible, maintain custody of the batterer's weapons and challenge all requests that they be returned.

Criminal justice professionals should also review the possibility that the batterer may be illegally possessing some of his weapons. The possession of sawed-off shotguns and various automatic weapons are considered violations of federal law. Local law enforcement personnel should refer all such violations to the Alcohol, Tobacco, and Firearms Division of the Federal Government for possible criminal charges. This should be done in conjunction with the batterer's arrest on all appropriate city and state violations.

An untold number of women and children could be saved each year if weapons were removed from the custody of Category Three batterers. If you have the legal authority to do so, don't hesitate.

• **Criminal justice experts should organize a task force that would review, revise, and rewrite their stalking laws so that they can be enforced without apprehension.** The less flawed these laws are, the more we can expect them to be utilized by law enforcement officials in their efforts to assist the battered woman.

As the battered woman tries to physically withdraw from the relationship, her abuser will undoubtedly intimidate and terrorize her from a distance. He will sit in his car outside her home and let her see him watching as she leaves. He will follow her to work and will be there when she gets off. From a distance and without saying a word, he is showing her that he still has control; that he could harm and even kill her at will. Stalking is aggression without violence. It implies, however, that violence is imminent if she does not return to him. It is just another means of domination and control. The same qualities that he used to keep her in the relationship are simply used in a different form to force her return.

Many states have passed what have become known as stalking laws. The primary intent of these laws is to prevent an act of violence before it occurs. Stalking laws make the systematic and threatening pursuit of a victim, even in the absence of verbal and physical assault, a criminal offense. Many states, however, have prepared these laws in haste. As a result, they are often poorly written and have numerous technical flaws that make them difficult to enforce.

• **All members of the justice system should lobby to strengthen laws and penalties relative to spousal abuse.** Ask and lobby legislators to develop and pass laws that increase criminal penalties relative to the number of convictions that a batterer has for attacks on his wife or girlfriend.

Louisiana currently has a state law whereby someone who damages a soft drink machine can receive up to two years in prison;[78] however, a man who shatters the face of his wife, or threatens her with a loaded gun, is generally charged with a misdemeanor punishable by no more than five months in jail. Likewise, another Louisiana statute states that an individual who steals "an alligator, alligator skin, or part of an alligator, dead or alive," with a value of more than five hundred dollars, "shall be imprisoned for not more than ten years."[79] In contrast, no matter how many times an individual has been convicted in the City of New Orleans for breaking his wife's bones, if arrested on a city misdemeanor, he can receive only five months in jail for his crime.

• **The various agencies that make up the justice system should keep themselves stocked with literature relative to spousal abuse.** The literature should include information about local community resources for battered women, general information concerning the causes of and solutions to domestic violence, and materials that explain the laws and agencies that are available to assist victims of family violence. Pamphlets and resource information should be carried by police officers on patrol and should be made available in all waiting areas of the justice system where the public gathers.

• **All agencies of the justice system should use forms, rubber stamps, etc., that differentiate between cases of domestic violence and others.** While this does not imply that other types of offenses are not important, crimes of spousal abuse are potentially the most lethal that you will encounter.

Few criminal offenses possess the unique qualities of domestic violence cases; consequently, they warrant a unique and specialized means of reporting the data. Specialized forms for reporting, tracking, and prosecuting cases of domestic violence would create a higher level of continuity and efficiency. If the justice system can justify special forms for the reporting of traffic accidents, surely it can justify the same process for the reporting of cases that are potential homicides.

• **Members of the justice system should recognize the significant civil liability that exists if it can be proven that they did not provide the battered woman with what is considered to be equal protection under the law.** There should be no double standards when advising, assisting, and protecting the victim from the batterer. Such matters must not be handled any less diligently than incidents of violence that involve unrelated parties.

After examining the facts and the defendant's prior history of violence, law enforcement personnel should question the appropriateness of trying to mediate such a case or in referring it to a civil court. They should also question their quick and often uninformed reasoning in referring the defendant to treatment in lieu of other criminal penalties. Such inappropriate decisions and referrals are often made in haste in an attempt to arrive at a quick decision about an issue filled with time-consuming complexities.

While some professionals will argue that spousal abuse cases are handled differently than others in the spirit of trying to keep the family unit together, it is imperative that we challenge such ideologies. The fact is, the battered woman is generally in much greater danger than is the victim of a perfect stranger. Additionally, many battered women do not want to keep the family together. They want to be protected.

Instead of addressing spousal abuse as an act of private violence, criminal justice personnel should focus on the criminality of such matters. Violence inflicted on another is a crime, irrespective of the assailant's relationship to the victim. A battered woman should not be treated differently from any other victim of a violent crime.

Always remember that if you impose double standards when addressing the needs and safety of the battered woman, civil juries can impose enormous civil judgments that have the potential to place you in permanent financial bankruptcy. Civil courts have long arms that are capable of reaching deep into your pockets. Protect yourself from civil litigation and liability by doing what is right. There are only a small percentage of criminal justice professionals who possess immunity from civil liability. Treat all battered women in the same manner as you would treat any other victim of a violent crime.

Members of the Police Department

The Call

The police complaint operator is usually the first voice that the battered woman encounters when she reaches out to the justice system for protection. She is often very intimidated by the thought of making such a call and has probably endured considerable violence before acquiring the courage to do so.

The victim is generally in a crisis situation when she makes her call for assistance, and the last thing she needs to detect from the complaint operator is an attitude of indifference and callousness.

It is very important that you receive such calls in a manner and voice that suggests acceptance, support, interest, and concern.

You should also project tolerance and patience and must never appear critical or judgmental. The nature and volume of domestic calls often results in a complaint operator sounding robotic, mechanical, and sometimes hostile. Periodically listen to some of your taped conversations with callers to determine if your telephone demeanor is pleasant and professional.

• **It is important that you acquire and take control of the dialogue between you and the caller so that information can be collected quickly and effectively.** If the call warrants priority response, immediately dispatch a police car upon acquiring essential information. Supporting data can be obtained following your initial dispatch.

• **When receiving a call involving domestic violence, you should request the following information:**

- What is the caller's name? What is the victim's name?
- What is the caller's phone number? What is the victim's phone number?
- If the caller is too hysterical to give you clear information, ask that she place someone, if available, on the phone who can.
- What is the address from which the caller is calling?
- What is the exact address of the disturbance? Apartment number? Building number?
- What is the closest major intersection or landmark to the disturbance?
- Ask the caller to explain the problem.
- Is the disturbance still in progress?
- Are there any serious injuries? Is the caller physically okay?
- Does the caller need an ambulance? Is medical assistance needed?
- Did the assailant use a gun or a weapon in his assault?
- Does the assailant carry or have easy access to a gun or a weapon? What type of weapon?
- Does the assailant have a history of threats or assaults with a weapon? Does he have a history of violence?

- Is there a history of violence or disturbances at the address from which the caller is calling?
- What is the caller's relationship to the assailant? To the victim?
- What is the relationship of the victim to the assailant?
- Are there any other victims?
- What are their names?
- Is the assailant still at the scene of the disturbance?
- What is the name of the assailant? What is his address?
- If the assailant is no longer at the scene of the disturbance, where did he go?
- If the assailant fled the scene, is he on foot? Driving a car? What is the description of the car?
- What is the description of the assailant? What is he wearing?
- What are the names of the people currently at the scene of the disturbance?

• **If it is apparent that the victim is not in imminent danger, attempt to keep her on the phone and get as much information as possible.** The caller's statements and what is heard in the background may assist responding units and may also become useful as evidence should the batterer be arrested for a serious offense. If necessary, hold a conversation with the victim until the police arrive at the scene of the disturbance.

If it appears, however, that the caller may be in significant danger, ask her to leave the phone off the hook and, if possible, to flee the residence. Your suggestion should be made immediately after acquiring enough information to establish the identity of the assailant and the location of the disturbance. Leaving the phone off the hook is both a means of gathering evidence and a method of maintaining contact with the victim if she does not make it out of the residence safely. Should she flee the location of the disturbance, instruct her to remain within close proximity until the police arrive and to identify herself upon their arrival.

• **If possible, separate calls into priority and non-priority response categories.** In your attempt to prioritize domestic violence calls, the following factors should be considered. A police car should be sent to the scene of the disturbance immediately if:

- there is an assault in progress
- there have been threats of suicide
- there have been threats of homicide
- guns or other weapons are present
- the assailant is under the influence of drugs or alcohol
- anyone is injured
- the assailant has a history of violence
- screaming, crying, or yelling can be heard in the background
- the caller is incoherent or hysterical
- the caller is whispering to you cautiously or cannot openly answer your questions
- the caller is a young child and appears to be in great distress
- it is determined that the assailant fits the profile of a Category Three batterer
- the phone communication with the caller is broken or interrupted by the assailant
- someone is being held hostage

Never second-guess these factors when assigning a domestic call priority status. It is better to react and play it safe than to minimize the danger and allow the violence to escalate into a possible homicide. Let the caller know whether the call is being assigned priority or non-priority status and give the approximate time of arrival. If phone communication with the caller is interrupted or broken, attempt to return the victim's call to determine the status of the disturbance and to let her know that you are responding to the situation.

• **You should always refer a priority domestic call to the nearest available patrol car.** If the closest car is detained with another investigation, the call should be relayed to the next nearest available car. Under no circumstances should there be a delay in response time. Any delay could result in a homicide. If the patrol car receiving the dispatch is involved in a non-priority call, it should immediately proceed to the priority disturbance.[80]

If staffing patterns permit, you should always dispatch the assignment to a two-person unit.[81] If not available, refer the call to at least two single officer cars. It is very dangerous for only one officer to respond to domestic disturbances, particularly without a backup. Always alert the responding officers if the possibility exists that the disturbance involves the use of weapons.

Ask that the officer(s) immediately notify you upon their arrival at the scene of the disturbance.

• **If you receive a domestic call that has evolved into a hostage situation but you do not have experience in hostage negotiations, place someone on the phone who does.** All police complaint operators should acquire training and expertise in the area of hostage negotiations prior to assuming their roles. Such specialized training could make a difference in whether someone survives such a disturbance.

The Approach

Since domestic disturbances are high risk calls, at least two officers should approach the scene of the disturbance simultaneously. The responding officers should also alert the closest available backup of their approach. If, after reviewing and surveying the scene, you feel that the disturbance is more volatile than originally anticipated, immediately ask that the backup come to the scene to provide assistance.

Always solicit additional information from the complaint operator that may be needed prior to entering the scene. Never assume. If you do not have important details, always ask.

• **Whenever responding to a call involving domestic violence, always make certain that you have the following items and materials in your car:**

- a first aid kit
- specialized forms for the reporting of domestic violence
- a camera and film
- a bulletproof vest
- a flashlight
- pamphlets explaining community resources for victims of domestic violence
- literature explaining the victim's legal rights and her legal resources

- a comprehensive community resource directory
- all other standard police equipment

• **Consider the use of your police light and siren relative to the information that has been provided to you by the complaint operator.** While a more dramatic approach may make an assailant flee, thus leaving a victim safe, such an approach can also cause him to become more agitated and volatile. Never park your car directly in front of the residence in which the disturbance occurred.[82] This may make you an easy target for the assailant. If you have a bulletproof vest available, wear it. Although you may feel that wearing a vest is physically restrictive and somewhat of an inconvenience, it could save your life.

• **Upon your approach at the location of the disturbance, be alert and vigilant.** Recognize your potential vulnerability to the assailant and the possibility that he may have a gun. While he may be aware of your arrival, you may not be able to see him. Always keep your guard up. Remember that a significant number of police officers are killed or injured while making such calls.

Don't underestimate or minimize your risk of being injured or killed in a domestic disturbance. Always approach the scene as if the assailant is anticipating your arrival and has a weapon in his possession. In many cases he does. It doesn't take any additional time or effort to be careful and cautious. A change in attitude could save your life or that of your partner's.

• **Prior to leaving your patrol car, perform a visual inspection of the disturbance area for possible points of a surprise attack by the batterer.** Carefully scan your immediate environment. Visually inspect all shrubbery, sides of buildings, open entrances, or any area in which the assailant could be hiding. If the suspect is sighted during your visual inspection, order that he hold his hands high above his head. If he is not seen, slowly and carefully approach the scene of the disturbance while continuing to scan the immediate area.

• **If two or more officers are approaching the residence simultaneously, always approach from different directions where you can visually see one another.** This will make it difficult for the assailant to attack you without being seen.

If your approach is at night, never hold your flashlight directly in front of your body.[83] Always turn your flashlight off when not in use. The light will make you an easy target for a suspect who may have his gun focused on you. Remain hypervigilant and listen for screams, gunshots, or anything that may alert you to potential danger.

If it is not necessary for you to speak to a fellow officer as you approach the residence, it is best that you remain silent. If the disturbance is during the day, use hand motions to communicate with one another. The less exposure you have prior to your assessment of the situation, the safer you are.

• **As you approach the door, carefully listen for noise that may alert you to the volatility of the disturbance.** Advise your backup of any such information that may be helpful. Never stand directly in front of the door of the residence in which the incident is occurring. Always stand to the side. If possible, another officer should look through an available window to observe anyone who may approach the door.[84]

After you have carefully reviewed the scene, knock on the door and announce your presence. The resident should be ordered to open the door slowly. If no one answers your order to open the door, don't leave the scene without thoroughly investigating the complaint to the best of your ability. Knock on the doors of neighbors to determine if they heard or know of the disturbance. Stay at the scene until you are certain that there is no one in danger. Silence does not necessarily indicate that the caller no longer needs your assistance. On the contrary, it could mean that someone is still in considerable danger or is being held hostage.

• **If the suspect or victim responds to your request to open the door of the residence, it is safest to ask for the assailant to step out into a common hallway, patio area, porch, etc., for questioning.** By doing so, he cannot readily retrieve a weapon and it is much easier for you to keep your eyes focused on him. If the suspect answers the door and asserts that there is no problem, ask that you be allowed to enter. Most suspects will allow you to gain entrance on request.

Once you have identified and visually focused on the assailant, do not let him out of your sight. Do not turn your back to him at any time. Immediately frisk the suspect to ascertain whether he has a weapon. If in your initial questioning he becomes physically aggressive with you, consider charging him with resisting arrest or assault on an officer, etc., and handcuff him until you feel he is under control.

• **As you are frisking and questioning the suspect, have the second officer focus on and address the needs of the victim.** Recognize that the victim may not want you to question and challenge her abuser and may react aggressively to the situation.[85] It should be the responsibility of the second officer to assist and maintain control of the victim and other witnesses.

The Investigation

Whereas a battered woman may call for your assistance during or shortly following the commission of the offense, upon your arrival she may assure you that everything is fine. She may also insist that you leave without investigating further.

• **Recognize that such a victim often responds in the same manner as a hostage.** She fears that if she takes a position against her batterer, he may retaliate by torturing, injuring, or even killing her. Don't simply take her word that all is resolved. Scan the residence for signs of domestic violence such as shattered glass, broken furniture, or ransacked rooms. Question witnesses and neighbors who were near the scene of the disturbance when it took place. Visibly inspect the victim for any signs of physical abuse such as cuts, bruises, lacerations, and torn clothing.

Even in the absence of the victim's cooperation, if there are obvious signs of domestic violence, arrest the batterer if you have statutory authority to do so.

• **Restoring order and control should be a prerequisite to your investigation.** As you enter the residence, continue to be hypervigilant. Visually scan the premises for any signs of danger or vulnerability. Immediately ask those who were not part of the incident to leave the premises. Turn off radios, television sets, and remove all distractions from the residence. Determine which parties were involved in the disturbance and the relationship they have to each other. Inquire about the problem in an effort to determine whether an offense has been committed.

• **During your investigation of the domestic disturbance, you may find that the batterer is rather submissive and subdued, while the victim appears argumentative, demanding, and aggres-**

sive. Perception of such behavior may lead you to believe that the woman is actually the aggressor while the male is the one who has been assaulted.

Beware of misleading interactions that take place at the scene of the disturbance. Your presence has temporarily taken control out of the hands of the batterer and placed it into those of the victim. Fearing arrest, the batterer often goes into a mode of behavior that dramatically reduces his chances of being arrested and incarcerated. His somewhat sedate behavior also makes him appear as if he is being victimized by the woman. The battered woman, on the other hand, recognizes that she has temporary control over her abuser and begins to vent various emotions that may make her appear to be the assailant.

The possibility that a woman could be the lone aggressor or a co-aggressor in a domestic disturbance is not discounted. It is not suggested that you give blanket absolution to a woman from being responsible for her actions and behavior. You should be aware, however, that both parties may respond in a manner that causes you to misread the circumstances. Be careful not to misinterpret the behavior of a victim, who in many cases has experienced years of incomprehensible physical violence and domination. If you are in doubt as to what actually took place, acquire a criminal record on both parties. An arrest record that displays a perpetual pattern of aggression is an excellent means of interpreting questionable situations.

• **During the onset of the investigation, be certain that you have complete control of the situation.** Under no circumstances should you let the assailant out of your sight. Never permit him to roam freely around the residence during the investigation. In some cases he may be partially undressed. Never permit him to go into the bedroom to retrieve shoes or clothes. While this is frequently allowed, it is a very dangerous practice, since the bedroom is where guns are often kept.[86] If it is necessary to retrieve such items, send another officer to perform this function.

• **If you determine that a gun or a knife was used in the assault, immediately locate and confiscate the weapon.** Any weapon confiscated should be secured and removed from view. Never leave a gun or a knife where it is accessible to the assailant or his victim.

• **Immediately determine whether the victim has been injured. If she has, call an ambulance.** While many injuries received from blows to the head and body may not necessarily be visible, always play it safe and call for emergency medical personnel to examine the woman. Medical attention is particularly important if a head injury has occurred and the victim has been drinking.

If it is apparent that the victim has suffered only minor bruises and lacerations, perform first aid and indicate that you have done so in your report. Even if it appears that the victim has not been injured in the assault, offer to transport her to the hospital emergency room for a routine examination.

• **If small children are present, address their physical and emotional needs.** There is perhaps nothing more traumatic to children than to witness violence in the home. While they may need both your reassurance and support, also consider that they may have been physically abused as well. Closely check all children for signs of abuse and neglect. If any of the signs of child abuse are present, use proper procedures in addressing their needs and consider booking the suspect on appropriate charges. If a child protection agency exists in your area, call it for specialized support and assistance.

• **Identify and ask all witnesses to remain at the scene until they have been interviewed.** Interview all witnesses in your effort to establish whether a crime has been committed. Knock on the doors of the immediate neighbors to determine if they heard or witnessed what took place.

• **Never interview the victim, her children, or individual witnesses in front of the assailant.** If you do, the immediate presence of the assailant will dramatically inhibit their responses. Always take them into a separate room where the abuser cannot see or hear what they say to you.

• **Determine whether the victim has a documented peace bond, order of protection, or restraining order in her possession.** Read the order and establish whether it has been violated by the assailant's presence or behavior. Also check to see if the suspect has outstanding warrants for his arrest.

• **If the assailant has left the scene of the assault, you should make an immediate attempt to locate him.** If not, the victim may remain in considerable danger. If after a reasonable search he cannot be located, a report should be filed and a warrant issued for his arrest. Always consider transporting the victim and her children to a safe location.

The Report

Remember that the manner in which you document statements and related evidence may be the primary determinant as to whether the suspect is tried for his crime. Since many district attorneys review only the police report in reaching a decision to either accept or reject a case of domestic abuse for prosecution, the contents of your written narrative are critical to that decision-making process.

Many prosecutors have adopted the policy of bringing a batterer to trial even in the absence of the victim's testimony or cooperation. This policy is possible, however, only if the police report and related materials are accurate and comprehensive enough to do so.

• **A checklist of information and materials that may be included in the police report is as follows:**

- location of residence where disturbance occurred
- name of owner or inhabitant of residence where disturbance occurred
- number of prior calls made to residence
- relationship of the assailant and victim(s)
- name, address, and date of birth of the assailant and victim(s)
- probable cause documented
- "Miranda Rights" read
- description of the allegations
- offense that party is being charged with, if any
- corroborating statements of witnesses
- threatening behavior during investigation
- admissions of the assailant
- list of injuries and attention given
- multiple victims listed
- children's injuries addressed and documented
- assailant's history of violence

- visible signs of violence
- weapons used and how
- description of the assailant
- description of the assailant's car
- description of the evidence collected
- property damage
- condition of residence
- restraining order or protective order violation
- probation violation
- dialogue with complaint operator
- description of demeanor of persons interviewed
- accuracy of names, addresses, and phone numbers of victim and witnesses
- back-up address and phone number of the victim and witnesses
- names of all officers at the scene

• **Note in your report that the suspect's "Miranda Rights" have been explained to him on a timely basis and immediately after his arrest.** With such a high number of police calls being made, without putting that notation in writing, it may be very difficult to recall if this area was properly addressed during your investigation. If you have read the perpetrator his rights, state it in your report. Never take the chance of having the perpetrator's case dismissed or overturned on a technicality.

• **Clearly and accurately list the names, addresses and phone numbers of the victim and witnesses in your report.** Describe the personal demeanor of all parties interviewed. If it can be determined who actually made the emergency call and spoke to the complaint operator, always note the name, address, and phone number of the individual in your report. It is also a good idea to get a back-up address and phone number from witnesses, in the event that they change their locations between the time of the arrest and the trial. It is particularly important that you acquire an alternative phone number and address from the victim, since she may not be staying in the same residence in which the assault took place. Many cases are dismissed by the district attorney's office because of inability to locate the victim or an important witness.

• **The names, badge numbers, and addresses of all officers that came to the scene of the disturbance should be listed in the police report.** Even names of officers who only briefly appeared at the scene should be included in the report. If necessary, their corroborating statements could prove very beneficial to the case at the time of the trial.

• **List and describe all weapons used and confiscated relative to the assault.** Comment on all procedures utilized in the collection of the weapons. List and describe all other physical evidence gathered and confiscated at the scene. Make certain that you collect all evidence in a manner prescribed and dictated by law.

• **The police report should clearly and accurately state the detailed allegations made by the victim.** The victim's emotional state should be described as well. All corroborating statements made by the witnesses should also be included, along with the officers' personal observations that may support the claims.

Routinely request all primary victims and witnesses to submit a written statement as to what took place. All written statements should include the author's original signature, phone numbers, addresses, and date on which the statement was written and signed.

• **Obtain a complete statement from the alleged assailant only if he has waived his fifth amendment rights.** Describe his emotional state. Carefully observe and describe any threatening or abusive behavior made by the suspect during the course of the investigation. If an assault is made in your presence, it should be clearly noted in the report. If appropriate or necessary, additional charges should be considered if a secondary offense was committed after your arrival or during your investigation.

• **If the assailant fled on foot or in a car prior to your arrival on the scene, a full description of the suspect and the vehicle that he was driving should be included in the report.**

• **Always include the suspect's full name (middle initial included), address, and date of birth in the report.** Check closely for accuracy. This information is particularly important should the assailant fail to appear in court, or if he fled prior to your arrival and an arrest warrant has been issued. Without a correct name and date of birth, the suspect may never be arrested. Never accept as fact the verbal response of the assailant regarding his name and birth date. Always order him to provide a driver's license or a photo I.D. to substantiate that the information he provided to you was correct.

• **Clearly note the offense for which the suspect is being charged and/or arrested.** To justify all measures that you have taken before, during, and after the investigation, always include in your report the issue of "probable cause." Clearly explain in writing what led to your actions and decisions. Your reasoning may very well be challenged by a defense attorney. Your report, statements from witnesses, personal observations, and the physical evidence that you have gathered should always support your reasoning for addressing the disturbance in the manner that you employ.

Remember that "probable cause" is based on the totality of the circumstances and not necessarily on a single piece of evidence. It should ideally be based on more than mere suspicion. For example, while a victim's allegations alone may not be enough to establish "probable cause," a ripped blouse, the assailant's personal demeanor, history of violence, bruises on the victim's body, and statements from witnesses supporting her allegations certainly would. While "probable cause" is somewhat subjective, it must also be an objective determination that is free of bias, stereotypes, and preconceptions.

If the conversation between the complaint operator and you suggests and supports the issue of "probable cause," state the related dialogue in your written report.

The report should clearly define the relationship between the victim and her assailant. It should also include the relationship of the assailant to the witnesses, if any.

• **The report should list the exact address where the disturbance occurred and the name of the individual who owns, rents, or resides at that address.**

• **If the assailant has violated a peace bond, restraining order, protective order, condition of release, etc., note the violation and the related case number in the report.**

• **Your report should clearly describe all injuries incurred by any party at the scene of the disturbance. Any signs of child abuse should be stated in writing and a copy forwarded to your local child protection agency for review and follow-up.**

• **If you witness property damage or a residence in disarray**

during your investigation, describe what you saw in your report. Always give an estimated value of the damage and the types of property that were destroyed. Courts frequently award restitution to victims for property loss, and such detailed information is generally very helpful in the court's assessment of the damage.

• **Give the victim the number of the incident or police report for future reference and follow-up.** Her ability to locate information relative to the incident without a valid reference number may be extremely limited. Carry pocket-sized forms in your car on which the incident number can be easily listed and given to the victim. Such forms should also list the community resources that can assist her.

Many prosecutors have adopted the policy of bringing a batterer to trial even in the absence of the victim's testimony or cooperation. This policy is possible, however, only if the police report and related materials are accurate and comprehensive enough to do so.

The Collection of Evidence

The collection of evidence in a manner prescribed by law is an essential part of the prosecutorial process. If necessary, call your crime lab to the scene of the offense. As noted previously, many district attorneys are forced to go to trial without the assistance of the victim, particularly when the case is that of a homicide. All evidence should be collected in a manner that cannot be challenged on technical grounds by a defense attorney.

Evidence Checklist:

- medical report
- weapons used
- photographs of crime scene
- photographs of injuries
- fingerprints
- copies of restraining orders
- copies of conditions of probation
- written statements from witnesses
- broken glass

- broken furniture
- broken phones
- torn and bloodstained clothing
- pieces of splintered windows and doors
- burned property
- photographs of vehicular damage
- broken auto parts
- shredded clothing
- shredded or torn personal photographs
- empty gun shells
- 911 and dispatch tapes
- personal phone recorder tape
- threatening notes and letters

• **Since there is generally a lengthy period of time that elapses between the suspect's arrest and his trial, you should closely follow all legal procedures regarding the chain of evidence and its storage.** Store all evidence properly. This is particularly important if the suspect has fled the scene and is at large for several months before being apprehended. If not, the suspect's attorney will quickly seize the opportunity to declare the evidence as inadmissible or contaminated. Tag all evidence in a manner that will not cause confusion or disqualify its use by the prosecutor. The tags should accurately correspond with the evidence described and listed in the police report.

• **Any and all property or related material that has been used, damaged, destroyed, or left in disarray should be considered as possible evidence in a case of domestic violence.** Shattered glass, damaged furniture, bloodstained clothing, phones pulled from walls, splintered and damaged doors and windows, shredded photographs, burned possessions and damaged automobiles are the most common physical evidence of a domestic disturbance.

• **Any instrument that has been used as a weapon in the assault should be confiscated.** Guns, knives, clubs, rocks, or virtually any objects that have been used to assault or strike the victim and support the allegations of witnesses should be considered important physical evidence.

• **If there are physical signs of a disturbance, photograph the entire crime scene.** Take pictures of shattered glass, doors, and windows. Photograph ransacked rooms and broken contents. Bloodstained and splattered rooms and clothing in addition to the victim's visible injuries should also be documented in this manner.

You cannot exhaust this form of documentation. Photographing a crime scene is a powerful means of conveying to a prosecutor, judge, or jury the seriousness of what took place. A verbal description of a crime scene in the absence of photographs often creates little impact.

• **Secondary evidence should be acquired and included as valuable supporting documentation.** Secondary evidence should include copies of written restraining or protective orders, conditions of probations, statements written and submitted by witnesses, 911 and complaint operator tapes, threatening letters and notes, and personal answering machine tapes.

• **If the victim has been treated at the scene or transported to a medical facility for assistance, include a copy of the medical report as evidence.** Such documentation is extremely important to a prosecutor. In many cases, the information contained within the medical report will support the allegation and statements of the victim and her witnesses. It may also support the professional observations that you made during your investigation.

If the victim does not immediately seek medical attention, but decides to do so after you have left the scene, instruct her to forward a copy of the medical report to you as soon as possible. If your report has already been submitted to the district attorney's office for screening, forward the delayed medical report to the prosecutor for review.

• **If the domestic attack was of a very serious nature, take fingerprints of the crime scene.** If the suspect has fled the scene prior to your arrival and a felony has been committed, dust for prints that may link him to the assault. This is particularly important if there were no witness accounts of the crime, except for the testimony of the victim.

The Decision

Historically, police departments' preferred response to domestic disturbance calls was that of non-arrest. Officers were trained to break up the disturbance and to mediate between the batterer and his victim. Some police departments utilized teams of social workers who accompanied officers to the scene of the disturbance and assisted in the mediation. Training manuals actually instructed officers to avoid arresting the perpetrator and to counsel both the assailant and his victim. They were trained to believe that the domestic violence was related to marital problems and that the role of the police was to administer "psychological first aid." The assailant would often be told to simply take a walk and cool off.

Such policies are not only antiquated, they are also worthless in any attempts to get the batterer to stop beating his spouse. Although police departments that promote arrest avoidance and mediation procedures are being challenged around the country, there still remains a strong tendency for police officers to simply "break up" the disturbance and to order the assailant to leave the scene of the violence. Police officers are still inclined to view spousal abuse as something less than a crime, and generally they attempt to defuse the situation by counseling the parties involved.

Don't perpetuate these outdated and archaic policies. Mediation and counseling at the scene do nothing to deter the violence of a chronic batterer. Don't play social worker. Talking to a batterer about what he has done without imposing criminal sanctions and penalties will not modify his violence. If anything, mediation in the absence of arrest for the chronic batterer implies that his behavior is not considered criminal. It also suggests that he can do what he desires to his spouse without fear of consequences. Don't treat this crime any differently than violence against a stranger. If the assailant has committed a criminal act, arrest him. If the act that he has committed is a felony, book him on a felony, not a misdemeanor.

• **All police departments should develop and promote written policies making arrest the preferred response to cases involving domestic violence.** Recent studies have suggested that the arrest of the batterer reduces recidivism and is a strong deterrent to future acts of violence against his victim. While an arrest will not actually reshape the personality of the assailant, it will bring him into the realm of authority that can provide his victim with a support system.

Don't merely "talk to" an assailant who has committed an act of domestic violence. If you feel that a disturbance is too minor to execute an arrest, write the offender a summons. A summons will serve to bring him into the jurisdiction of the court where time can be spent exploring the severity and circumstances of his violence.

While an arrest or summons is certainly not the total solution to domestic violence, it is in most cases the only route to a solution. An arrest or summons will not only make him responsible for what he has done, it will also bring him into a system that can set boundaries and impose sanctions.

• **Many factors may affect your decision to arrest the batterer for his actions.** While some of these determinants are conscious ones, others may be less obvious. The following variables should not influence your decision regarding the arrest of the batterer for an act of domestic violence.

- *Marital or intimate relationship status*: Totally remove the issue of relationship from the decision-making process. There is a general reluctance to arrest an assailant when he is married to or intimate with the victim.
- *Cohabitation*: The fact that the batterer is still living with his victim should not affect your decision to arrest him. Living with her does not give him the right to beat her.
- *Location of the offense*: You should not hesitate to arrest the assailant merely because the battery took place at his own residence. Would you not arrest a neighbor who assaulted another neighbor merely because the attack took place in the assailant's home? Such an offense is a crime regardless of where it takes place.
- *Signed rental lease*: Although the assailant may show you that his name is on the lease of the residence where the assault took place, this does not give him the right to assault his victim. This is especially true if a restraining or protective order has been previously issued and is currently valid.
- *Charming, friendly, "nice guy" appearance*: The batterer can be very charming and manipulative. He may convincingly promise you that it will never happen again. If you find yourself questioning whether he could have committed what is alleged, run a criminal record check on the suspect. You will be surprised how many "nice guys" have extensive criminal records for acts of violence.

- *Victim's prior resistance in filing charges*: While the victim may have refused to cooperate with you in the past, try not to let her previous resistance affect your current decision. There are many reasons why she may have refused to cooperate with you before. Always be objective and concentrate on the current offense.
- *Victim's current resistance to filing charges*: If it is apparent that an act of domestic violence has been committed, you should make an arrest even if the victim is reluctant to cooperate and refuses to press charges. In many jurisdictions, an arrest without the consent of the victim is permissible. The victim is actually considered as a witness of the state, and the state is considered the entity filing the charges.
- *Batterer's need for medical assistance*: If it is appropriate to make an arrest but the batterer requires medical attention because of injuries received in the disturbance, transport him to a hospital and stay with him until he is treated. Do not let the long wait that you anticipate at the hospital influence your decision about whether or not to arrest him. Don't give him a summons only because you don't wish to be delayed.
- *Batterer's attempt to discredit the victim*: Don't allow the assailant's attempt to assassinate the character of the victim take your focus off what he has done. One of his most cunning ploys is to place his victim into a defensive posture. The batterer will frequently claim that she is an unfaithful wife, a terrible mother, a whore, or whatever it takes to discredit her and to justify his actions.

• **If "probable cause" exists along with any of the following factors, the batterer should be arrested without hesitation:**

- if the victim(s) has been injured
- if a weapon was used by the assailant in the attack
- if the assailant has a history of violence
- if there is evidence of physical violence and it is ascertained that it was committed by the assailant
- if significant damage was done to personal property
- if the assailant is a recurring domestic offender
- if past reports and current information suggest that the suspect may be a continued threat to the victim

- if threats were made to the victim by the assailant in the presence of the investigating officer
- if the assailant is under the influence of drugs or alcohol
- if the assailant has a history of stalking his victim
- if threats were made to kill the victim
- if the assailant threatened to commit suicide
- if the disturbance was committed by a Category Three batterer
- if a peace bond, restraining order, probation, etc., has been violated
- if a felony has been committed

• **If none of the above factors exist, and if you elect not to arrest the batterer even though it is apparent that he has violated a criminal statute, execute a summons.** A summons, however, should never be seen as an alternative to the arrest of a batterer who fits the profile of a Category Three abuser.

Recognize that such a batterer is capable of turning a minor disturbance into a multiple homicide immediately after you leave the scene of the disturbance. If a Category Three assailant has caused a domestic disturbance or committed an act of violence, he should be arrested and removed. A summons gives him an opportunity to immediately return to the scene and resume his attack. In most cases, he will.

• **If the suspect is neither arrested nor given a summons to appear in court, you should at least file an incident report with your office.** Such documentation is extremely valuable should future events call for written substantiation of previous assaults.

Never close the investigation of a domestic disturbance without doing a report. Even if the volume of domestic calls to your department is overwhelming, an incident report is recommended, which lists the date, time, address, names of the assailant and victim, and the issue addressed.

• **If you choose not to arrest the suspect, but he does not have the apparent right to be at the location of the disturbance, instruct him to leave and to stay away from the premises.** Let him know that if he returns to the location upon your departure, he will be immediately arrested for trespassing.

• **If you cannot or choose not to arrest the assailant, the victim may desire to vacate the premises in which the disturbance took place.** Do not leave the residence until the woman has retrieved her immediate personal belongings and has safely left the area. Leaving the scene prior to the departure of the battered woman places her in a very volatile and vulnerable position. Let the suspect know that if he pursues the victim upon your departure, you will return and he will be immediately arrested.

Even in the event that you decide to arrest the assailant, advise the victim that he may post bond and be out within hours. If she feels that she may be in continued danger, suggest that she seek safe shelter until the court has imposed boundaries. If she chooses to leave the residence but needs help in locating and getting to a safe shelter, assist her in the acquisition of, and transportation to, the shelter.

• **Clearly explain to the battered woman that she has the right to charge her abuser if an act of domestic violence has taken place.** If, however, you have valid reasons not to charge the assailant, explain to the victim that she may be able to file a complaint through the local justice of the peace, civil court, city court, or district attorney's office. Many states have laws making it your responsibility to advise a battered woman of her legal rights.

• **Unless it is apparent that the woman was also an aggressor in the incident, never suggest that if you arrest the assailant, you will have to arrest her as well.** Such a response is like telling a tourist who has been mugged on the street that if he/she files charges against the mugger, the tourist will also have to be charged. It is unfortunate that in most cities where mandatory and pro-arrest policies relative to domestic violence have been adopted, dual arrest has risen significantly.

In your attempt to get control of a domestic situation, you need not, and should not, practice dual arrest unless both parties are obviously at fault. Arrest only the individual who has committed the violence. In most cases it is not difficult to identify the actual assailant.

• **Prior to leaving the scene of the disturbance, clearly explain to the victim what she is to do and where she is to go to follow through with any of the charges that may have resulted from your**

investigation. The criminal justice system is a very complex and intimidating bureaucracy to any victim, particularly to a battered woman. Unless you clarify to the victim what her options and responsibilities are relative to charges against the batterer, she may become easily confused and overwhelmed and is less likely to follow through with the process.

The Screening, Prosecution, and Follow-up Process

Submit your report to the prosecutor's office on a timely basis. While some district attorneys place time limits and restraints on how long an officer can take to submit a police report, others leave the process somewhat open-ended.

Nevertheless, it is suggested that you self-impose a short and structured time period in which to submit your report. If not, you will begin to have one case piled up on another, and it is unlikely that you will do an adequate job on any of them. There will also be a defense attorney speaking for the assailant and lobbying against the victim immediately following the arrest. A delayed report places the prosecutor in a situation in which he or she has little or no information to counter the defense attorney's position.

- **You will often find it necessary to make supplemental reports that include medical examinations, newfound evidence, estimates of property damage, and phone numbers and addresses that were changed or were not available to you during the initial investigation.** If, after filing your report with the district attorney's office, additional documents or information becomes available, immediately forward it to the prosecutor so it can be included in the screening of the case.
- **Always keep lines of communication open with the prosecutor's office.** Speak up for the victim and be assertive in your efforts to see the defendant brought to trial for what he has done. Never display an attitude of indifference or apathy. If asked by the prosecutor if you have any professional interest in seeing the case prosecuted, respond in the affirmative even when it appears that the victim herself is not interested.

If it is apparent that the victim's charges against the assailant will not be prosecuted, request that all police charges (resisting arrest, battery on an officer, etc.) be prosecuted on behalf of the police department.

• **If a new domestic disturbance occurs while an old case is still pending, forward the information along with the new report to the prosecutor's office for review.** This will show a pattern that may make a difference in how the prosecutor addresses the defendant's original case. It also reinforces the evidence and information that was initially provided.

• **Never ignore a court subpoena, especially one involving domestic violence.** In many such cases, yours is the only testimony other than that of the victim. If the victim sees that you do not support her in the courtroom, she will hesitate calling you in the future for assistance.

Responding to court subpoenas shows interest and concern. Not responding displays apathy and indifference. While it is a legal requirement for all of us to respond to court subpoenas, it is most unfortunate that many police officers often fail to do so. If your inability to respond to a subpoena is due to a time conflict, call the prosecutor and ask that the case be reset. In most instances the district attorney will do so without question.

• **Make yourself available and accessible to the victim in case of future domestic assaults.** Let her know how to contact you in case of future assaults. Share with her your name, card, phone number, and the address of your office.

• **Periodically contact the victim by phone to show support and to determine whether the batterer has left her alone.** As you patrol her neighborhood, occasionally stop by her residence to see if she and her family are safe. Making periodic contact with the victim is a strong deterrent to the batterer's continued assaults.

• **If, following the assailant's arrest and prior to his trial, he violates a condition of release or restraining order, immediately enforce the violation.** If you do not have statutory authority to act on the violation of the court order, explain to his victim where to go to have the matter addressed. If he has committed a new offense while violating the court order, book him accordingly.

Prosecutors

Adopt a policy of pro-prosecution with cases that involve domestic violence. Many district attorneys have a tendency to avoid prosecution in cases of spousal abuse and address them only as civil matters. Prosecute the domestic batterer in the same manner that you would if the two parties were unrelated. In matters of criminal violence, there should be no double standards.

• **Always counsel and advocate for a victim to go forward with her charges.** Let her know that you support her efforts and will do whatever is necessary to assist and protect her. Even in the absence of her cooperation and testimony, if documentation, police testimony, and physical evidence support a conviction, bring the case to trial.

• **Let the battered woman who is intimidated and reluctant to prosecute her abuser know that it is the state (if statutory authority permits) and not the victim who ultimately decides whether a case is accepted and brought to trial.** She is merely a witness for the state. Let the defendant know that it is your decision, not his victim's, to prosecute him for his crime.

• **Adopt a no-drop policy in cases of spousal abuse.** If the victim refuses to cooperate with your efforts to prosecute, and you do not have enough documented evidence to go to trial without her testimony, require that she attend a domestic violence program. Request that she receive professional counseling prior to being given consideration to withdraw her charges. Under no circumstances should consideration be given prior to, or at the time of, arraignment. In many instances, involvement with a family violence agency, along with your support, will be enough to convince and encourage a battered woman to follow through with her case.

• **You may find that many victims are reluctant to cooperate because they don't want their abusers to go to jail.** In such cases, explain to the battered woman that alternatives to incarceration, such as a suspended jail sentence, supervised probation and diversion, mandated community service work, and financial restitution payments, are creative sentencing possibilities that don't require the incarceration of the defendant. Such information often turns a reluctant witness into a cooperative one.

• **In your attempt to prosecute the batterer, you may find it necessary to assist and stabilize the circumstances of his victim.** Consider referring her to family violence or advocacy programs for guidance, counseling, and support. Aligning yourself with such agencies may provide you with the means of addressing the many fears and apprehensions that the battered woman has in pursuing her case. Since many of these agencies have advocates who will accompany the victim to court hearings, it is also a method of giving the case focus.

• **If the victim exhibits outward signs of physical abuse such as bruises, abrasions, stitches, etc., inquire as to whether photographs were taken at the time of the incident.** If they were, acquire a set for your file. If they were not, have someone on your staff immediately photograph the victim and, if possible, include the pictures as evidence.

If the injuries are relatively fresh, schedule the victim to return to your office two or three days later and take a second set of photographs. Bruises are generally more pronounced several days after a beating than immediately following the incident.

Consider your camera as essential to your office as the computer. Don't assume that the police will provide you with such photographs; in most cases, they will not. Without visual aids, you will never be able to create in the minds of a judge or a jury the significance of the victim's injuries following the attack.

• **Train members of your local police department to know what you need as a prosecutor to convict a batterer for the offense of which he has been accused.** Police expertise in investigatory procedures is particularly important in cases of domestic violence when you do not have the cooperation of the victim or if the woman has been killed.

• **The prosecutor who initiates a particular case should always be the one who follows it through to its conclusion.** Such prosecution is imperative if case continuity is to be preserved.

Assigning a single case to a different attorney each time that it is reset results in lost information, confusion, and fragmented insight. Unfortunately, this may be the rule rather than the exception in most jurisdictions.

• **Recognize that your primary duty is to focus on the criminal actions of the defendant, not on the claims made by his attorney against the victim, whether true or not.** In issues of domestic violence, always remember who the defendant is.

A defense attorney will frequently try to buffer a defendant from what he has done by blatantly attacking and assassinating the character of the victim. Some of the issues that he/she alleges in pretrial conferences will be without validation. The defense attorney routinely tries to discredit the battered woman in a desperate attempt to make the defendant's violent behavior more palatable. Never reinforce these efforts by accepting unsubstantiated allegations as absolute fact.

• **Challenge defense attorneys or assailants who insist that the victim wants to withdraw her charges.** Such claims will frequently be made in the victim's absence and will occasionally be supported with an affidavit signed by the woman expressing her desire to drop the case.

Always recognize that such self-serving declarations made by the defense may not be accurate. Even with a notarized document signed by the victim, you should consider the possibility that she did so under much duress. After all, if she lives in absolute fear of her abuser, it becomes even more threatening when he arms himself with an attorney who coerces her to sign a release.

Never assume that the documents the defense presents, or the statements the defense makes relative to a dismissal, are consistent with the victim's personal desires or intent. Always invite the victim in and discuss the matter with her privately. The discussions should never take place within the presence of the assailant or his attorney.

• **If you have enough evidence to convict a Category Three batterer, never agree to or support a diversionary process as an alternative to formal prosecution.** Diversion for the chronic batterer is not only inappropriate, it also suggests that his actions were less than criminal.

Most diversionary processes require the defendant to fulfill specific court mandates in lieu of being prosecuted. Batterers who fail to comply with terms of diversion should not be given a second chance and should be immediately prosecuted for the offense for which they were initially charged.

Always prosecute first and make secondary decisions and agreements within the context of a conviction, whereby penalties can be imposed if the defendant fails to comply. Diversion in the absence of strong sanctions does not work with the chronic batterer.

• **Never allow the chronic batterer to plea bargain a lesser**

charge if you have enough evidence to get a conviction on the more serious offense. If a defendant is charged with a felony and your evidence supports the offense, don't allow him to plea bargain relative to a misdemeanor.

While heavy caseloads may motivate and even dictate the need to negotiate the terms and conditions of a plea, you should do so without reducing the charge to one of relative insignificance. In no case should a plea bargain undermine the seriousness of the offense or place the victim in continued jeopardy.

Your assertiveness in the plea bargain process will serve as a strong deterrent to further acts of violence directed at the victim. The deterrent can be as strong as or stronger than an arrest.

• **Recognize that you do not have to get a conviction each time you go to trial to accomplish the victim's primary objectives.** Most battered women simply want the beatings to stop and for their batterers to leave them alone.

Like arrest, prosecution—even in the absence of a conviction—is a strong catalyst in meeting these objectives. It leaves a strong message with the batterer that spousal abuse is not only intolerable, it could also lead to his incarceration.

• **Recognize that the battered woman may make a terrible witness and may jeopardize the trial process.** Always be prepared for the worst and utilize an expert witness, if necessary, in your efforts to rehabilitate the testimony of the battered woman.

There is a strong probability that at some time during your dialogue with the victim, she will begin to recant. While recanting may begin to occur early in the screening process as she experiences the "honeymoon phase" with her abuser, it is most likely to occur immediately prior to trial or during the trial itself.

Even within the context of much support, the victim often remains intimidated and terrorized by her batterer, particularly when it comes to testifying in his presence. During testimony, she may begin to totally contradict earlier statements made to investigators and support personnel. She may minimize, rationalize, and even deny her earlier circumstances.

• **As a prosecutor, your case file may include, but should not be limited to, the following information, documents, and evidence:**

- the police report
- verbal and written statements of the victim
- verbal and written statements of the witnesses
- medical reports and doctors' statements
- admissions and confession of the defendant
- defendant's criminal record
- photographs of the victim's injuries
- photographs of the crime scene
- property broken or damaged by the assailant
- professional estimate of the damaged property
- bloodstained or torn clothing
- 911 or dispatch tapes
- video and audio tapes relevant to the offense
- threatening letters and notes
- fingerprints
- copies of technical reports that may substantiate the offense, such as home security system reports of intrusions, caller identification systems, etc.
- prior copies of conviction relative to domestic violence

Judges and Prosecutors

There are no cases that present a greater danger to court personnel and witnesses than those involving domestic violence. The media reports with stunning frequency episodes of courtroom violence in which batterers have shot and slain judges, bailiffs, attorneys, witnesses, and members of the public. Yet, in light of what we know, courts continue to display great laxity when it comes to protecting their staffs and the public against such assailants.

An informal review of several New Orleans courthouses revealed that all were easily accessible by the domestic offender, with little or no security measures taken. Defendants and others were generally allowed to walk in and out of the courtrooms and buildings without question. They were permitted to bring in purses, duffel bags, briefcases, and other containers without being searched or scanned by a metal detector. More shocking than the recent epidemic of courtroom violence is the lack of attention and security measures taken to prevent it.

• **Take the lead in securing your building and courtroom against the potential assault of a domestic batterer.** Contract with a security firm that specializes in courthouse security to research and implement the procedures necessary in securing your premises. Generally speaking, the following measures should be taken against such intrusions:

- *Secure Entrances and Exits of the Building:* Within the framework of fire codes, allow as few entrances into the court building as possible and have them monitored by uniformed security guards. The security guards should use a metal detector to scan all people entering the premises. Bags, briefcases, and other containers should also be closely checked.
- *Secure Building During Non-operating Hours:* During non-operating hours, the court building should be locked and secured, and the public should not be allowed to enter the premises. Immediately prior to opening the building each day, security should carefully check the premises for possible intruders.
- *Secure Entrances and Exits of Individual Courtrooms:* It is recommended that each court appoint an individual to stand at the courtroom's entrance to provide a second check and scan of the individuals entering. All individuals who leave the courtroom while it is still in session should be rechecked upon their reentry.
- *Provide for Safe Storage of Weapons:* All law enforcement and quasi-law enforcement personnel should be mandated to secure their weapons in a locker area near the entrance of the court building. At no time should they be allowed to carry their weapons into the courtroom.
- *Provide Courtroom Security:* All individual courtrooms should be secured by a uniformed law enforcement official. The security guard should never leave the courtroom unattended.
- *Post Signs Relative to the Illegal Carrying of Weapons:* Without exception, anyone found to be illegally bringing a weapon into the court building should be arrested on a felony violation. Prominently post signs at the main entrance of the building alerting the public to the existence of such penalties.

While these very basic areas of security should be of primary concern, never limit yourself to the above. All buildings and systems are somewhat unique and should be comprehensively reviewed relative to their security needs. Through reassignment and the use of existing resources, many of the steps necessary in securing your building and courtroom can be accomplished with only moderate additional cost. Recognize that both you and the public are at high risk in unsecured settings and the cost of security measures is worth the return. Stop minimizing the risk and take action.

• **Never ask a battered woman or her witness to sit in the same waiting area as that of the assailant.** Such a practice is not only traumatic to the victim, it is also very dangerous. Courts frequently ignore this critical safety issue and place the woman in a position where she occupies the same bench or waiting area as her batterer.

Always designate a section of the court for victims that is safe, well lit, and significantly removed from where the assailant must wait. Prohibit the defendant from entering this area. Even in the absence of weapons, batterers are frequently known to attack their victims in courtroom settings. All precautionary measures should be taken to prevent such an assault.

• **Designate a special court and judge to handle only cases of domestic violence.** Courts traditionally address a wide variety of criminal cases. While this may logistically serve a useful purpose, it is a detriment in cases of domestic violence. It dilutes the interest that needs to be placed on such matters and diverts time and energy into other criminal cases that are not life-threatening.

The special court should address these cases from arraignment and bond placement to the trial and its final disposition, appeal, and related follow-up. As in vertical prosecution, a single court assigned to such cases enhances expertise, case continuity, efficiency, and the safety of the victim.

• **Within constitutional boundaries, implement policies and procedures whereby the batterer is not allowed to post a bond until he is formally arraigned.** While the general rule is that an assailant can make bond shortly after he is booked, this is a dangerous practice, since it does not take into consideration the immediate danger that he presents to his victim. The minimum policy should be that no bond should be fixed in a domestic violence matter without a judge or magistrate having the defendant's previous record and some information concerning the facts of the case.

Until the court is able to adequately assess the lethality of a particular defendant, his ability to make bond should be suspended. It is incumbent on the judiciary, however, to hold a hearing promptly, since the defendant would be remanded into custody until the arraignment is held.

• **If the defendant's case is to be heard by a jury, carefully screen all jurors for bias, prejudice, or opinions that perceive women as occupying subordinate positions in society.** It is very difficult to find individuals who do not place some element of blame on the battered woman for what has occurred. She is often seen as an adult who has freely chosen to stay in the relationship with the abuser. Many jurors have never been exposed to the concept of the Battered Women's Syndrome and do not comprehend its significance. Jury selection is a critical element of the trial process. Screen potential jurors carefully and dismiss those who project any degree of prejudice.

• **Don't allow politics or close friendships to enter the plea-bargaining, prosecution, or sentencing process, whereby you reduce or sacrifice the safety of the victim.** While you may feel obligated to recommend or accept treatment or leniency because of peer relationships, doing so may jeopardize the lives of the parties involved. Always treat a case of Category Three violence as a potential homicide, and address it appropriately, not as politics may dictate.

Your primary responsibility in cases of domestic violence is to protect the battered woman and her children. Their safety should be paramount to any and all other considerations.

• **If a defendant has been placed under a bond and is consequently held in custody, always alert the victim to the possibility of her assailant's release, if and when the bond is posted.** Never allow her to leave the court with a false sense of security. Let her know that you have no control over his release if he should make bond, and that she will probably not be notified.

The amount of the bond should be consistent with the scope of the current offense and the defendant's prior history of domestic violence.

• **An assailant should never be released on his own recognizance if one or more of the following factors exist:**

- the victim is seriously injured
- a weapon was used in the assault
- the defendant is a continued threat to the victim
- the defendant continued to threaten his victim following his arrest or while in your presence
- an act of child abuse was committed
- the defendant is a Category Three batterer
- the defendant is a Serial Batterer
- the defendant exhibits the Battering Male Syndrome
- the defendant rates high on the Lethality Index
- the defendant is a multiple offender
- the defendant does not have a local or permanent address
- the defendant has threatened suicide
- the defendant has a history of drug abuse
- the defendant is actively psychotic

• **Never continue a case of domestic violence that has been scheduled for trial unless you have a valid or strategic reason for doing so.** Defense attorneys will frequently approach the court with a multitude of reasons why they would like to have their case rescheduled. The assailant's attorney knows that time is often his/her best defense.

Challenge all requests for continuances and require some degree of validation if consideration is to be given. While heavy dockets, personal agendas, and other factors may motivate you to grant such requests, recognize the anguish that a victim feels each time a case is delayed. Expedite cases of spousal abuse quickly and avoid agreeing to continuances unless it is in the best interest of the victims.

• **Children should never be asked or allowed to testify against the assailant unless it is absolutely necessary.** This is particularly true if a child lives with the batterer or remains under his immediate control.

Mandating children to testify will only further jeopardize their safety and well-being. They are generally terrified of the batterer, and the need to testify will traumatize them further. If a child's testimony is critical to a case, design a safety plan whereby the danger that a defendant may present to a young witness is greatly reduced.

• **Whenever necessary, introduce and allow the use of expert testimony.** While such testimony is generally used in cases where the victim has slain her abuser, it is strongly recommended that experts be used in cases where men have seriously beaten, injured, or killed their wives or girlfriends.

Juries have difficulty in recognizing pathological batterers from those who are relatively normal. They have difficulty distinguishing between lethal assailants and those who present no further threat to their victim. Jury members often perceive men who commit incomprehensible acts of domestic violence as "emotionally disturbed" or "mentally ill."

Defense attorneys capitalize on such perceptions and ignorance. They assert that their clients are no longer a continued threat to their victims or that they should be mandated to treatment programs in lieu of incarceration. They insist that the defendants need counseling as an alternative to punishment and that sending them to jail will only make their "problems" worse.

In an effort to neutralize such perceptions and arguments, expert testimony regarding the profile of the batterer is necessary. It is important to dispel the belief that the defendant is not fully responsible for his behavior because of "emotional problems." It is important to explain that the chronic batterer has a personality disorder and knows right from wrong. Expert witnesses can convince a jury that a man who ruthlessly beats his spouse is rarely psychotic and is fully responsible for what he has done. Experts can substantially reduce the possibility that a jury will accept the argument that the batterer is a victim in his own right and that his sentence should be modified in order to accommodate his treatment needs.

Experts should be encouraged to utilize the terms and concepts of the Batterer's Continuum, the Battering Male Syndrome, and the Serial Batterer. The use of such information will enhance the insight of jurors and may help them overcome fixed perceptions. Without the use of such conceptualizations, it is likely that a juror's perception will remain as it was at the outset of the trial.

• **If a victim fails to honor her subpoena, do not issue a warrant for her arrest.** If you desire to go forward with the case, have someone on your staff contact the battered woman and assertively request that she come in. Always remember that she is the victim and recognize the many reasons why she may fear or choose not to follow through with her case. Unless there is a valid reason for doing so, never issue a warrant for her non-appearance. When you do, you victimize her a second time.

• **Restraining orders, peace bonds, and conditions of release should be routinely issued in cases of domestic violence.** You should carefully explain to the defendant that violating such orders will result in his recognizance bond being revoked, contempt of court, or whatever potential consequences were levied at the time of his release.

Since the inception of stalking laws, these restraints are of particular importance, since they validate that the defendant has been placed on notice to stay away from his victim. Many stalking laws also accelerate penalties if restraining orders are violated within the context of the stalking incident.

Unless the battered woman is a legitimate co-defendant, never issue dual restraints. When you do, as in dual arrest, it insinuates equal blame for the violence that occurred. It also empowers the batterer with a document that he will strategically use against his victim. If you do not have probable cause, never issue documents which suggest that the victim is mutually to blame for what took place. After restraining orders have been issued, make certain that the victim receives a copy prior to her departure from the courtroom.

Under most circumstances and within constitutional boundaries, it is recommended that you schedule such court orders for periodic status hearings. These hearings should be held to ascertain whether compliance has been maintained. While status reviews should be held at intervals of thirty, sixty, and ninety days, the time lapse for such conferences should never be extended beyond ninety days. These reviews are a powerful deterrent in getting the defendant to leave his victim alone. The fact that the battered woman will be allowed regular dialogue in the presence of court officials is an excellent means of ensuring compliance to court mandates. Never underestimate the value of status hearings; while they take only minutes to review, they ensure the ultimate in compliance.

If there is considerable evidence that restraining orders and other court mandates have been violated, immediately schedule a hearing to determine the validity of the allegations. If the hearing determines that a violation has occurred, don't hesitate to hold the defendant in contempt of court or to take appropriate punitive actions against him.

• **Be fully advised and familiar with the victim's circumstances and the defendant's history of violence prior to his sentencing.** If victim-assistance or probation programs exist within your jurisdiction, they can acquire much of the information that you may need. These agencies can perform a pre-sentence investigation whereby a comprehensive review of the victim's needs and the defendant's social history and potential to re-offend can be adequately assessed.

You should always have a criminal record available for your review prior to sentencing the batterer. Most accessible records, however, reflect only the assailant's criminal history as it relates to your local community. It is important to set up procedures whereby you can receive national record checks from the National Crime Information Center. Category Three batterers do not batter in one locale only. They have abused women in most communities in which they have lived. It is important that you obtain this information. The defendant's past is one of the best predictors of whether he will re-assault his victim.

• **Batterers who are multiple offenders should never be shown leniency.** Judges and prosecutors, however, are noticeably reluctant to sentence repeat offenders to significant or maximum jail sentences for their crimes. Courts generally impose only a fraction of the penalties allowed by law on such defendants. Additionally, chronic offenders who regularly attack victims with guns and weapons are generally charged with only misdemeanor crimes.

If evidence supports the offense for which the batterer is charged, don't reduce it. If he is convicted, never hesitate to impose significant penalties and consider incarcerating the offender, if appropriate. Penalties and consequences should be accelerated according to the number of domestic violence convictions that an assailant has. Under no circumstances should a multiple offender receive a diversionary or probationary sentence in lieu of more serious penalties. Never be manipulated by a defense attorney who argues that incarceration will do nothing to deter further violence. The fact is, strict penalties imposed on multiple offenders are a significant deterrent to repeat violence against specific victims.

• **Do not accept the argument that you have a responsibility to treat and assist the chronic batterer in overcoming his history of domestic violence.** While a defense attorney will frequently argue that jail will only make matters worse, research actually suggests that incarceration is a strong deterrent to future violence on the victim in question. While it would be unrealistic to suggest that a defendant's confinement will bring about a personality change, it does alert the batterer that attacking his victim results in the loss of his freedom.

Your primary responsibility is the safety and protection of the battered woman and her children. If a Category Three batterer is ordered into treatment for his violence, set rigid boundaries and conditions and immediately enforce penalties if they are violated. Always make the defendant pay for services that he may receive as an outgrowth of the crime that he committed.

• **If a chronic batterer is convicted for his crime, strongly consider incarcerating him if any of the following factors exist:**

- he is a multiple offender
- the victim was seriously injured
- a weapon was used in his attack
- he remains a serious threat to his victim
- he has threatened to retaliate against his victim
- he shows no remorse and tries to justify what he has done
- he has a significant history of violent acts
- he threatens the victim while in your presence
- he has a history of violating court orders relative to domestic violence
- he is considered to be a Serial batterer
- he possesses the Battering Male Syndrome
- he is considered to be a Category Three batterer
- he has a high number of unfavorable responses on the Lethality Questionnaire

• **In cases of domestic violence, the court should forfeit and destroy all guns and weapons that do not have to be legally returned to the defendant.**

• **Carefully utilize the Batterer's Continuum and Lethality Questionnaire whenever making a decision relative to the sentencing of a domestic batterer.** Soft sentencing alternatives such as diversion, community service work, probation, and house arrest should not be considered for batterers on the right side of the continuum or the high end of the lethality scale.

• **All batterers who are given soft sentencing alternatives, such as probation, diversion, community service, etc., should be closely monitored for compliance.** Their soft sentences should be immediately revoked for any violation of court mandates or nonperformance.

• **Be very selective and cautious when utilizing treatment and intervention programs that solicit referrals of defendants charged with spousal abuse.** While some may have well-trained staffs, others may use unqualified employees who have little or no experience in the treatment of batterers.

• **Recognize that the concepts involved in the Battered Women's Syndrome come into play if you are dealing with a battered woman who has slain her assailant because she saw no reasonable solution or escape from her violent plight.** If the woman has significant documentation and validation that she was chronically and systematically abused by the slain party, review the case with consideration being given to this syndrome. If the batterer continued to abuse his victim after she had taken every legal and safety precaution necessary in preventing it, consider that she did what any reasonable person would do under the circumstances. No reasonable individual would allow herself to be violently and systematically attacked on an ongoing basis without taking a defensive posture. The battered woman should be allowed no less of a response.

Accept the Battered Women's Syndrome as a potential factor in cases of domestic homicide, and consider such an issue in the screening phase, the prosecution, and the sentencing process of her case. If the syndrome is validated and circumstances justify her actions, the battered woman should be given every consideration relative to her actions.

• **Finally, advocate for and assist in the implementation of in-house victim assistance and probationary services.** Such programs are an excellent means by which to gather information, records, and evidence pertinent to domestic violence cases. These in-house services can be employed to screen and interview victims and witnesses. They can be used to provide the court with informed recommendations regarding bond amounts, pre-sentence investigations, and suggestions relative to peace bonds, restraining orders, and conditions of release. These services can also provide an overseer of court mandates who can assume the responsibility for petitioning the court in the event that such orders are violated. Additionally, victim-assistance and probationary services can provide a battered woman with information, emotional support, and a safety net that she may need prior to, during, and following the disposition of her case.

The expense of such services should be incurred by defendants who have been convicted of crimes of domestic violence. Courts should mandate the batterer to pay fines and court costs that are dedicated to the operation of programs that provide safety and services to his victim. Such revenue generating measures are not only practical, they also make the man who is a threat to his victim responsible for paying salaries of those who seek to protect her.

Victim Assistance Workers and Probation Officers

Dealing with the Battered Woman

If it is your job to assist the victim of domestic abuse, your best approach is to serve as her advocate. The judicial process is intimidating. It is likely that she will withdraw her case prior to its conclusion if she has no one to turn to when in distress. You may be one of the few professionals in the justice system she can depend on for emotional and technical support.

Always explain the court process to her. In many instances, it is assumed that she understands what is going on around her. In most cases, she does not. During each step of the process, describe to her what is occurring, why, and how she should respond. Never assume that she understands what you may perceive as routine.

If it is apparent that the battered woman needs assistance from civil court relative to property disputes, child custody, and divorce proceedings, clearly explain the process to her or refer her to someone who can.

Many domestic violence programs offer assistance to the victim in civil court. Utilize these programs for the purpose of acquiring legal services for the battered woman relative to civil litigation. Having civil courts simultaneously impose boundaries on the batterer will reinforce those established within the context of the criminal proceedings.

Most battered women make poor witnesses in the courtroom. They become easily intimidated by defense attorneys and often make mistakes that are detrimental to the prosecutors' efforts. Help prepare the battered woman for her testimony in court. You may consider role-playing to give her a better grasp of the trial process.

Orienting the battered woman in the art of testifying is critical to success. Never underestimate her need for such assistance. Without it, the victim will frequently flounder and make errors that jeopardize her case.

• **Work closely with the victim in an attempt to ensure her presence in court on the date of her assailant's hearing or trial.** Many battered women are hesitant to proceed because they feel that they are alone in confronting their abusers. Your support, along with that of other advocacy groups, is essential to the successful conclusion of a victim's case.

• **Always involve the battered woman in the investigatory and follow-up phases of her case.** During all pretrial, prosecutorial, or post-prosecutorial proceedings, she should be allowed quick and easy access to you.

Early in your involvement with the victim, provide her with an office phone number and address where you can be reached. It is suggested, however, that you do not use your actual name since it may be acquired by the defendant. Instead, give the victim a business card that lists your initials and case worker number. While such a system allows the victim easy access to you, it establishes some degree of anonymity relative to your exposure to the batterer.

It is suggested that you do not place your name on your office door. You should also acquire a private residential phone number and never list your name in the public telephone directory. A public directory may give the assailant both your home phone number and your residential address. Why take such risks?

• **On the day in which the defendant reports to you, always contact the victim by phone to determine if the batterer has complied with all conditions of release or terms of probation.** If the victim is not easily accessible by phone, make arrangements with her to call you immediately prior to the day of supervision.

While it may be tempting to skip this process altogether, recognize the significant deterrent value of having ongoing and regular dialogue with the victim. The batterer becomes keenly aware that such communications exist and that any violation of a court order can be immediately addressed.

Batterers who are not monitored traditionally re-offend. Those who are closely supervised are much less likely to do so.

• **Recognize that the victim of a Category Three batterer is in considerable danger.** This is particularly true prior to, during, and immediately following the trial of her abuser. Her vulnerability also increases significantly during the period in which she tries to terminate the relationship.

Assist the battered woman in developing a well-defined and structured safety plan. Having pre-planned responses to the batterer's quick and often unexpected attacks may be essential to her survival and that of her children. In your efforts to protect the battered woman, it is suggested that you utilize and review the comprehensive safety plan outlined in the Appendix. While the victim should address many of the listed suggestions prior to leaving the relationship with her batterer, others should be addressed after she has left.

• **Many states maintain and operate victim compensation programs that reimburse victims of violent crime for some of their financial loss incurred as a result of the attack.** There are certain prerequisites, however, that must be met for a victim to qualify. While some battered women may not qualify, others will. The prerequisites vary considerably from one state to another.

Contact your local Department of Corrections, District Attorney's Office, etc., and inquire about such benefits. If battered women are not included in their programs, lobby that they be added to the list of potential candidates.

Dealing with the Batterer

Your assessment of the spouse abuser is one of the most important functions that you will perform as a victim assistance worker or probation officer.

In an effort to ascertain where an assailant falls on the Batterer's Continuum, it is suggested that you utilize the Lethality Questionnaire included in the Appendix. The questionnaire is presented in the first person and is directed at the victim. It can also be administered to a family member or informed party.

Responses to the questionnaire will provide you with the insight necessary in determining the batterer's potential for treatment and his propensity to re-assault his victim. It is suggested that the greater the number of unfavorable responses received, the less likely it is that he is treatable and the more likely he is to re-offend. Spouse abusers with an extremely high number of unfavorable responses should be recognized as potentially homicidal.

• **If the court requires that you consider the batterer for diversion or that you perform a pre-sentencing investigation, your assessment and evaluation should diagnostically include the Batterer's Continuum, the Lethality Questionnaire, the Battering Male Syndrome, and the Serial Batterer.**

Since all of these concepts are closely associated with one another, if he is found to be highly deficient in one area, the probability is that he is deficient in the others as well. For example, a Category Three batterer who falls to the far right of the continuum possesses the Battering Male Syndrome. He is also very likely to be a potentially lethal Serial Batterer.

Batterers whose personality and behavioral profiles rate negatively in any of the above areas should be addressed in a consequential and punitive manner. Never hesitate to recommend incarceration for a Category Three batterer who has committed a serious offense against his victim.

Chronic abusers whose profiles fit the above conceptualizations should not be considered, nor should they be eligible, for diversionary or probationary services. On the other hand, batterers who fall on the left side of the continuum (i.e., Category One abusers) should be liberally considered for such alternatives. Those in the middle (i.e., Category Two batterers) should be given such consideration only after cautious scrutiny.

• If you are ordered to perform a pre-sentencing investigation of the batterer, such a process may include but not limit itself to the following documentation and information:

- the assessment of the batterer as reported by the victim
- interviews with witnesses
- interviews with victims
- interviews with family members
- medical records of the victim
- medical bills of the victim
- estimate of property damage
- photographs of the victim's injuries
- threatening messages on answering machine tapes, letters, notes, etc.
- criminal record of the defendant
- police report of the current offense
- whether a weapon was used in the offense
- whether he still owns or possesses a firearm
- history of assault with a weapon
- history of violence
- history of suicide threats or attempts
- history of threats to kill his victim
- history of stalking his victim
- history of drug usage or drinking
- number of times the police have responded to calls of domestic violence
- whether there are other domestic violence cases pending
- whether restraining or protective orders were violated or issued in the past
- history of child abuse committed by the defendant
- social history of defendant
- a psychiatric evaluation
- location on the Batterer's Continuum
- whether or not he is a Serial Batterer
- whether or not he exhibits the Battering Male Syndrome

- remorse level
- motivation to change behavior

• **If your pre-sentence investigation determines that it is appropriate to recommend probation for the batterer, there are numerous special conditions of probation that may be imposed.** All special mandates, however, should be relative to, and consistent with, the individual case that you are addressing.

• **Depending on the issues involved, it is suggested that any one or more of the following conditions be considered:**

- *community service work*: the court mandates that he perform a specific number of hours of free labor for a nonprofit or public agency.
- *symbolic restitution*: the court mandates that he perform community service work with an agency that directly addresses the offense for which he has been convicted (e.g., a defendant who is convicted of spousal abuse may be ordered to assist in the construction of a shelter for abused children).
- *financial restitution*: the court mandates the defendant to pay the victim for all out-of-pocket medical expenses, property damage, etc.
- *weekend incarceration*: the court mandates that the batterer serve time on the weekends (Friday afternoon until Sunday afternoon).
- *no contact with victim*: the court prohibits the defendant from communicating with his victim in any manner. Peace bonds and restraining orders should be signed by the batterer acknowledging the warning.
- *treatment*: the court orders the batterer into treatment for his substance abuse, psychiatric problems, or those problems associated with his abusive behavior.
- *surrendering his weapon*: the court mandates that he surrender and forfeit his handgun or rifle.
- *special officer commission hearing*: if the batterer is commissioned and authorized to carry a gun, the court should mandate that he appear before the regulatory agency that governs his gun permit.
- *urine screens*: the court mandates the batterer to take and

pass periodic drug screens.

- *fee payment*: the court mandates that the batterer pay a regular fee each time that he reports to the probation officer. Such fees should be dedicated for probation services or treatment programs for battered women and children.
- *status hearings*: the court mandates the batterer to report to the judge for quarterly reviews to determine whether there has been total compliance with all conditions of probation.
- *probation appointments*: the court mandates the batterer to report to the office of his probation officer on a structured and regular basis.

• **If a batterer is mandated by the court to report for monitoring and supervision, these should be performed with complete structure.** After providing him with the dates and times of his supervision, terms of release, and the conditions in which he can or cannot communicate with his victim, hold him to the specific terms agreed upon in open court. If a valid reason exists for terms to be altered or modified, always formally agree to any changes in writing and do so in the presence of the judge who presided over the case.

The Category Three abuser is notoriously cunning in evading and confusing structure. Given an inch, he will take a mile. If he is allowed any flexibility in the conditions originally levied, he will sabotage your efforts to monitor him. The chronic batterer has a way of transforming a lack of structure into a means of manipulating court-imposed boundaries and mandates.

• **If the batterer fails to comply with a court mandate, immediately petition for a hearing relative to his noncompliance.**

If he has been released on his own recognizance but has violated conditions of release, ask the court to revoke his recognizance bond and to place him into custody. If he has been diverted to a treatment program in lieu of prosecution but failed to comply, ask the court to set his case for immediate prosecution. If he has been placed on probation but has violated its terms, file for a probation revocation hearing. If he is found guilty of the probation violation, request that he be incarcerated for the length of time that was originally suspended. Never hesitate to recommend to the court incarceration of the batterer if and when he violates the court mandates.

While structured and closely monitored court mandates are very effective deterrents to future attacks by the batterer, penalties that are imposed for violation or noncompliance are imperative if such a process is to work. The single most counterproductive response that a probation officer or a victim assistance worker can exhibit is complacency or inaction when the batterer tries to test the boundaries and orders imposed by a court.

• **If the batterer is court-ordered to enter a treatment program, never refer him to one with which you are not familiar.** It is most unfortunate that many agencies that proclaim to treat the batterer employ staff members who are virtually unfamiliar with the dynamics of spousal abuse. Such programs often interpret the violence as being caused by stress or marital discord. Their lack of insight into the etiologies of such behavior actually serves to perpetuate the problem.

If you are mandated by the court to refer the batterer for treatment services, always be familiar with the agency in which you place him. Inquire about such issues as fees charged, staffing patterns and credentials, training and experience in the area of domestic violence, and the types of treatment used.

• **If the batterer is not immediately prosecuted or held in custody for his offense, but remains a possible threat to his victim, recommend that the court set the case for periodic status reviews.** Such hearings are particularly beneficial in cases where the prosecutor agrees to diversion, restraining orders, or other conditions of release. The actual length of time between hearings should be relative to the potential lethality of the individual offender.

At the onset of the case, appropriate conditions of release and restraining orders should be imposed on the defendant. Always request that the court subpoena both the batterer and his victim to all status reviews.

Your role at these reviews should be to ascertain whether or not the defendant has continued to threaten, assault, or abuse his victim. On the day in which the defendant and victim appear, always speak to the victim privately to determine if any violations have occurred since the previous hearing. If the batterer has been compliant, recommend that the court release him conditionally and also request that the court schedule another status hearing. If it is determined, however, that the batterer has not been compliant, recommend that he be placed into custody and be referred to the district attorney for possible prosecution.

Monitoring the batterer within the context in which he originally appeared and before the same judge and prosecutor proves to be a powerful deterrent in the reduction of assaults on his victim.

• **Never allow yourself to be inappropriately used by the public defender or the defendant's private defense attorney.** Defense lawyers are notorious for trying to convince judges and prosecutors to refer chronic batterers to programs such as yours for diversion, treatment, and other sentencing alternatives.

Be aware of the fact that a defense attorney's primary objective is to get his client's case dismissed, or, if the batterer is convicted, to see that he does not go to jail. Regardless of how serious the case, or how dangerous the batterer, the assailant's attorney will advocate for him to be placed on probation or given treatment for his crime.

Always resist such referrals from defense attorneys. Advocate for the victim and what is in her best interest. Don't allow yourself to be a dumping ground for lawyers who inappropriately try to use your program as a conduit for a chronic batterer's freedom. Assert yourself by asking the court to reconsider such referrals while suggesting that it consider a punitive approach.

• **While soft sentencing alternatives such as community service, diversion, restitution, and probation are frequently appropriate for Category One and Category Two abusers, the Category Three batterer is a poor choice for such consideration.** If an assailant exhibits some of the following personality traits or behaviors, and has committed a serious offense against his victim, you should consider excluding him as a candidate for such sentencing alternatives:

- he has a history of using weapons
- he is homicidal
- he has no remorse
- he justifies what he did to his victim
- he has no motivation to change his behavior

- he has a history of violence
- he is a multiple domestic offender
- he has a chronic pattern of stalking his victim
- he is a Serial Batterer
- he is a Category Three batterer
- he has had multiple violent relationships with women
- he has a history of torturing and mutilating his victim
- he continues to threaten, assault, or intimidate his victim during the course of his trial or sentencing
- he has seriously injured his victim
- he has been convicted for beating his pregnant spouse
- he remains a continued and ongoing threat to his victim
- he violated a restraining order or was on probation for domestic violence when the current offense took place

• **If your department offers direct counseling or treatment programs to the batterer, adopt a policy whereby Category Three abusers are deemed inappropriate and unacceptable for such services.** While it is recommended that Category One and Category Two batterers be considered for therapeutic alternatives in lieu of incarceration, the Category Three assailant should not be afforded such an opportunity. Although the chronic batterer will generally agree to any terms that will keep him from going to jail, it is merely a ploy to avoid incarceration or other punitive consequences.

Safety Precautions

As a member of a victim assistance or probationary service, your physical safety should always be considered an issue of concern. You will be required to assume investigatory and supervisory functions relative to the chronic batterer. In doing so, your exposure to the abuser over an extended period of time may be significant. In most cases, you will be perceived by the defendant as an adversary in the relationship with his spouse.

All professionals who routinely investigate and supervise Category Three batterers should consider acquiring a commission to possess and carry a firearm. The permission to carry a firearm should not be granted, however, until a certified firearms training program has been fully completed.

• **Remain hypervigilant and at no time let your guard down.** Most of the abusers whom you supervise will resent that you are intruding in the relationships with their wives or girlfriends. The batterers who went to jail for beating their victims will eventually be released and may recall that you recommended their incarceration. While it is not suggested that you become paranoid, it is recommended that you recognize and accept the reality of your profession. The potential for a chronic batterer to harm you is always present. His retaliatory responses are not limited only to the battered woman. As you sit in your office, be aware of who is approaching. As you enter the courtroom, be aware of what is going on around you. As you leave work for the day and begin walking toward your car, be alert for people sitting in nearby cars or standing on nearby sidewalks, and so on.

• **The main entrance of your office area should include a metal detector and a security guard that can scan batterers who are reporting for an interview or supervision.** It is recommended that many of the security procedures suggested for the court system be applied to your office as well. While you may be addressing the assailant within a different context than the court does, you are still interacting with the same individual. As stated earlier, don't let your guard down. There is no reason to become passive when supervising the chronic batterer.

• **If the defendant has been ordered by the court to be routinely monitored, the supervision should never be performed through the process of home visits.** Reduce your exposure to danger by requiring the defendant to report to your office on the day that his supervision is scheduled. Probation officers should never make home visits in such cases. Since the batterer frequently possesses weapons in his residence, such exposure carries significant and unnecessary risks.

• **Finally, when interviewing or supervising the batterer, never disclose or discuss information with him relative to his victim.** Never lay his case file where it is easily accessible to him. Many files contain the victim's phone number, address, and other confidential information that, if acquired, may place the victim in unnecessary danger.

Chapter X

Battered Women's Programs and Shelters: Keeping Victims Safe

It is very difficult to fully comprehend the plight of the battered woman prior to the emergence of battered women's programs and shelters. More the rule than the exception, the victim chose to stay in the closet. She was keenly aware that without resources, assertive responses to her batterer's aggression only placed her in more volatile and dangerous circumstances.

Even with the emergence of spousal abuse programs, the battered woman remains in considerable danger. While society has come to recognize her dilemma, its response still does not correspond to the magnitude of her problems. Laws, funding, and resources are still grossly inadequate in addressing one of society's most devastating social problems.

The Five Priorities

In an effort to address society's lax attitudes and response to the ruthless violence of the batterer, it is incumbent on spousal abuse programs to place a priority on the issues of advocacy, education, referral, counseling, and protection.

Advocacy

Programs should advocate for the rights of the battered woman. As an advocate you should assist her in certain police matters and should always attend court proceedings relative to her batterer. Your simple presence often makes criminal justice personnel more responsive to the victim's needs. While you should never appear as uncompromisingly demanding, intervene with criminal justice personnel in an assertively professional manner.

Prior to your direct involvement with police and court personnel, however, you should always be well trained and versed in legal protocol and procedures. If legal advocacy is performed properly, the criminal justice system can become your greatest ally..

Programs should also lobby the legislative branches of government in passing laws that further criminalize the act of spousal abuse. At present, laws are dramatically remiss in conveying the seriousness of such violence.

Finally, it is incumbent on spousal abuse programs to advocate for the battered woman's right to housing, financial assistance, food stamps, victim's compensation, or virtually any resource that she needs but has been inappropriately denied.

Education

Educate the general public on the topic of spousal abuse by utilizing the mass media. Newspapers, magazines, radio, and T.V. have enormous influence on how we perceive and respond to an issue. Use the media to alter and modify perceptions.

Host and sponsor training sessions and seminars at hospitals, universities, churches, community and government agencies, etc. Educating individual professions on the dynamics of spousal abuse is essential in bringing about appropriate change.

Referral

Operate as a clearinghouse for the many needs of the battered woman. She will come to you with her sick and hungry children. They will often be penniless and without adequate clothing. The victim may be uneducated and have few job skills. Her needs will be vast and may be in areas that you cannot directly assist.

Become knowledgeable and acquainted with the various community agencies available to the battered woman. Become familiar with the staff of such agencies and the eligibility criteria that they require of the battered woman if she is to receive services. Your comprehensive knowledge and relationship with outside agencies is essential to your efforts to assist the victim in ending her cycle of violence.

Counseling

Provide individual and group counseling to the battered woman. To reduce the risk that she will return to her abuser or develop a new relationship similar to the old, it is critical that she address issues relative to self-esteem, co-dependency, denial, and factors that bond and attract her to the batterer. Counseling should always include a frank discussion of the dynamics of the man who abuses her. Insight into the personality of her assailant is a critical factor in her attempt to make reasonable and appropriate decisions.

As a condition of receiving services from your agency, the battered woman should be required to participate in counseling. If she does not, it is unlikely that the issues that brought and kept her in the relationship with her abuser will be resolved. The time that you have with the victim is very limited. Use it wisely and productively.

Protection

The foremost and basic service that you should provide to the battered woman is that of safety. Without this issue being addressed first, none of the other services can be appropriately implemented.

If you are in a program not directly affiliated with a shelter, explore the possibility of housing the victim and her children in "safe homes" (homes of volunteers), motels and hotels, and other non-domestic shelter facilities. Before you and your program become involved in outside housing resources, the issue of liability should be researched and addressed. In many cases the batterer will pursue and locate his victim, and the possibility of the assailant harming others is always present.

Shelter Programs: Three Stages to Assimilation

If you are directly affiliated with or operate a shelter program, recognize that a battered woman will need more than just a few weeks to get her life in order. Many shelter programs offer the victim fewer than thirty days in which to resolve her problems. Since many victims' problems have developed over the course of a lifetime, it is unreasonable to think that such programs can resolve them in less than a month.

If shelter programs are to be truly effective in assisting the battered woman with her vast and very complex problems and needs, it is recommended that three levels of residential services be considered and implemented.

• **The first stage should be considered as crisis resolution and intervention.** Victims who are in immediate danger should be allowed access to the program without delay. The first stage should include screening whereby the shelter staff can adequately address her needs, problems, and immediate danger. The first stage should be for a period of not more than thirty days.

• **The second stage should be more comprehensive and should involve not only the stabilization of the victim, but also time in which she can assert her independence.** She should be encouraged and assisted in searching for a job, locating child care, acquiring financial assistance, entering vocational counseling, and doing all the tasks that will essentially foster her independence. The second stage should last for a period not to exceed four months.

• **Finally, the third stage is one in which she leaves the structured residential setting of the second to enter a more independent multiple family complex or compound.** While the third stage should be separate and physically independent of the primary shelter, it should be closely monitored and administered by the parent program. This third stage will allow the battered woman an opportunity to put into motion the many resources and contacts she developed during her stay in the second stage shelter. The third stage should not exceed a period of one year from the time she leaves the second stage.

Programs that rush victims through are generally subject to failure from the outset, since they do not allow enough time for the woman to restructure her life's priorities. It is strongly recommended that if you do not have a third stage component in your program, you advocate and lobby for its establishment.

Essential or Recommended Programs

• **As an adjunct to your program, operate a twenty-four hour crisis line.** The battered woman is more likely to reach out to you while in crisis or immediately following a beating than she is when things are relatively normal. The batterer knows no time restraints. He is more likely to assault his victim during non-traditional work hours, such as late evening and weekends. It is imperative that the victim has access to you during these times.

While a twenty-four hour crisis line will demand much attention, the majority of the extra work can be accomplished through a staff of trained volunteers. In addition, if you program your phone to include call forwarding, evening and weekend calls can be transferred to the home of the volunteers on duty.

• **Offer an array of children's services that address the emotional and physical needs of the child.** Nutritional, child care, and counseling services should be integral components of your program. If the seeds of dysfunction are planted within the violent experiences of the child's early environment, it is incumbent on all domestic violence agencies to prioritize those services that may stabilize and address the child's trauma. Without a comprehensive children's program, the intergenerational transmission of family violence will continue to flourish.

• **Establish an educational or vocational component to your program.** Assist the client in acquiring a G.E.D. or the vocational skills that will be necessary for her to join the workforce. If your agency cannot provide such services directly, refer her to one that can.

• **Develop a working relationship with your local housing authority or "Section Eight" program.** Governmental agencies that administer and regulate public housing generally allow for the emergency placement of families who are in crisis situations. While such a policy may not mean immediate placement, it does allow for priority status. If battered women are not included in the priority status policy of the housing administrator, advocate for their inclusion.

• **During the pretrial, trial, or post-trial processes, establish a system that will offer the victim emotional support.** Offer to assist with transportation to court and with child care. Offer to assist prosecutors in developing a safety plan, in the acquisition of expert testimony and language interpreters, or whatever is appropriate. While you should never appear intrusive, there are many areas in which you can assist the court. Such an offer of assistance, if done properly, will win you both credibility and respect.

• **Train all staff members in the dynamics of the batterer's personality profile.** If staff workers are going to assist the battered woman in escaping the violence that engulfs her, it is imperative that they fully understand her assailant. Without such training and insight, suggestions that are well intended but ill-advised may endanger the well-being and safety of the victim.

The fact remains that a victim of Category Three violence is in considerable danger. She is often in denial and must be educated as to the true risks that she faces unless she asserts her full independence from the assailant. You should take the brief time in which you have to work with the victim to assist her in recognizing the need for terminating the relationship; without such assistance, the odds are significant that she will eventually return to her assailant.

If you were a hotel employee, wouldn't you counsel tourists to avoid the high crime areas of the city which they are visiting? As a family violence caseworker, you should assertively and convincingly advise the victim that returning to a chronic batterer could be as deadly. While you cannot make her final decision, the manner in which you counsel her may make the difference in whether she returns to the relationship. It is not suggested that you force her into her decision. It is only recommended that you not sit passively by while she makes the wrong choice.

• **Educate your staff that client records might not be completely confidential.** Even the darkest secrets and admissions made and recorded during client counseling sessions are subject to the subpoena process and can be used during the course of legal proceedings.

Defense attorneys often have a field day with "confidential client records" seized by the court during civil and criminal litigation. Never reduce anything to writing that the victim may say in a counseling session if it could be embarrassing or detrimental to her well-being.

Program Components

• **Networking should be considered as a very critical function of spousal abuse programs.** While there may be numerous independent programs in your community that address domestic violence, they may rarely interact with each other and may not fully recognize what the other does.

Take it upon yourself to contact all other community-based programs in an effort to create a task force. Such networking should include all agencies that are interested in or that provide some level of direct care or service to the battered woman. The primary objective of such a task force should be to provide better service and protection to the victim. The best way to accomplish this is for one agency to know exactly what the other is doing.

• **Consider approaching the following groups in an effort to acquire the free assistance that could not otherwise be acquired through regular funding sources.** Search out businesses and companies in your community that would provide free services, care, and products to the battered woman. While some would give out of sheer empathy, others would donate as a public relations statement. While these groups are considered priority, your appeal for assistance should not be limited to them alone:

- cab companies: transportation
- hotels/ motels: shelter
- restaurants: food
- law offices: legal assistance
- hospitals: medical care
- doctors' offices: medical care
- dental offices: dental care
- clothing stores: clothing
- supermarkets: food
- pharmacies: medicine
- shoe stores: shoes
- business schools: vocational training
- banks: checking and savings accounts

Security Measures

All battered women's shelters and programs should prioritize the issue of security. The chronic batterer presents a potential threat to any individual who he perceives is an adversary in his relationship with his spouse. In the context of your interaction and services to the battered woman, always consider the implementation of the following security measures:

Staff Security Measures

- The address and phone number of your program should be unlisted and kept confidential. Stress the importance of such confidentiality to clients, volunteers, and staff members. Battered women should be able to locate and access your program through second-party agencies (i.e., parent programs, social service programs, courts, police department, church groups, etc.). If you are contacted by the batterer, never acknowledge that his victim is receiving assistance from you.

- Your program should not provide services to the victim's assailant. If you feel obligated to address the "needs" of the batterer, suggest that an agency independent of your own provide such services. Mixing the two groups (i.e., victims and batterers) within the context of the same agency is a dangerous practice.
- Batterers should never be allowed to access or visit the premises used for your program.
- Lobby for the implementation and enforcement of laws that make it a felony for a batterer to trespass on or near the premises of your program.
- Lobby for the implementation and enforcement of laws that make it a felony for a batterer to assault, threaten, or intimidate any member of your staff.
- All staff members should be properly trained in the method of addressing an intruder. Never verbally or physically confront a batterer who appears on the premises of your program. Immediately alert the police by calling 911.
- Develop a close working relationship with your local police department. Invite your police chief or a high-ranking officer to meet with your staff and board of directors. The meeting should be held on the premises of your program and should address concerns and needs relative to security and safety.
- When you enter or leave the premises of your program, always be aware of anyone sitting or loitering on or near your property. Proceed with vigilance. Never take unnecessary risks. If something appears to be suspicious, alert the police.
- Always post emergency numbers next to your phone. If it can be programmed for single digit dialing, program all emergency numbers for that purpose. If you don't have such a phone service, acquire it. Such a service could save your life.

- Acquire a caller identification system that can give you the direct source of harassing or threatening phone calls. Such a service can enhance your position in court should you have to bring charges against the batterer.
- As a measure of acquiring greater program anonymity, acquire and maintain a post office box.
- At no time, and for no reason, should staff members and clients be allowed to bring or possess guns or weapons on the premises of your program.
- In an effort to avoid allowing keys to fall into the hands of the batterer, those receiving program keys should be kept to a minimum. They should be of a type that cannot be duplicated. The distribution of keys should be carefully recorded. Only authorized personnel should be allowed to possess keys to the program's entrance. All keys should be returned immediately upon the staff member's resignation.
- The issue of fire safety should be regularly practiced and monitored. Fire drills which include proper evacuation routes and procedures should be implemented. Smoke alarms, fire extinguishers, rope ladders, and other fire safety equipment should be purchased and installed.
- Your program should hold special training sessions for all staff relative to safety and security needs.

Physical Security

- deadbolts on all main entrance doors
- peepholes on all entrance doors
- window locks that prevent windows from being opened from outside
- bulletproof glass
- motion sensitive lights on the outside of your building
- video surveillance cameras near strategic areas of your building
- an emergency button located near the desk of the receptionist or other staff member that may alert others of impending danger
- an alarm system that will detect and alert your staff to unauthorized intrusions into the shelter

Client Security

- Each client should be required to have, or to immediately acquire, a restraining order against her assailant upon her admittance to the residential program.
- If child visitation for the batterer has been court ordered, such visitation should never take place on the premises of the shelter. In such circumstances, the child should be brought to a third-party residence or facility that has no direct affiliation with your program.
- Young children should never be left at the shelter without appropriate staff supervision.
- Clients should be prohibited from directly contacting their batterers while residing at the shelter. This includes phone communication and personal meetings. Recognize that if your client calls her abuser from your phone, a caller identification system may tell him your phone number and address. Alert your phone company of this problem and ask that a "block" be placed on your line.
- Clients should be required to "check in" with a designated staff member on a daily basis.
- Clients should be required to notify a designated staff member of any planned overnight absences from the shelter. Notification should include the date and time of the client's expected return.
- Clients should practice the "buddy system." They should notify staff members or fellow clients of their intended destinations each time they leave the cluster. They should also notify their "buddies" as to the time they expect to return. If times and circumstances change, notification of such changes should be promptly given.
- A structured curfew should be established and enforced.
- Any intentional and ongoing violation of shelter safety rules by the client should be immediate grounds for discharge. Violations of security rules endanger all individuals who reside and work on the premises of the shelter. Such violations should not be tolerated.

Chapter XI

Advice for Therapists and Social Workers

As a caseworker, clinical social worker, or therapist, always employ the Batterer's Continuum and the Lethality Questionnaire in your attempt to design a treatment program for the batterer or a safety plan for his victim. This is not to imply that all battered women need a safety plan or that all abusers should be clinically treated in lieu of criminal sanctions. This simply provides you with a standard from which to make professionally sound decisions.

In your diagnostic efforts, refer to the Appendix for several assessment tools that will aid you in determining an individual batterer's lethality or potential for treatment. As stated throughout this book, your response to any batterer should be relative to where he falls on the continuum. These assessment tools will serve you as a means of determining the type of assailant that you are addressing. Upon your evaluation of an individual batterer, the following models should be considered.

Category One Batterer

The design of a safety plan is rarely needed for a victim of Category One violence. The focus of your intervention, provided that the victim is interested, should be reconciliation.

- **In your clinical work with the Category One batterer, you should consider the following treatment modalities:**
  - *Individual counseling*: One-on-one counseling should focus on the external issues or trauma that brought his aggression to the surface. If you do not have the expertise to address such issues as grief, substance abuse, stress, or the causative factors of his aggression, refer the client to a clinician who can.
  - *Marriage counseling*: While marriage counseling is generally inappropriate in cases of chronic violence, this is not true in

matters of Category One abuse. The issue or trauma that has caused his violence has also affected the quality of his relationship with his spouse. The wounds and emotional pain of his victim have to be addressed if she is going to remain in the relationship with her assailant.

- *Support groups*: One-on-one counseling and marriage counseling are very limited in the time that a client spends in therapy. Support groups that focus on the specific issues or trauma that caused his violence are excellent means of reducing isolation, giving him exposure to others who understand his trauma, and providing him with an opportunity to establish peer relationships and fellowship. Support groups that address issues of stress, grief, substance abuse, etc., and that employ a twelve-step program modality, such as Alcoholics Anonymous, are excellent resources for such clients. If alcoholism is an issue of concern, victims should be simultaneously referred to Al-Anon.
- *Spiritual needs*: In your efforts to utilize a holistic approach in your treatment design, the batterer's spiritual leanings, if any, should be appropriately addressed.
- *Boundary setting*: The Category One abuser responds well to spouse and court-imposed mandates. A spouse who is ready to end the relationship with her abuser and a court which is ready to prosecute him can create significant levels of motivation relative to clinical intervention for this batterer.

Category Two Batterer

The Category Two batterer is a modified version of the Category Three batterer. Since he is capable of committing some of the same criminal acts as the Category Three batterer, including homicide, a safety plan for the victim is generally recommended.

While it may be politically correct to suggest treatment for the batterer, extreme caution must be taken with the Category Two abuser. Experienced professionals report very low success rates with these individuals.

A victim of Category Two violence should never be coerced or manipulated into counseling sessions with her batterer. In fact, even if she is interested in participating, she should not do so until her abuser has successfully completed an extended treatment program relative to his violence.

In addition, victims of Category Two violence should never be given false hope and should be informed of the relatively poor prognosis for this group. It is not unethical nor is it inappropriate for a professional to work toward the termination of a Category Two relationship.

Since his violence is based more in internal issues and defective character traits than it is in external trauma, the treatment modalities for a Category Two batterer should be of a different format than those of the Category One batterer.

• **Unless a holistic approach is taken with the Category Two abuser wherein most of the following approaches are employed, there is little chance for positive change:**

- *Individual counseling*: One-on-one counseling should focus on the many defective character traits and internal issues of the Category Two abuser. If you do not have the knowledge or expertise to address relative issues of concern, refer him to a clinician who does.
- *Group counseling*: As you know, individual counseling can be very expensive. Therapy performed within the context of a group, however, can reduce cost significantly. Since many of your clients will have limited financial resources, keeping costs to a minimum should be a primary objective.

Group counseling will also provide the batterer with an atmosphere of confrontive intervention, whereby his negative behaviors and violence can be challenged by his peers. Violence and related behaviors are somewhat learned. The group process, through the use of peer pressure and feedback, can be an effective tool in reshaping and modifying such behavior.

It is not uncommon, however, for members of such a peer group to get into behavioral collusion with one another whereby negative traits are actually reinforced. A trained therapist should be aware of such a possibility and should counter peer collusion appropriately.

- *Educational groups*: Since much of the violence of the Category Two assailant is associated with learned behavior, an educational component to your group is essential to its success. If you are to be successful in reshaping the attitudes of this batterer while modifying elements of his socialization, he must be reeducated on matters involving gender roles, control, and sexism. Educational groups should explore the legal consequences of his behavior, child trauma relative to his violence, and virtually anything he needs to recognize in his attempts to become non-abusive.

- *Support groups*: As with the Category One client, individual and group counseling time is very limited. While you may spend only one or two hours weekly with this client, it is essential that he address his sense of isolation and other issues that will arise between sessions.

Category Two abusers respond well to support groups that practice a twelve-step program such as Alcoholics Anonymous, Narcotics Anonymous, and Batterers Anonymous. The availability and accessibility of many of these programs are endless and can help him fill the emotional voids that the Category Two batterer frequently experiences. While such groups are not equipped to address the deep-seated problems of the batterer, they will provide a healthy balance to your clinical intervention.

- *Spiritual needs*: In your effort to utilize a holistic approach to your treatment design, if the batterer has spiritual leanings, such needs should be appropriately addressed.
- *Boundary setting*: The Category Two batterer responds moderately well to spouse and court-imposed mandates. A spouse who temporarily leaves her assailant and a court which is poised to prosecute him for his criminal acts provide in some cases enough leverage to motivate him into a treatment program.

Suggestions for the Category Two Victim

• **If a Category Two victim has filed criminal charges against her assailant and intends to continue a relationship with him, she should ask the court to mandate her batterer into a treatment program for a period of not less than twelve months.** She should also ask the court to schedule periodic status hearings in an attempt to determine compliancy.

• **If the Category Two batterer enters treatment and his victim desires to work toward reconciliation, she should physically sep-**

arate from him for a period of approximately twelve months. This will give her time to determine her batterer's motivation toward continuing in treatment and in changing his violent behaviors.

• **If criminal charges are pending and the victim is temporarily separated from her batterer, she should ask for a restraining order that limits or restricts his personal contact with her.**

• **Within the structure and boundaries of spouse and court-imposed mandates, time becomes the victim's ally.** If this batterer is motivated to enter treatment only as a means of having criminal charges dropped or as an attempt to manipulate his spouse back into a relationship, he will not endure treatment over an extended period of time.

• **A victim of Category Two violence, irrespective of whether her batterer has entered treatment, should periodically review her safety plan as a precautionary measure.**

• **If this batterer successfully completes a treatment program relative to his violence and his victim makes the decision to reconcile, she should also:**

- enter into joint counseling for a brief period of time
- contract to see a therapist with her batterer at least once a year for a "checkup"
- attend Al-Anon if her batterer has a history of alcoholism
- always be aware that there is a significant possibility that his violent behaviors will return
- periodically review her safety plan

• **If this batterer fails to enter or complete a treatment program relative to his violence, his victim should:**

- develop a strong support system
- develop and implement a comprehensive safety plan
- terminate her relationship with him

Category Three Batterer

Two of the most idealistic statements made by clinicians and social workers are, "Anyone can change," and "If I can help even one family to stay together, it has all been worth the effort." Never apply this ideology to the treatment of the chronic batterer. Never allow your idealism to impair your judgment. Each time that you advocate to treat the Category Three abuser, you endanger the lives of his victim and her children.

• **Don't rescue the Category Three batterer from the consequences of his behavior.** If you find yourself advocating for his "needs," recognize the inappropriateness of your actions. To advocate for the chronic batterer is to advocate against his victim.

Category Three assailants who enter treatment generally do so in an effort to avoid criminal prosecution or in an attempt to lure their victims back into relationships. Your advocacy for the batterer serves to reinforce his manipulation of others. Both the court and the victim will be misled into believing that you are the solution to their problems. Consequently, they will let their guards down and you will have given control back to the batterer.

• **Instead of promoting treatment for the Category Three batterer, promote boundaries such as court mandates, restraining orders, and restrictions that serve to protect his victim.** Properly monitored restraining orders are powerful deterrents to continued violence against a specific victim.

• **Recognize that the criminal justice system refers batterers to treatment programs indiscriminately.** Independent assessments are rarely performed by court personnel, and it is likely that you will have a significant number of Category Three batterers referred to you for treatment. This is particularly true since the largest number of batterers seen by the courts fall in the range between Category Two and Three.

While you may feel obligated to treat all batterers referred to you by court mandates, question your ideology. If you feel that a referral has been inappropriately made, assert yourself and inform the person who made the referral of your apprehension. If you do not, you may end up with a group of sociopathic batterers who will turn your clinical practice into a clinical nightmare. Never allow yourself to become a dumping ground for court-mandated referrals.

• **Recognize that the chronic batterer has extensive levels of denial.** He will minimize, externalize, and rationalize all of his behaviors and violence. If you have absolute validation that he has committed certain acts of violence, he will minimize them. If you have no real validation, he will deny them altogether. He will also try to convince you that he was provoked into his violence by issues external to himself.

Victims also exhibit high levels of denial. Her minimization of what actually took place often parallels that of her abuser. In an effort to survive her abusive relationship, she will often try to justify its occurrence.

• **If you do provide treatment to the chronic batterer, never allow him to portray himself as a victim.** While in some cases it may be true that he had a horrendous childhood, he is now the perpetrator and should be confronted as such. Always remind him that his behavior is unacceptable, immoral, criminal, and could result in his incarceration.

While you may treat the pain of his past, you should always confront the actions of the present. In your attempts to address the emotional scars that lie deep within, under no circumstances should you reinforce the batterer's sense of victimization.

Addressing the Needs of the Category Three Victim

• **In addressing the needs of a victim of chronic abuse, never imply that you "know how she feels."** The pain of being tortured or mutilated by her assailant is anguish that only a victim can fully understand. Being stalked, kidnapped, and threatened with guns and other weapons are terrors that only she can appreciate. I have personally interviewed and assisted thousands of battered women over the years, yet I still cannot comprehend their plight.

The danger of believing that you fully understand her situation lies in minimizing its occurrence. The consequence of such a perception is to become reactive rather than proactive, to become passive when you should become responsive. Always respond to such a victim as if it is a life and death situation. In matters involving Category Three violence, that is generally the case.

• **If you are treating the battered woman who is a victim of Category Three abuse, never suggest that she enter into marriage counseling with her assailant.** Category Three violence has nothing to do with the quality of the relationship. She does not cause his violence and should not be placed in a position that implies she does. Marriage counseling suggests that as the relationship improves, the violence will cease.

Such a perception is dangerously erroneous. As long as the victim of chronic abuse stays in the relationship with her assailant, regardless of what measures are taken to improve it, he will continue to beat her. Instead of promoting marital therapy, suggest divorce counseling. Instead of promoting reconciliation, suggest termination. In matters of Category Three violence, there are no other solutions.

• **Accept the fact that many relationships need to end, particularly those in which the woman and her children have been in considerable danger.** There is no value in trying to keep a family together when there has been chronic and ongoing violence. An attempt to reunite a family that has suffered chronic abuse merely perpetuates the transmission of family violence. Little girls grow up to be battered women while little boys grow up to be batterers.

Never try to reconcile or preserve a family unit in which chronic violence has been the norm. Instead, work toward the termination of such a relationship. Always recognize that a broken home is better than a violent one.

• **Beware of misleading the victim into believing that counseling will stop the abuse of a Category Three batterer.** The thought of therapy conjures up a sense of security to those who have been victimized. The battered woman begins to feel safe within the context of hope. If she sees that you are promoting treatment, she will believe that things will change and reconciliation may occur. Never enter into passive collusion with the chronic batterer.

There is no room for clinical heroes in the field of domestic violence. While it may be politically correct to consider treatment for all batterers, question such an ideology. Acknowledge your limitations and those of the men you are treating. Recognize your own co-dependency and related tendency to rescue the assailant. No matter how qualified you may be, a Category Three batterer is incapable of productive change. His condition is malignant. He cannot bond with others nor can he feel remorse for his actions. You cannot successfully treat a serial killer or serial rapist. Likewise, you cannot treat the Serial Batterer.

While you are able to treat the Category One abuser, and sometimes the Category Two, trying to assist the Category Three batterer is fruitless and may only result in the death of his victim. Instead of treatment and reconciliation of Category Three batterer relationships, suggest to the victim that she run for her life.

• **Since the Category Three assailant is a predator, stalker, and Serial Batterer, it is imperative that you assist his victim in developing and implementing a comprehensive safety plan.** He is potentially homicidal, and she and her children are in extreme danger.

• **If children are at high risk and living with the chronic batterer, advocate for their removal.** Suggest to the victim that if she does not want to get out of the relationship for herself, she should do so for the sake of her kids. If child abuse is occurring and the battered woman refuses to take appropriate action, refer the matter to the police or a child protection agency for proper intervention. It is likely that all states have laws that mandate such reporting. If you know child abuse is taking place and do not report it to the proper authorities, you could assume both criminal and civil liability.

It is unfortunate that while most clinicians are aware of the irreversible emotional damage done to children reared in environments of chronic violence, appropriate preventive measures are seldom taken. The impact of family violence on children is indisputable. If you are going to have any impact relative to family violence, you must first address the needs of the children. If such needs are not addressed, the transmission of family violence will continue to spread like an incurable virus.

• **If the batterer was referred to you by the courts, but fails to comply with all legal mandates, immediately notify his probation officer or the individual responsible for his supervision.** While courts frequently refer batterers for treatment, they are generally very lackadaisical in the follow-up of their referrals. It is therefore incumbent on you to take the lead in communicating with appropriate personnel.

Providing feedback to the court concerning noncompliance is particularly important since mandates relative to criminal charges will eventually reach prescription. Prescription is a legal time boundary that, when passed, makes all criminal charges and court orders unenforceable. If you fail to report the batterer's nonparticipation on a timely basis, he will no longer be able to be held accountable for his behavior.

• **The batterer's criminal behavior should never be allowed to conceal itself behind the shield of client confidentiality.** While the privacy and confidentiality of the client is protected under civil law, this should not extend to overt threats that he may make or disclose to you during counseling sessions.

If you are treating the batterer and he openly makes a threat to seriously harm his victim, you have the ethical, moral, and, in many cases, legal responsibility to notify both his victim and the authorities. Failure to do so could result in significant civil liability should his threats become reality.

• **Never allow yourself to become a dumping ground for defense attorneys.** Such lawyers conveniently subscribe to the theory that everyone is a victim and has an inalienable right to treatment. Their primary intent is to achieve their client's freedom at any cost.

• **Even if you possess academic credentials as a clinical therapist, never treat the batterer without first acquiring specialized training in the area of domestic violence.** Treating the batterer is a very complex process that requires unique skills and knowledge.

If you are treating the battered woman, always remember that the notes you keep relative to your counseling sessions with her are not necessarily private and confidential. They are generally subject to the subpoena process and may be ordered released to the batterer's attorney if requested.

Never keep notes, documents, or material in the victim's file that are not in her best interest. Never reduce to writing information that may enable the batterer's attorney to discredit the victim while buffering his client from consequences.

• **Never allow symbols to blur reality.** The fact that an individual batterer is an articulate, well-dressed, and affluent professional does not reduce his responsibility for his violent attack. Batterers come in all types of symbolic packaging. Never allow your perception of a batterer to cloud the truth.

• **Know the difference between remorse and manipulation.** While the Category One abuser is genuinely remorseful for what he has done to his victim, the Category Three assailant is cunningly manipulative and cold. Although the Category Two batterer can be manipulative as well, he may possess some degree of remorse for his action.

The motivation that a batterer has for seeking your assistance can be induced by either internal or external factors. In some instances, it can be induced by both. The Category One abuser will generally come to you as a result of internal motivation. He wants to change because he doesn't like who he is or what he has done. On the other hand, the Category Three batterer will come to you as a result of external coercion or duress. His participation is usually a result of court mandates or of the fact that his spouse has left him and refuses to return unless he "gets help." He will come to you not because he wants to, but because he has to. He will almost always withdraw from treatment once his wife or girlfriend returns or the criminal charges against him have been withdrawn or dismissed. While the Category Two assailant's motivation to change is largely external, he may possess enough internal motivation to make productive change possible, if boundaries are appropriately set and enforced.

Your assessment of the batterer's level and source of motivation will usually correlate with his position on the Batterer's Continuum. The general rule is, the farther he is to the right of the continuum, or the higher he is on the index, the less remorse he will possess and the greater the possibility that he entered treatment as a result of external coercion.

His motivation for coming to you should affect not only the modality you utilize in treating him, but in some cases, it should impact whether you assist him at all. While you may feel professionally obligated to treat any batterer who seeks your services, be aware that he may be trying only to evade the consequences of his behavior.

• **In some cases, it may be very difficult for you to distinguish between Category Two and Category Three violence.** This is particularly true when the Category Two batterer's abuse has been triggered by stress, substance abuse, estrangement, or a combination of all three. In fact, under such circumstances, the Category Two batterer begins to take on the profile of the Category Three. Such triggers can cause the boundaries between Category Two and Category Three to become blurred.

One of the best means of distinguishing between the two types is through the utilization of the questionnaire located in the Appendix. Another general rule to remember is that the difference between Category Two and Three abuse lies in the degree of the violence, how often it occurs, and the level at which it is sustained. Always remember that while the Category One abuser's violence is isolated, the Category Two batterer's abuse is sporadic and reoccurring. The abuse of the Category Three assailant, on the other hand, is always ongoing, systematic, and chronic.

A batterer may not necessarily exhibit a perfect profile of Category Two or Three. He may fall somewhere between these two primary points of reference and may therefore be more difficult to define and diagnose.

• **You will rarely encounter a batterer who is psychotic or out of touch with reality.** In the screening of approximately 20,000 cases of domestic violence by the New Orleans Municipal Court Probation Office, only a dozen or so assailants appeared to be psychotic.

Most chronic batterers have a personality disorder and know exactly what they are doing when they commit their crimes of violence. They know right from wrong—but just don't care.

• **Never consider the alcoholism or drug addiction of the Category Three batterer as the reason for his aggression.** Substance abuse is not a direct causative factor of his violence. For chronic batterers, it is just one of the many symptoms of the personality disorder itself. Even in the absence of his substance abuse, the violence will continue.

If, however, you are treating a Category One or Two abuser who is also addicted to drugs or alcohol, always address the substance abuse first. You must assist him in his efforts to recover from substance abuse if you are going to be capable of addressing the other dynamics of his personality and socialization that are bringing about his aggression. Under no circumstances should he be allowed to attend sessions while under the influence.

All Batterers

• **Before you begin to treat batterers, be aware of the civil liability that both you and your agency assume.** If the batterer should seriously injure or kill his spouse, and it can be shown that you do not have the academic credentials or training necessary for treating him, you may increase your exposure to liability.

• **Under no circumstances should lay volunteers enter into a counselor-client relationship with a batterer.** Volunteers and staff members who are without academic credentials and training in the areas of social science and domestic violence should never attempt to serve in the capacity of a professional therapist. The dynamics of battering are complex and should not be addressed by staff members who have no relevant expertise. Such a scenario is like a mechanic opening up a medical practice.

Many self-proclaimed counselors who insist on treating the Category Three batterer have little or no insight into the batterer's personality disorders. They want to treat the batterer without having essential knowledge of the dynamics and complexities of his rage.

• **Recognize the responsibility that is associated with the treatment of the batterer.** Never provide such a service unless you are qualified to do so. The victim's life could depend on the expertise that you have in addressing her abuser.

Chapter XII

An Intervention Protocol for Medical Personnel

Protocol

All medical facilities should develop and implement proper protocol in addressing the needs of the battered woman. The desired protocol should be adopted as policy and closely monitored for staff compliance.

Protocol helps to set the standards by which a battered woman is received and treated. It serves to reduce the discretionary authority that many staff members exhibit while treating a victim of abuse. It reduces the ability of personnel to allow their opinions, prejudices, and misconceptions to cloud the manner in which they provide care.

Regardless of the type of medical facility that you operate, if you provide services to the battered woman, consider establishing the following protocol:

Expedient Service to Police Officers

Establish proper procedures that ensure police officers priority response when they bring a victim of domestic violence to your facility for assistance. Police officers are generally very reluctant to transport the battered woman to a medical facility for an examination. Much of their resistance comes as a result of the time-consuming nature of the medical process.

It is not unusual for an officer to receive ten to twenty calls a shift involving domestic violence. If he/she encounters bureaucratic red tape each time a victim is transported for treatment, the police officer may begin to ignore the process altogether.

Ensure all officers that your response will be as quick and efficient as possible. If they recognize that your facility will not delay them in resuming their regular routine, there is a greater probability that they will transport the battered woman to you when she is injured.

Multidisciplinary Team

Your emergency room or reception area should be staffed with a multidisciplinary team that has special skills and expertise in the area of domestic violence. When a battered woman comes to your facility for assistance, she is much like a victim of rape. She has been violently attacked and violated. The crisis and trauma she has endured are similar to those experienced by a victim of sexual assault. In many cases, she *has* been sexually assaulted.

It is best if the multidisciplinary team is made up of a cross section of professionals such as a doctor, nurse, social worker, technician, and receptionist. Upon the arrival of a victim of spousal abuse, all should work together in providing the type of care and service that is unique to the needs of the battered woman.

The team concept ensures a greater level of efficiency, consistency, and continuity. It ensures that the processing and treatment of a victim will be appropriate and consistent from one staff member to the next and that it will be provided in a nonthreatening manner.

It is a good practice to have those professionals who work in the treatment of the battered woman volunteer for this assignment. Those who exhibit special interest in this field generally make empathetic caretakers and listeners. Since the victim is generally in trauma upon her arrival at your facility, sensitivity to her needs is essential to her stabilization.

Expedient Service to Victim

Once a woman has been identified as a victim of spousal abuse, immediately attend to her emotional and physical needs. All needless delays in service delivery should be avoided. Most battered women are reluctant to come to you for treatment. They are embarrassed, humiliated, intimidated, and fear that their abusers will kill them if they seek help. They usually have been battered on many occasions before they find the courage to seek medical assistance. In many cases they have been seriously injured and have no choice.

All unnecessary red tape and paperwork should be postponed

until the victim has been properly received and reassured. Make her feel as comfortable and relaxed as possible. While expedient and conscientious service can motivate the battered woman to address her problems further, long delays and indifference will often result in her leaving your facility before treatment is completed. In many such cases, she will not return and will permanently surrender to the control of her assailant.

Do Not Examine the Victim in the Presence of Her Batterer

Always separate the victim from her abuser. Never allow the woman's batterer to escort her into the examination room. Under no circumstance should he be allowed to participate in the treatment process. Even if she suggests that it be permitted, explain that it is policy to speak with her alone. If you discover that he is the assailant only after you have begun her examination, immediately ask the batterer to leave.

If he refuses to comply with your first request, calmly make your request a second time. If he still refuses to comply, immediately notify hospital security or the police, if necessary. Never get into a personal confrontation with the victim's batterer. Any confrontation could prove dangerous for you, his victim, and those in the immediate area.

The physical presence of the batterer during the medical interview and examination is a very intrusive and intimidating experience for the battered woman. Without saying a word, he is able to control her responses and statements to you. He will try to intercede in the examination because it is in his best interest to do so. He doesn't want his victim to tell you the truth. He doesn't want her to tell you what he has done.

Preserve the Victim's Right to Privacy

Always respect the battered woman's right to privacy. Even in your initial stages of questioning, the victim should be afforded a private area in which to provide her responses. Doing so not only protects her confidentiality, it also places her at ease and ensures you a greater degree of openness concerning her injuries and related problems. The staffs of many medical facilities frequently interview and question battered women within hearing distance and in view of the general public. This is particularly true in the common receiving and waiting areas of large hospitals. It is not unusual to hear a receiving clerk question a patient as to the cause of her injury. Nurses and other medical personnel routinely ask the victim in the presence of others detailed questions regarding the nature of her problems.

Questioning the battered woman in public is both humiliating and embarrassing to the victim. It also restricts and inhibits her responses to you. It is very difficult for her to confide in others under normal circumstances. To ask her to do so in a public waiting area is unreasonable, and it violates her right to confidentiality.

Address the Victim in a Nonjudgmental and Supportive Manner

During your interview and examination of the battered woman, always be attuned to the manner in which you address her. It is not unusual for medical personnel to become frustrated with such victims and to come across as callous and indifferent.

Recognize that you may be the first professional that the battered woman approaches relative to her abuse. Your personal demeanor may very well dictate whether she takes her problems beyond medical intervention. Treating her with care and sensitivity may motivate her to address her issues further. Treating her with insensitivity and indifference will cause her to withdraw.

- **It is recommended that the following considerations be observed during your treatment of the battered woman:**
  - Always speak to the victim in a nonjudgmental manner. While it may be difficult for you to understand the relationship that she has with the abuser, appearing critical will only alienate her.
  - Let her know that she is not alone. Explain that medical facilities treat tens of thousands of spousal abuse victims each year and that there are professionals willing to assist her in escaping the violence.
  - Your tone of voice with the battered woman is very important. Always address and question her in a tone that is gentle and caring. Never appear abrasive, defensive, or dogmatic. Tone of voice is crucial to the establishment of patient trust.
  - Let the victim know that you support her efforts to stop the abuse. Display intolerance for what the batterer has done,

and assist her in acquiring the community and legal resources that can address her needs. Always let the victim know that either you or members of your staff will be available to her in the future should she need your assistance.

- Always make eye contact with the victim and call her by her first name. Such techniques demonstrate personal attention and validation. Calling the woman by her last name while avoiding eye contact suggests that you are distant and indifferent to her plight.
- Never make it appear that you are rushing the victim through the examination and interview process. If your caseload is too large to spend the time with her that she needs, find someone on your staff who can. It is a good idea to have a staff member pre-selected for this assignment.

The Interview and Examination

The assistance that you provide to the battered woman should go beyond medical care. Such care should be comprehensive and all-encompassing and should address her emotional, medical, and safety needs. It should include those areas of concern that, if not met, will make her more vulnerable to her assailant's coercion and physical assaults. If you are to effectively assist a victim of spousal abuse, the following areas should always be addressed:

Identifying Her as a Battered Woman

Always question a woman as to the origin of her injuries. Let her know of your suspicion that she has been battered. Your questions should be direct, specific, and to the point.

Crisis Intervention

After you have identified a patient as a battered woman, be prepared to intervene in her emotional state. On some occasions she may appear depressed and lethargic. On other visits she may be hysterical and overcome with anxiety. Always be prepared and equipped to intervene in her emotional state, regardless of the demeanor that she presents.

Medical Examination

Always give the victim a complete physical exam. There may be residual injuries that resulted from previous beatings. Check her closely for fractures, internal injuries, bruises, and abrasions that may not be immediately detected in a routine examination.

Treatment

Always take a holistic approach in your treatment of the battered woman. Treat her for more than the physical symptoms of spousal abuse. Address their causes as well.

All too often, doctors see battered women and prescribe medication as a means of masking the pain that they feel. Antidepressants, tranquilizers, and other drugs are frequently given in an attempt to make the problem go away. In some cases, the battered woman solicits the medication; in many cases, she does not.

The addictive qualities of the medication that you prescribe should be of significant concern. The battered woman is vulnerable to becoming addicted to any drug that provides immediate gratification and relief from the stress, anxiety, and pain that she feels.

Before prescribing medication to any woman, be certain that you are not simply covering up the symptoms of a larger problem. If you discover that she is being physically abused, avoid the use of prescription drugs and turn more appropriately to counseling and those agencies that specialize in the treatment and assistance of the battered woman. While drugs may reduce the victim's anxiety, drugs will not stop her abuse.

Documentation

Always document your medical findings of a battered woman in an accurate and legible manner. Your handwriting and word usage should be such that others can read and understand it. If your records are subpoenaed as a result of litigation, those trying to read them should not have difficulty in doing so.

Counsel and Support

Once you have physically treated and stabilized your patient, address her fears and apprehension. Explore alternatives with her in seeking a resolution to her abuse. Let her know that you care and that she is not alone. If a victim feels support at your level of intervention, there is a greater probability that she will take measures to do something about her problem.

Education

Educate the battered woman on what specific options are available to her. Give her as much information as possible relative to legal remedies and social service programs. Provide her with reading material on the dynamics of spousal abuse. Even if it appears that the victim is not motivated to address her problem further, educate her about community resources and domestic violence. Education is a building block to recovery.

Referral

Never allow a battered woman to leave your facility without offering to refer her to those legal and social service programs that can further address her problems. Even if she appears disinterested in such a referral, provide her with the name and phone number of a domestic violence program should she later change her mind.

Follow-up

Always let the battered woman know that you are available to her should the need arise. Let her know that your door is open to her in the event of future attacks and crises. If she has a phone number independent of the abuser's, periodically contact her to see how she is doing. Such follow-up will remind her that you are there in the event that she needs you. It may also encourage her to take control of the situation.

Identifying the Battered Woman

It is most unfortunate that many members of the medical profession treat the wounds of the battered woman without questioning the victim as to the nature of her injuries. They stitch wounds, mend broken bones, and clean abrasions and lacerations without questioning the victim's unlikely explanation of their origin. She is quickly treated and released, only to have the entire scenario repeat itself over and over again.

Your role as a medical professional includes identifying victims of domestic violence. If a woman presents herself with any of the injuries noted in the next section, consider that she may have been battered. Perform a thorough inquiry into the cause of her injuries. While your questioning of her should not be intimidating, it should be direct and specific relative to your suspicions. Avoid being abrasive, but let her know that you believe she has been battered. While you may want to formulate your own questions, it is suggested that you review and utilize many of those listed in the Lethality Questionnaire located in the Appendix.

Also recognize the possible liability that you may assume for not properly identifying and diagnosing blatant signs of spousal abuse.[87] If your patient is subsequently injured or killed by her abuser and it can be shown that your previous exam did not question or address the obvious, civil juries could perceive your inaction as negligence.

Protect both yourself and your patient. If your exam suggests that she is a victim of spousal abuse, treat and counsel her and refer her to community agencies that can assist further.

The physical injuries that the batterer inflicts on his victim are often very similar in type and scope. The injuries are also generally found on specific areas of the woman's body.

• **A medical practitioner who sees any of the following injuries should view them as red flags and explore the possibility of spousal abuse:**

- black and swollen eyes
- swollen lips
- broken or loose teeth
- facial bruising
- hearing loss
- virtually any injury to the head or facial area
- scratches or bruises around the neck
- bite marks
- large bruises on various parts of the woman's torso and/or

extremities
- lacerations, abrasions, and burns
- puncture wounds
- broken ribs
- fractured and broken bones, particularly in the areas of the arms, legs, and face
- spontaneous abortions and premature labor

While it is possible for a woman to receive these injuries in many ways other than by being battered, if you find that she has numerous injuries on various parts of her body, the likelihood that spousal abuse exists is significant. Likewise, if a woman comes to you for treatment on a regular basis with such injuries, it is very likely that she is being physically battered.

If a pregnant woman comes to you with bruises, black eyes, abrasions, cuts, or broken bones, or she is in premature labor, immediately consider the possibility of spousal abuse. Always question her regarding the origin of her injuries. While appearing both supportive and nonjudgmental, explore this possibility until you are satisfied that it is not an issue of concern.

Battered women frequently report that their beatings accelerate when they are pregnant. They also describe attacks that are directed at the abdominal region. It is not unusual for a victim to be punched or kicked in her stomach during the late stages of pregnancy. This may be a direct attempt by the batterer to murder the fetus. He may feel that he is incapable of competing with the baby once it is born.

Documentation

Always consider your documentation of the battered woman's injuries as an important adjunct to the treatment that you provide. Your diagnosis and the manner in which you compile your medical report could become essential evidence, should the assailant be civilly or criminally prosecuted for his crimes.[88]

Likewise, if the victim kills her abuser in self-defense, your medical report, particularly if it illustrates ongoing and perpetual abuse, serves to validate her position.

• In compiling your report of the battered woman, always consider the following issues and elements of concern:

Confidentiality

The information contained within your report might not be entirely confidential. Practically all medical records are subject to the subpoena process. The manner in which you document your observations and the statements of the battered woman may be essential in substantiating her credibility.

Legibility

Your report should be clearly and legibly written. Your signature on the medical report should be recognizable. It is suggested that you sign and also print your name. In the event that subpoenas have to be issued in your name, the court will be able to determine who you are.

Origin of Patient's Injury

Your report should include a statement from your patient explaining the cause of her injuries. Also include a statement as to how you believe her injuries occurred.

The Need to Testify

The litigation process will not always dictate a personal court appearance or the need to give testimony in a formal deposition. This is particularly true if your report can be easily read without further explanation. Most litigation is resolved through out-of-court settlements and through the plea-bargaining process, and it will not necessarily require your physical presence.

Appearance of Irrationality

Never inappropriately give the impression in your report that the battered woman is irrational and unstable. Such documented statements can destroy the victim's credibility and her attempts to seek relief from her assailant through the courts. While she may appear to be hysterical and overwhelmed with anxiety, such symptoms are often a normal response to being physically battered.

The Batterer's Presence

If the victim's batterer escorts her to your facility, note his presence. If he refuses to leave the treatment area when asked, or tries to control the statements of his victim, note such behavior in your report. You should also document any utterances, threats, or statements made in your presence by the assailant that may validate the victim's claims of being battered.

The Patient's Testimony of Abuse

If a patient describes to you a history of being abused by her assailant, note it in your report. Any utterances or statements that she makes relative to her assailant's recent attack should also be included in your report.

If Police Were Involved

If the police escorted the victim to your facility or if you contacted them for assistance, state it in your report. If you have direct knowledge that the batterer was arrested for his attack, such information should also be recorded.

If the Victim is Pregnant

If you determine that the victim is pregnant, include such information in your report. While the beating of any woman is serious, it will be viewed by the courts and others as even more serious if it involves a pregnant woman and her unborn child. If you determine that the fetus is at risk due to the physical trauma of the beating, clearly state your findings in the medical report.

Size of Bruises and Lacerations

Measure the size of your patient's bruises and lacerations and note them in your report. Also indicate their approximate number and the locations of such injuries.

Photographic and Imaging Documentation

Whenever possible, your medical records should also include photographic and imaging documentation.[89] If the victim pursues a divorce or files criminal charges against her assailant, it may be weeks or months before her case is heard by the courts. Your medical records, in addition to visual evidence, preserve and provide strong substantiation that the beating took place.

Physical Diagram of the Patient's Anatomy

Include with your report a special form that outlines the human anatomy. Illustrate on the diagram the specific locations of the patient's bruises, lacerations, puncture wounds, broken bones, and other injuries that she suffered as a result of the beating. Such a diagram will give those receiving your evaluation a clear and precise illustration of the victim's injuries.

Diagnosis and Prognosis

Your report should include a summary of your medical findings, laboratory and test results, and a complete diagnostic and prognostic profile of the victim. If she has suffered a permanent or disabling injury as a result of the attack, such information should also be included.

General Suggestions

Report the Crime

All states now have laws that mandate you to report the crime of child abuse. The mandatory reporting of spousal and elder abuse, however, varies from state to state. Unfortunately, such reporting remains highly controversial. To mandate medical professionals to report cases of spousal abuse to the police creates significant dilemmas in the area of liability and safety. Doctors and nurses who fail to recognize a borderline case could face malpractice suits. Battered women, on the other hand, knowing that the police would be notified by medical authorities, may not seek the help they need since they may fear retaliation by their assailants.

Review local and state laws to determine your responsibility relative to reporting crimes of spousal abuse and family violence.[90] While the state in which you practice may not mandate such reporting, always encourage a victim to allow you to notify the authorities. This is of particular importance when she is pregnant.

Educate the Victim

The battered woman should never be simply treated and released. She should also be educated and referred to those programs that can assist her with financial, legal, safety, emotional, and housing needs. Upon treating the victim for her physical injuries, always provide her with a referral to those criminal justice and community service agencies that can further address her problems.

Provide her with a comprehensive list of domestic violence programs along with their phone numbers, addresses, and contact personnel. Give your patient literature relative to spousal abuse and family violence. Many of these materials can be acquired free of charge at family violence agencies.

If you are to be effective in making appropriate referrals for the battered woman, it is important that you become familiar with those agencies that are available in your community. Volunteer to sit on their advisory boards or to participate in their training. Such participation breeds familiarity with the staffs of these programs and makes the proper referral of the victim easier to accomplish.

Implement Hospital-Based Treatment Programs

It is recommended that medical facilities consider the implementation and operation of hospital-based treatment programs for battered women.[91] Second only to the police, medical professionals are likely to see the battered woman more frequently than any other group. Since she is often very reluctant to address her problem further, you may also be the last. Intervention at your level is therefore critical if many victims are to enter the road to recovery.

Hospital-based programs can be inpatient, outpatient, or both. Such programs should include a multidisciplinary team approach consisting of a staff of doctors, nurses, social workers, technicians, and other support personnel. All members of the team should be expertly trained in the dynamics of domestic violence and spousal abuse. Under no circumstances should a professional be allowed to join the team unless he/she possesses the proper credentials. The multidisciplinary team approach will enhance treatment continuity, efficiency, and competency.

Since many battered women will also be in financial crisis when they come to your facility, cost factors should be given major consideration. Always consider linking the service that you provide to her insurance benefits, if she has any. Other means of reducing costs to the victim are through sliding scale fees, federal and state grants, private and corporate donations, and so on. If you are to maximize services to the greatest number of battered women possible, keeping costs to a minimum is essential to that objective.

• **Hospital-based programs for the battered woman should include, but not be limited to, the following services:**

- consultation
- evaluation
- identification
- crisis intervention
- medical examination and treatment
- individual counseling
- group counseling
- emotional support
- development of a safety plan
- assistance in applying for crime victim's compensation
- legal advocacy
- referral services

Provide Formal Training and Education to Medical Students and Personnel

The American Medical Association should mandate all medical schools and residency programs to provide formal training and education on the subject of domestic violence.[92] Such training should take the form of credit courses and should include outside speakers.

Doctors, nurses, and other medical practitioners who are required to participate in ongoing certification programs should be required to periodically attend seminars and conferences that focus on family violence. Such conferences have proliferated over the last few years, and the opportunities for such in-service training are vast and comprehensive.

Chapter XIII

A Plan for Educators: Dealing With Date Violence

As an educator, school counselor, or school administrator, you have assumed the responsibility of assisting students in their search for emotional stability and an adult identity. You will play the role of their parent, teacher, disciplinarian, and counselor. You will become both their friend and their adversary. Second only to their parents, you will become their role model. Sensitivity to the needs of your students will dictate that you address areas and provide services which were once the sole responsibility of the parents.

In your personal interactions with students, you will come upon drug problems, teen parents, alcoholism, sexually transmitted diseases, mental illness, eating disorders, and, of course, the tragedy of domestic violence. You will encounter teenagers who are being abused by a parent or who are witnessing violence in the home. You will meet young girls who are being abused by boyfriends, and young boys who are the abusers.

Normal Adolescence or a Personality Disorder?

If you have read those chapters that describe various personality disorders, be careful not to confuse symptoms commonly associated with adolescent immaturity with those of adult disorders. While teenagers frequently go through periods when they may commit petty theft, vandalize personal property, experiment with drugs, exhibit extreme jealousy and self-centeredness, experience an identity disturbance, and are sexually promiscuous, such traits within the context of adolescence are not necessarily indicative of a personality disorder.

The primary method of assessing "normal" adolescent immaturity from a personality disorder is by examining the onset, duration, longevity, and magnitude of such behaviors and symptoms. If, for example, the symptoms have no longevity and the onset was only recent, chances are you are addressing adolescent immaturity and nothing more. If, however, you find that the origin of the behaviors was in early childhood and they have great longevity in addition to magnitude, you may be addressing a student with a fully developed personality disorder.

Of course, if you are not a psychotherapist or clinician, you should always acquire a diagnostic opinion from such professionals. As is the case with adult batterers, the manner in which you address adolescent assailants should be relative to their locations on the Batterer's Continuum.

Teenage batterers and their victims vary according to degree. While some teenage assailants' behaviors may simply be related to external stress or adolescent immaturity, the violence of others may be rooted in a well-developed personality disorder. While some victims may not need the services of a therapist, others may exhibit the Battered Women's Syndrome and should be addressed clinically.

Never minimize the traits and characteristics of teenage batterers or their victims. The fact that they are very young is no guarantee that a personality disorder or the Battered Women's Syndrome is not present. The fact is, such a disorder or syndrome develops very early in life and often becomes clearly visible in early adolescence.

The School and Date Violence

It is interesting that while date rape has been a recent focus of concern by professional educators, the issue of date violence, which is far more prevalent, remains virtually ignored. Whereas the two behaviors closely correlate with one another, those associated with date rape are notoriously blatant. Date violence, however, is often more subtle: slapping, pushing, pulling of hair, pinching, and stalking.

It is imperative that educators begin to assertively address date violence by developing policies that would declare such behaviors unacceptable and reprimandable by school standards.

In matters of date violence, you will have to address the aggression of the perpetrator and the needs of his victim. While preserving some degree of student confidentiality, ideally parents should be consulted. Although some assailants will respond to a reprimand and warning, others may need to be suspended, expelled, or even criminally charged.

Of course, the measures you take are dependent on where the offense took place. If the act occurred on the school grounds and was committed by one student on another, you should take appropriate administrative action. If, however, the offense took place off school property, while you may not be able to reprimand, suspend, or expel the assailant, your liaison should consider advising the victim and her parents how to seek relief through the criminal justice system.

Establishing Policies

While your school may already have a strict policy relative to violence on campus, a written statement concerning date violence will indicate that such offenses will be investigated by the school liaison and, if appropriate, reported to authorities. In your policy handbook, define such violence as any aggression directed by one student toward another when there has been an intimate or dating relationship. The uniqueness of behaviors associated with date violence calls for a specialized policy designed by school districts.

• **Within the context of your date violence policy, adopt a secondary policy relative to one student stalking another on campus.** If the teenage stalker is not associated with your school and appears on your campus, call the police and have him charged with criminal trespassing. If one student stalks another while on school grounds or at a school-sponsored function, address the assailant administratively or, if necessary, by filing criminal charges. If the stalking activities occur off the school grounds, advise the victim's parents of the various legal remedies and community resources that are available to them and suggest that they take appropriate action. Adolescent stalking can be as serious as stalking committed by adult offenders and should be addressed appropriately.

• **Your policies should advocate the use of the police and the courts in the same manner as if the domestic violence involved adults.** The criminal justice system has the ability to provide you with the leverage necessary in getting an adolescent assailant to stay away from his victim. In more serious cases of date violence, court mandates may be your only means of controlling such situations. Courts have the authority to issue restraining orders, stay away orders, etc., that if properly monitored, serve as powerful deterrents to future assaults.

• **Policies requiring documentation of incidents are essential. All aggressive activities of the adolescent assailant should be well documented.** If the victim has been bruised, cut, lacerated, etc., photograph her injuries and, if appropriate, acquire a copy of her medical records. Advise the victim to keep a daily log relative to all aggressive acts of her assailant. Such logs will not only aid her in recalling specific events, if necessary, but will also assist her in convincing others that her concern is valid.

Such documentation will prove very valuable to you as an educator or administrator should you have to assist in action against the aggressor.

• **Acts of violence directed by one student toward another, regardless of the relationship, should not be tolerated.** Policies should indicate no double standards.

Your school probably has a zero tolerance policy regarding weapons, drugs, and campus violence. Adopt a zero tolerance policy relative to date violence as well.

• **Policies regarding the possession or use of weapons are also essential.** Any student who commits an act of date violence on the school grounds or at a school-sponsored function while in possession of a lethal weapon should be promptly expelled, arrested, and prosecuted for the offense. Under no circumstances should there be exceptions.

Increasing Student Awareness

As part of the student's academic curriculum, utilize courses in sociology and psychology that address the dynamics of interpersonal relationships. Such courses should provide the student with a significant level of information relative to domestic violence.

• **Specific focus should be given to the following areas:**

- elder, child, and spousal abuse
- dynamics and profiles of assailants
- dynamics and profiles of victims
- warning signs; "red flags"
- community resources

- social and legal remedies and dynamics

• **Invite professionals from various agencies such as the police department, courts, and domestic violence programs to participate as guest lecturers.** Most students enjoy having guest speakers visit their class. You should time their presentations relative to the information that you are providing in class.

• **Require students to complete term papers on various aspects of relationships and domestic violence.** Provide them with a list of topics from which to choose. Each student should select a different topic and be required to give an oral presentation to the class. Such a format will provide students with significant exposure to a wide range of issues.

• **Ask your school librarian to include in the library's inventory books, videos, and materials on a broad range of topics concerning relationships and domestic violence.** Effort should be made to keep all resource material current and consistent with modern research findings.

• **Survey your students with a formal questionnaire as to what information and course material they would like to see offered relative to domestic violence and relationship issues.** Have them prioritize the topics that they list.

• **As part of your school's academic curriculum, encourage and allow students to perform internships at local domestic violence agencies.** Prior to implementing such a program, always seek your governing school district's approval. Students who perform such community service work should be required to submit written reports on their experiences and could possibly receive academic credits for their participation. Internships provide students with an environment in which they can apply what they have learned in the classroom.

The Role of Your School's Counseling Department

• **If you discover that a student is being battered by a dating or intimate partner, refer her to the school's counseling office or appointed liaison for appropriate intervention.** If you do not have such resources available to you in the school, or if the victim has a specialized problem that you are not equipped to address, refer her to outside community agencies that can provide assistance.

Your school's counseling department should give priority response to the issue of date violence. If your school does not have an established counseling office, it should appoint a specific staff member to serve as a liaison between students and the school relative to such problems.

Any staff member, regardless of credentials, should receive special training in the area of domestic violence prior to assuming such liaison responsibilities.

• **The counseling department or assigned liaison should become familiar with all local domestic violence programs.** A good means of acquiring such knowledge is by participating on a local task force or by joining the advisory board of a local domestic violence program or shelter.

Such involvement provides professional educators with an excellent way of networking with community resources and individuals that can assist students who are victims of domestic violence.

Providing Information and Referral

• **School districts should consider establishing domestic violence/date violence hotlines within the framework of their counseling departments.** Such hotlines would provide information and assistance to those students who desire anonymity. Students should be informed of the specific times that the hotline would be in service and a trained counselor should be made available to assist such callers.

• **Pamphlets about domestic violence and community resources should be placed in common areas where students gather; your school's counseling or administrative offices are also good locations for such material.** Most local domestic violence programs will provide you with literature free of charge.

• **Open communication should always be encouraged between home and school.** The school should assume a tenacious role in the informational and promotional aspects of various offerings to parents regarding date violence. Speakers, graphics, pamphlets, etc., could be made available during regularly scheduled parent/teacher meetings. This may help parents to identify their daughter as a victim or their son as a batterer. The school should also offer confidential support services to parents on request.

• **Parents must be made aware that they share a unique re-**

sponsibility in the total education and well-being of their children. You should utilize the school and its many resources to inform and educate the parents of your students. This joint effort is imperative if your mission as an educator is to be fully attained.

Chapter XIV

When Domestic Abuse Disrupts the Workplace

As a personnel manager or supervisor, you will routinely find yourself confronted by the personal problems of your employees. During any given day, you may assist them in the capacity of a counselor, advisor, mediator, negotiator, financial consultant, or social worker. More specifically, you will interact, assist, and negotiate with employees who have problems related to substance abuse, mental illness, emotional upsets, or physical disabilities, or who may be experiencing a family crisis.

Perhaps the most serious problem you may face is that of an employee who is a victim of spousal abuse. She may not only present a concern related to absenteeism and job production, but her assailant could also be a physical threat to everyone in your employ, including yourself. It is not uncommon for an estranged husband to appear at the office of his victim while in possession of a lethal weapon. Domestic violence at home often presents a safety concern at the workplace. Employers frequently find themselves trapped between the privacy rights of an employee and the safety of co-workers.

For example, as a supervisor, there is perhaps no issue that will evoke more of an empathetic response than that of a woman who comes to work battered and bruised. While it is strongly recommended that you respond to her needs and that you take specific steps to intervene, it is also suggested that you do so in a manner that limits both financial liability and physical danger.

Many women who are battered by Category Two or Category Three assailants are also threatened and assaulted at work while they are trying to leave the relationship or immediately after they have left.

A victim's place of employment can be extremely intimidating to her batterer because it offers her the social contacts and financial means to independence. Job harassment is a blatant attempt to eliminate both and to regain control of the victim. Batterers know that a victim without social and financial resources is also a victim without alternatives.

When Domestic Abuse Impacts Your Workplace

Identifying a battered woman in your employ may be somewhat difficult. Some of the symptoms may actually mimic problems commonly associated with substance abuse. She may have a pattern of tardiness and unplanned absenteeism, and unreasonable explanations and excuses for both. She may also appear anxiety ridden, be sensitive to criticism, and have low production levels.

There are, however, issues related directly to the behavior of her batterer that may make it easier for you to identify such an employee. She may come to work with visible bruises on her face, limbs, and torso. Black eyes and large circular bruises on her arms and legs are common. She will frequently try to camouflage such telltale signs with makeup, sunglasses, and long-sleeved blouses or ankle-length dresses.

Female employees who are battered may also experience frequent harassing phone calls, cars that are vandalized, and episodes of stalking on or near their places of employment. In your effort to identify such a victim, always assess the totality of her symptoms and circumstances.

If you currently employ a victim who is being terrorized or harassed by an ex-husband or ex-boyfriend, it is highly likely that he will threaten her by telephone and will stalk her as she enters or leaves your place of employment. If so, your assertive response to his actions is essential to modifying his behaviors relative to your workplace.

- **If he is intimidating her by phone, the following responses are recommended:**
  - have a supervisor verbally advise him that he is not to call your office
  - have someone witness and/or screen the victim's calls
  - if possible, have the telephone company place a trace on incoming calls to determine their points of origin; this may be difficult, however, if you have multiple business lines

- install caller identification devices to determine the origins of calls and document each call relative to time and date
- with the victim's permission, tape all incoming calls made to your office by the assailant
- if he continues to call, file criminal charges through the police department or local courts relative to telephone harassment

• **If he is seen intimidating, threatening, assaulting, or stalking her on or near your place of employment:**

- never view it as a personal matter; consider it to be a criminal offense
- avoid getting into a personal verbal exchange with the assailant
- if he enters your premises and requests the location of his victim, calmly avoid providing such information to him
- if you have a security department within your business or agency, notify its officers of his presence and request that they take appropriate action
- if you do not have a security department, call the police and alert them of the intrusion
- go to court and ask that restraining orders be issued restricting him from verbally contacting his victim at or near work and from physically trespassing on or near your business premises

• **In conjunction with the above, the following technical and preventive measures should be taken if it is practical to do so:**

- eliminate as many entrances and exits into your business as possible; always do so, however, within the bounds of fire codes
- install an electric door lock and buzzer that allow you to restrict those who wish to enter your work area
- if you have an alarm system, install a secret buzzer that will alert the alarm company of a possible emergency
- establish a "secret code word" that would alert other employees to notify the police that you need immediate assistance
- install a closed-circuit camera system

- have the victim go to lunch with co-workers or have the victim carry the company's cellular phone
- document everything sent to you or the victim by the assailant; keep letters, notes, phone tapes, etc., in your efforts to substantiate the problem
- keep a daily diary documenting his activities that involve your business premises
- as you enter and exit your place of business, always be very vigilant

• **If the batterer comes on your place of business and is charged with criminal trespassing or assault on his victim, it is important that you follow through with the criminal charges.** Attend all court hearings and ask that a restraining order be issued. Your non-appearance suggests a lack of interest and will result in little or nothing being done relative to the batterer's behavior. It could also subject you to a counterclaim from the batterer relative to defamation, etc.

Your appearance in court is a powerful statement. It tells the judge that the batterer not only presents a threat to his primary victim, but also to her co-workers. Your presence provides a victim with the credibility and support that she needs and gives her case focus.

Avoid the Role of Counselor

If you have an employee who is a victim of spousal abuse, there are several reasons why you should avoid entering into a counseling role with her.

Confidentiality and privacy laws restrict specific types of discussions with employees, and it will be difficult for you to determine when you are violating those restrictions. Secondly, while you may be an excellent advisor, mediator, and listener, it is highly unlikely that you have the knowledge or expertise to advise such a victim. Incorrect or inappropriate advice could place her in great jeopardy. It could also present both you and your company with civil liability should something go wrong and should it be shown that you overstepped your boundaries. Finally, getting intimately involved with a victim places you in a conflict of interest.

Should you have to discipline the employee for reasons unrelated to her domestic violence issues, you will find it almost impossible to remain objective.

• **Once you have assessed the fact that your employee is a victim of spousal abuse, refer her to an agency that can address her needs and remove you from becoming involved in a counseling scenario.** After acquiring information about available community resources, provide the information to her and ask that she make her own appointment. You should never make the appointment for her.

All referral information should be discreetly provided to the employee. You want to not only preserve her confidentiality and reduce your civil liability, but also limit your exposure to her assailant. As previously stated, her job presents a significant threat to the batterer. It is in your best interest and in the best interest of other employees not to reinforce the threat that he already feels by your needlessly playing a high profile role in intervention efforts. If at all possible, a discreet referral is the best way to reduce your exposure to her batterer.

If, however, her assailant has already intruded on your place of business, it may be important to assert yourself through the courts.

How to Support the Battered Woman

While you may get frustrated and even consider discharging an employee as a result of poor work performance related to the harassing behaviors of her abuser, recognize that such a response fulfills the assailant's objectives. He is very aware that if he causes her to lose her job, she is also without the social and financial resources that provide her with an identity and economic independence. His primary goal is to force her return through the loss of resources that empower her.

It is highly unlikely that you would consider firing an employee who was constantly being physically and verbally harassed by a co-worker. As most company policies dictate, you would probably reprimand, suspend, or discharge the harasser. While a victim's batterer may not be in your administrative control to take such action, you should address his behavior through the criminal justice system, if necessary, while supporting your employee's attempt to remove herself from the situation.

• **If an employee who is also a battered woman attempts to take positive measures in addressing her issues, try to be somewhat flexible regarding various company policies relative to tardiness, absenteeism, production, and so on.**

While it is not suggested that you ignore the policies and standards of your business, recognize that during her transition, such work-related issues may continue to be areas of concern.

Recognize that if she were being assaulted or stalked by a perfect stranger, you would treat her as a victim. If she is taking appropriate measures to prevent the activities and intrusions of her batterer, support her and treat her as a victim as well. Without your support, particularly if you terminate her, she has little hope of eluding her assailant.

• **As you become involved with employees who are victims of spousal abuse, seek the advice of professionals in the social services, law enforcement, and security fields.** Since many technical questions will arise relative to legal boundaries, always consult with a labor lawyer for specific guidance.

A reminder: The Family and Medical Leave Act and the Americans with Disabilities Act are very broad and loosely interpreted. Employees who are also victims of domestic violence, particularly those who have been diagnosed as having the Battered Women's Syndrome, may be protected within the context of both federal laws.

Always consider such circumstances within the context and restrictions of those regulations. Your assistance, intervention, and methods of discipline with such an employee should always be consistent with the federal, state, and local laws that regulate your business.

When Your Employee Is the Batterer

You may find it necessary to suspend or to terminate an employee who fits the description of a Category Two or Category Three batterer. Co-workers, particularly those who have an intimate relationship with such an employee, may complain that he has threatened or assaulted them. It is without question that your not taking action to deal with such allegations, should an employee be injured or killed, exposes you and your company to significant civil liability.

• **If your initial investigation supports such claims, call the alleged assailant into your office.** With proper security present or nearby, address him in an assertive but non-threatening manner. If he denies such claims, advise him of your concern and tell him that aggression directed to anyone in your employ will not be tolerated. Document your conversation with the employee and the related allegation and place the document into his personal file. Explain to him that if he chooses to give you a written statement relative to his claims, you will include it as well. For the sake of both physical safety and civil liability, ask a supervisor to witness your conversations with the employee who has been accused.

• **If such problems persist and his continued activities can be substantiated, practice appropriate progressive discipline.** If necessary, suspend or even terminate him. If, however, you feel that other employees are in imminent danger, terminate him immediately. If necessary, call the police and ask for assistance in removing him from your premises.

Conclusion

While it may be fashionable to suggest that we as professionals have come a long way in addressing the needs of the battered woman, perception is not necessarily reality.

My twenty years of experience in this area suggest that the issue of relationship is still used as the primary determinant factor as to how the criminal justice system responds to acts of violence between two parties. It still appears that if you beat your neighbor, the police want to arrest you. If you beat your spouse, however, they want to mediate your problem. If you beat your neighbor once with a club, it is likely that you will be booked on a felony. If, however, you beat your wife five times with the same club, you are likely to be booked on a misdemeanor. If you are convicted for beating your neighbor with a club, they want to send you to jail. If you are convicted for beating your wife with a club, they want to provide you with treatment. While many professionals may argue that this scenario is overly dramatized, I assert that they are wrong and that it is imperative for us to recognize the truth. Violence is violence, regardless of whom it is inflicted upon. There is no room for double standards, yet in many cases they still exist.

My assertion that the response of the American justice system to the needs of the battered woman has been a token one, at best, is supported by the following facts. At present, there are still more animal shelters in this country than there are shelters for battered women and their children. Some municipalities have considered legislation that would place the statement "it is a criminal offense to batter your spouse" on marriage licenses as a subtle attempt to inhibit such behavior. In many cities, the beating of your spouse carries the same penalty as the violation of a litter ordinance. In the State of Illinois, an appellate court returned two young daughters to their father after the man served twenty months for the beating and strangulation death of their mother while the children watched. The charge had been reduced to manslaughter in a plea bargain agreement. In an outlandish civil decision, a judge granted visitation rights to a father released from prison after serving time for setting his son on fire with gasoline during a custody dispute with his estranged wife. Such decisions and facts suggest that many professionals are still in passive collusion with the batterer. While I do not suggest that it is conscious collusion, it is collusion just the same.

I do not make such assertions through the eyes of a feminist nor the idealism of a democrat. In fact, in this area I subscribe to no specific political ideology. I speak only the truth. Women should not go to bed each night in fear of dying at the hands of intimate partners, yet millions do.

It seems so very ironic to me that many of those individuals who advocate for the safety and protection of the victim are the same parties who promote treatment for the Serial Batterer. Perhaps they do so out of the desire to appear politically correct. Perhaps they do so out of naiveté. Advocating for both parties, however, seems not only paradoxical but extremely dangerous.

It is all too apparent to me that the same double standards that have been employed in the past relative to police intervention are now being used in the courtroom. Unless such a scenario is recognized by all professionals, Serial Batterers, using the ploy of treatment, will continue to evade true consequences, and victims will continue to die needlessly.

APPENDIX

Tools for Assessment and Safety Planning

Profile Assessment Chart

The following chart is a comprehensive description of characteristics displayed by all domestic abusers, relative to their location on the Batterer's Continuum. The list contains not only the most common behavioral patterns of the male batterer, but also the most universal personality and psychological traits of all groups.

It is stressed that these traits should not be perceived as being absolute in their occurrence, degree, or position on the continuum. There are always exceptions to the rule, particularly if the physical violence is caused by issues not relative to the continuum, such as psychosis, a brain tumor, nutritional deficiencies, chemical imbalances, or other diagnostic categories described and defined in the D.S.M. IV. While exceptions may be a reality, however, the following profile chart describes the majority of all men who batter women in American society.

Profile Assessment Chart

Common Behaviors, Traits & Characteristics

	Category One	Category Two	Category Three
Carries out ongoing, systematic physical abuse of spouse	Does not exist	Moderate	High
Shows premarital physical abuse of spouse	Does not exist	Moderate	High
Has multiple physically abusive relationships with women	Does not exist	Moderate	High
Physically injures his victim	Low	Moderate	High
Assaults his spouse with weapons	Low	Moderate	High

	Category One	Category Two	Category Three
Has potential to commit a domestic homicide	Low	Moderate	High
Uses economic deprivation to control his spouse	Low	Moderate	High
Uses terrorism in an effort to control his spouse	Low	Moderate	High
Uses intimidation in an effort to control his spouse	Low	Moderate	High
Attempts to isolate his spouse from others	Low	Moderate	High
Tortures and mutilates his spouse	Low	Moderate	High
Beats his spouse while she is pregnant	Low	Moderate	High
Follows and stalks his spouse	Low	Moderate	High
Damages his spouse's car, personal property, etc.	Low	Moderate	High
Kidnaps and threatens his victim's children	Low	Moderate	High
Bites his spouse during his assaults	Low	Moderate	High
Cuts his spouse's electrical and phone wires	Low	Moderate	High
Harasses his spouse by phone and mail	Low	Moderate	High
Has potential to harm, injure, or kill those who assist his spouse	Low	Moderate	High
Performs and throws childlike tantrums	Low	Moderate	High
Intrudes and interferes with spouse's job	Low	Moderate	High
Sexually assaults his spouse	Low	Moderate	High
Threatens to commit suicide	Low	Moderate	High
Displays pathological and intense jealousy	Low	Moderate	High

	Category One	Category Two	Category Three
Is in contact with the criminal justice system; has criminal record	Low	Moderate	High
Is unable to maintain employment	Low	Moderate	High
Devaluates his spouse	Low	Moderate	High
Is dogmatic; dominates his spouse	Low	Moderate	High
Exploits his spouse physically and emotionally	Low	Moderate	High
Is emotionally dependent on his spouse; possessive	Low	Moderate	High
Feels inadequate, insecure	Low	Moderate	High
Has recurring emotional intensity	Low	Moderate	High
Manipulates spouse and others	Low	Moderate	High
Has potential to re-assault and injure his victim	Low	Moderate	High
Remains a continued and ongoing threat to his victim	Low	Moderate	High

Treatment Assessment

The decision as to whether one should advocate for the clinical treatment of a spouse abuser should be based on an honest and reliable assessment of his history of violence, and should be in accordance with his position on the Batterer's Continuum.

Professionals must recognize that men do not batter for the same reasons. The decision to push for treatment or, when an individual batterer has been arrested, for sentencing leniency should be made only after professionals determine the motivation of the batterer toward change and the potential for the change to be successful. Since motivation can be fabricated by an abuser in an attempt to avoid prosecution, or in his efforts to manipulate his spouse back into the relationship, the roots of his motivation should be closely examined.

Those making decisions as to how to address a batterer should also consider whether he presents an ongoing threat to the safety of his spouse and her children. To ignore the reality of his past history and his potential for future violence is a very dangerous practice. We must never minimize what he has done to his spouse or what he is capable of doing. Always remember that it is very easy to advocate for a man who has terrorized and physically attacked his family when you are not his victim.

The following chart expands the Batterer's Continuum as it relates to his treatment potential. As previously suggested, the ability of the batterer to cease his violence and to work toward positive change is in direct relation to his position on the continuum. The Category One abuser located on the far left of the chart, for example, is the most likely to be rehabilitated, while the prospect of rehabilitation for the Category Three assailant is extremely dismal and remote. The prognosis for the Category Two batterer should be considered guarded at best.

The Treatment Assessment Chart provides you with a list of psychological traits that are very relevant in determining a batterer's therapeutic potential. It is suggested that these traits, in addition to those described in the profile chart and lethality questionnaire, be closely examined in your attempt to determine an individual abuser's potential for clinical intervention.

Treatment Assessment Chart

For All Battering Profiles

	Category One	Category Two	Category Three
Prognosis	Good	Guarded	Poor
Presence of psychopathology	Does not exist	Moderate	High
The ability to bond with his spouse, others	High	Moderate	Low
Feels a sense of remorse and guilt following his assaults on his spouse	High	Moderate	Low
Has insight into his personal problems and dynamics	High	Moderate	Low
Has internal motivation to change his behavior	High	Moderate	Low
Is able to separate and understand various emotions	High	Moderate	Low

	Category One	Category Two	Category Three
Has problems with substance abuse, use, or addiction	Low	Moderate	High
Rationalizes and externalizes his physical violence	Low	Moderate	High
Minimizes his physical violence	Low	Moderate	High
Denies his physical violence	Low	Moderate	High
Has therapeutic potential	High	Moderate	Low
Uses physical violence in relation to external conflicts	High	Moderate	Low

Lethality Questionnaire

While you may not be able to predict a specific act of domestic violence, a proper assessment of an individual batterer will clearly reveal those men who are most likely to continue attacking their intimate partners. In your determination of a batterer's lethality, generally consider the following factors.

-The past is an excellent predictor of the future. If the male has a long history of violence, the probability that it will continue is very high. The longer the history, the greater is the probability for its continuance.

-If the batterer has a personality disorder and a history of violence, you can be assured that his violence will continue. The visibility and blatancy of such violence may be relative to the type and degree of the disorder in which it is embedded. For example, while antisocial batterers overtly act out their violence, obsessive-compulsive batterers may be more discreet and less obvious. Don't allow your assessment of the batterer to be influenced only by his outward appearance.

-The greater the number of psychological and behavioral commonalities that he possesses (see Chapter V), the greater his potential for continued violence or homicide. The commonalities that have been described, if embedded within the context of a personality disorder, can be a lethal combination. Commonalities in the absence of a disorder are less lethal.

-The possession of weapons and the abuse of alcohol or drugs are two major predictors. This is not to suggest that normal males who drink and have guns are potential killers. This is obviously not the case. Those with personality disorders, however, who possess the multiple commonalities described in Chapter V, and who also abuse alcohol and drugs and possess guns, should be considered extremely lethal.

The following questionnaire closely parallels the Profile Assessment Chart. While this questionnaire may be considered somewhat subjective in its design, it will clearly define a profile of the batterer that will lead you to an informed judgment of the batterer's potential to harm his victim.

Questionnaires that produce a high number of unfavorable responses indicate that a victim is associated with a Category Three batterer and is in significant danger. Those that produce a moderate number of unfavorable responses suggest that the association is with a Category Two batterer, and the victim's danger is marginal. Those that result in few or no unfavorable responses indicate a relationship with a Category One abuser and the victim is in no ongoing danger. Unlike victims of Category Two and Category Three abuse, those involved with a Category One abuser do not generally need a safety plan.

Professionals should always administer this questionnaire to a battered woman or her informants in an effort to assess the lethality of an individual batterer. Because of its first-person and checklist format, it can be easily administered with little or no instruction.

Lethality Questionnaire

01) How long have you been intimate with your batterer? _____

02) How many times do you estimate that he has put his hands on you in any manner? _____

03) Does he stalk you? Yes ___ No ___

04) Does he follow you? Yes ___ No ___

05) Does he monitor your behavior? Yes ___ No ___

06) Does he accuse you of being unfaithful? Yes ___ No ___

07) Does he exhibit jealousy? Yes ___ No ___

08) Is he frequently concerned with the issue of infidelity? Yes ___ No ___

09) Is he dependent on you? Yes ___ No ___
10) Does he have difficulty being alone? Yes ___ No ___
11) Does he try to isolate you from others? Yes ___ No ___
12) Does he try to dominate you? Yes ___ No ___
13) Does he have intense mood swings? Yes ___ No ___
14) Does he experience depression? Yes ___ No ___
15) Does he threaten to commit suicide? Yes ___ No ___
16) Has he ever attempted suicide? Yes ___ No ___
17) Does he abuse drugs or alcohol? Yes ___ No ___
18) Does he harass you by mail or phone? Yes ___ No ___
19) Does he intrude on your job? Yes ___ No ___
20) Does he have a history of premarital abuse? Yes ___ No ___
21) Does he have a history of violent relationships? Yes ___ No ___
22) Does he beat you on an ongoing and frequent basis? Yes ___ No ___
23) Has he ever injured you? Yes ___ No ___
24) Has he ever violated a restraining order? Yes ___ No ___
25) Does he refuse to show up for court appearances? Yes ___ No ___
26) Has he ever been diagnosed with a personality disorder? Yes ___ No ___
27) Has he ever been diagnosed as psychotic? Yes ___ No ___
28) Have you ever received medical attention or hospitalization because of his beatings? Yes ___ No ___
29) Has he ever threatened you with a weapon? Yes ___ No ___
30) Has he ever attacked you with a weapon? Yes ___ No ___
31) Does he have an obsession with weapons? Yes ___ No ___
32) Has he ever threatened to kill you? Yes ___ No ___
33) Has he ever threatened to kill others? Yes ___ No ___
34) Does he threaten you in front of others? Yes ___ No ___

35) Does he have a history of violence? Yes ___ No ___
36) Has he beat you when you were pregnant? Yes ___ No ___
37) Has he ever kidnapped you? Yes ___ No ___
38) Has he ever kidnapped your children? Yes ___ No ___
39) Has he ever threatened to harm your children? Yes ___ No ___
40) Does he bite you? Yes ___ No ___
41) Does he physically beat your children? Yes ___ No ___
42) Has he ever threatened to set you or your house on fire? Yes ___ No ___
43) Has he ever tortured or mutilated you? Yes ___ No ___
44) Has he ever burned you with cigarettes? Yes ___ No ___
45) Does he try to terrorize you? Yes ___ No ___
46) Does he use intimidation and fear to control you? Yes ___ No ___
47) Does he have outbursts of anger? Yes ___ No ___
48) Is he often angry? Yes ___ No ___
49) Does he throw childlike tantrums? Yes ___ No ___
50) Does he sexually assault you? Yes ___ No ___
51) Does his emotional intensity scare you? Yes ___ No ___
52) Does he mutilate himself? Yes ___ No ___
53) Has he ever held you hostage? Yes ___ No ___
54) Does he damage your personal property? Yes ___ No ___
Your car? Yes ___ No ___
55) Has he ever burned your personal property? Yes ___ No ___
56) Does he break into your home when you are asleep? Yes ___ No ___
57) Does he break down your front door? Yes ___ No ___
58) Does he break through your windows? Yes ___ No ___
59) Does he cut electrical and telephone wires connected to your residence? Yes ___ No ___
60) Does he have a criminal record? Yes ___ No ___
61) Does he have difficulty holding a regular job? Yes ___ No ___

62) Have you previously called the police because he was assaulting you? Yes ___ No ___

63) Have you previously charged him for assaulting you? Yes ___ No ___

64) Does he show any remorse after beating you? Yes ___ No ___

65) Does he try to justify his beatings? Yes ___ No ___

66) Does he ever show motivation to change his behavior? Yes ___ No ___

67) Have you ever placed him under a restraining order? Yes ___ No ___

A Professional's Guide to Victim Safety

Advise the victim of chronic violence to develop and implement a safety plan before leaving her batterer. The guidelines below provide the basis for three important aspects of such a plan: what to do before leaving, what to do after leaving, and court-related safety strategies.

Remind her that the period of estrangement is the most dangerous phase of her relationship with the batterer. Those victims who develop and activate a safety plan, however, are in much less danger than those who try to leave without taking precautionary measures. While the following plan does not guarantee the safety of the battered woman, it most definitely enhances it.

The Safety Plan
Part One: Before Leaving

____ 01) Establish a comprehensive support system.

____ 02) Get to know professionals who can serve as your advocate.

____ 03) Pre-plan safe shelter; if possible, plan to go to a location unfamiliar to your batterer.

____ 04) Do not allow your batterer to isolate you from friends and family who can provide essential resources once you leave.

____ 05) Pre-plan child care resources and alternatives.

____ 06) Acquire vocational training and begin to search for a job.

____ 07) Enter counseling alone; do not participate in marriage counseling with a chronic batterer.

____ 08) Make certain that your therapist has proper credentials.

____ 09) Beware of the "Honeymoon Phase" of the relationship with your batterer.

____ 10) Read books and literature about domestic violence.

____ 11) Avoid arguments; avoid being verbally provocative.

____ 12) Gradually and discreetly remove essential items that you will need so your batterer will not recognize your intentions.

____ 13) Immediately preceding your departure, collect your batterer's guns and turn them in to the police or court officials.

____ 14) Educate your children as to what to do if your batterer physically attacks you.

____ 15) Post emergency phone numbers next to phones.

____ 16) Document everything relative to your abuse; keep a diary, letters, tapes, medical reports, police reports, court affidavits, photographs, and virtually anything that substantiates your claims of being battered.

____ 17) Acquire and keep all documentation in a safety deposit box or at the home of a friend or relative.

____ 18) Pack an emergency bag that includes anything you may need if you have to leave quickly.

____ 19) Open a secret checking and savings account.

____ 20) Secretly stockpile cash.

____ 21) Secretly acquire credit cards.

____ 22) Stockpile food and clothes at the home of a friend or relative.

____ 23) Make a copy of your personal keys and leave them at the home of a friend or relative.

____ 24) Discreetly acquire a post office box.

The Safety Plan
Part Two: After Leaving

____ 01) Live or move to an area where there is a comprehensive support system.

____ 02) Offer to do volunteer work with domestic violence programs; it will give you exposure to professionals who can assist you.

____ 03) Implement a "buddy system"; always tell a friend where you are going and when you expect to return.

____ 04) Always remain hypervigilant; when you leave your home or office, or walk in a parking lot, be aware of who is around you.

____ 05) If possible, have others walk you to your car.

____ 06) Never walk alone in isolated areas.

____ 07) Take a self-defense class, which does not necessarily mean learning the use of weapons; self-defense training can teach you how to respond to provocative situations.

____ 08) Advise school officials and your children's teachers of who specifically is allowed to pick them up from school.

____ 09) Never allow your batterer to visit your children at the residence in which you live; arrange for child visitation to be at the home of a neutral third party.

____ 10) If your batterer is under a restraining order, ask your neighbors to notify you and the police if he is seen on your property.

____ 11) If possible, seek refuge in a residence or shelter that is unfamiliar to your batterer; never disclose its location.

____ 12) Try to conceal your car in a garage or in an area not visible to your batterer.

____ 13) Try to avoid giving a house key to your children; if you do, your batterer may have an opportunity to acquire and copy it.

____ 14) Consider moving from the residence which you once shared with your batterer; your abuser is very familiar with how to gain entry.

____ 15) Consider installing and acquiring the following technical equipment to enhance your physical safety:

____ alarm system
____ deadbolts on doors
____ lock devices on windows
____ motion lights
____ door peephole
____ smoke detectors
____ fire ladders for second floors
____ closed-circuit camera and monitor
____ cellular phone
____ cordless phone
____ caller identification device, one-digit dialing
____ telephone answering machine

____ 16) Acquire an unlisted telephone number.

____ 17) Never call your batterer from your residence; caller identification devices may tell him your location.

____ 18) Practice fire drills with your children.

____ 19) Pre-plan emergency exit procedures with your children.

____ 20) Get a dog that will bark if someone comes on your property.

The Safety Plan
Part Three: Court-Related Safety Strategies

____ 01) Acquire restraining orders from both criminal and civil courts.

____ 02) Ask the court to set your case for a status hearing in which restraining orders can be reviewed for compliance by the batterer.

____ 03) If restraining orders are violated, assert yourself and insist on their enforcement.

____ 04) Ask an advocate to accompany you to all court hearings.

____ 05) Ask someone to walk you to your car following each court appearance.

____ 06) Honor all subpoenas; cooperate with court officials.

____ 07) Never suggest that the chronic batterer "needs help"; if you do, you will sacrifice your issues of safety.

____ 08) Don't be led into believing that mandatory counseling for your batterer is the solution to your problems.

____ 09) Ask that you be allowed to sit in an area of the courtroom that is not in close proximity to your batterer.

____ 10) Ask to initially speak to the court officials alone.

____ 11) Never suggest that you want to drop your charges against your batterer.

____ 12) If a restraining order has been issued against your batterer, never destroy its sanctions by attempting to communicate with him.

____ 13) Send a certified letter to the warden of the jail in which your batterer is detained and ask that you be notified of his release.

____ 14) Request that your private address and private phone number be kept in a court file not accessible to your batterer.

Endnotes

1. U.S. Department of Justice, Bureau of Justice Statistics, *Sourcebook of Criminal Justice Statistics* (Washington, D.C.: U.S. Government Printing Office, 1995), 334.
2. U.S. Department of Justice, Federal Bureau of Investigation, *Crime in the United States* (Washington, D.C.: U.S. Government Printing Office, 1991), 13.
3. Murray A. Straus, "Wife Beating: How Common and Why?," *Victimology: An International Journal* 2(3-4), 1977-78, 445.
4. Bureau of Justice Statistics, *Sourcebook of Criminal Justice Statistics,* 334.
5. Neal Pierce, *New Orleans Times Picayune,* 4 Mar. 1985, sec. A: 13.
6. American Psychiatric Association, *Diagnostic and Statistical Manual of Mental Disorders, 4th ed.* (Washington, D.C.: American Psychiatric Association, 1994), 629.
7. *New Orleans Times Picayune,* 31 Aug. 1982, sec. A: 1.
8. Richard Boyd, *New Orleans Times Picayune,* 26 Jan. 1989, sec. B: 1.
9. Bob Ussery, *New Orleans Times Picayune,* 16 Dec. 1990, sec. B: 10.
10. American Psychiatric Association, *Diagnostic and Statistical Manual of Mental Disorders, 4th ed.,* 629-73.
11. Ibid., 658.
12. Ibid.
13. Ibid., 659.
14. Ibid.
15. Ibid.
16. Ibid.
17. Ibid., 646.
18. Ibid., 645.
19. Ibid., 647.
20. Ibid., 646.
21. Ibid.

22. Ibid.
23. Ibid.
24. Ibid., 651.
25. Alvin L. Bertrand, *Basic Sociology: An Introduction to Theory and Method* (New York: Meredith Publishing Company, 1967), 230.
26. American Psychiatric Association, *Diagnostic and Statistical Manual of Mental Disorders, 4th ed.,* 656.
27. American Psychiatric Association, *Diagnostic and Statistical Manual of Mental Disorders, 3rd ed.* (Washington, D.C.: American Psychiatric Association, 1980), 321.
28. American Psychiatric Association, *Diagnostic and Statistical Manual of Mental Disorders, 4th ed.,* 651.
29. Ibid.
30. Ibid., 655.
31. Ibid., 657.
32. Ibid., 656.
33. Ibid., 655.
34. Ibid.
35. American Psychiatric Association, *Diagnostic and Statistical Manual of Mental Disorders, 3rd ed.,* 315.
36. American Psychiatric Association, *Diagnostic and Statistical Manual of Mental Disorders, 4th ed.,* 655.
37. American Psychiatric Association, *Diagnostic and Statistical Manual of Mental Disorders, 3rd ed.,* 315.
38. American Psychiatric Association, *Diagnostic and Statistical Manual of Mental Disorders, 4th ed.,* 635.
39. Ibid.
40. American Psychiatric Association, *Diagnostic and Statistical Manual of Mental Disorders, 3rd ed.,* 309.
41. American Psychiatric Association, *Diagnostic and Statistical Manual of Mental Disorders, 4th ed.,* 634.
42. American Psychiatric Association, *Diagnostic and Statistical Manual of Mental Disorders, 3rd ed.,* 307.
43. Ibid.

44. Ibid., 309.
45. Ibid.
46. American Psychiatric Association, *Diagnostic and Statistical Manual of Mental Disorders, 4th ed.*, 669.
47. Ibid.
48. Ibid.
49. Ibid.
50. Ibid.
51. Ibid.
52. American Psychiatric Association, *Diagnostic and Statistical Manual of Mental Disorders, 3rd ed.*, 327.
53. Ibid., 330.
54. Ibid.
55. American Psychiatric Association, *Diagnostic and Statistical Manual of Mental Disorders, 4th ed.*, 650.
56. Ibid., 672.
57. Erich Fromm, *The Art of Loving* (New York: Harper and Row, 1974), 22.
58. Ibid., 17.
59. Ibid., 15.
60. Ibid.
61. Peter Neidig, Dale Friedman, and Barbara Collins, "Attitudinal Characteristics of Males Who Have Engaged in Spouse Abuse," *Journal of Family Violence* 1(3), 1986, 227.
62. Ibid.
63. Michael Groetsch, Unpublished Study (New Orleans: New Orleans Municipal Court, Probation Office, 1988).
64. Ibid.
65. Glenda Kaufman Kantor and Murray A. Straus, "The Drunken Bum Theory of Wife Beating," paper presented at the National Alcoholism Forum Conference, San Francisco, CA, 24 August 1986, 11.
66. Diane Hoshall Coleman and Murray A. Straus, "Alcohol Abuse and Family Violence," paper presented at the annual meeting of the American Sociological Association, Boston, MA, August

1979.

67. Ibid., 108.

68. Kantor and Straus, 11.

69. U.S. Department of Justice, *Sourcebook of Criminal Justice Statistics,* 334.

70. Lenore E. Walker, "Battered Women and Learned Helplessness," *Victimology: An International Journal* 2(3-4), 1977-78, 527.

71. Ibid., 526-27.

72. Ibid., 526.

73. U.S. Department of Justice, *Law Enforcement Officers Killed and Assaulted* (Washington, D.C.: Federal Bureau of Investigation, 1994), 31.

74. Ibid., 39.

75. Mark A. Wynn, "Arrest: Victim's Assistance at the Scene of Family Violence," paper presented at the National Conference on Domestic Violence, Williamsburg, VA, 11 Oct. 1992, 20.

76. Tricia Fritsch, "The Paradox of Violence Protection: The Challenge of Awareness, Action, and Accountability," paper presented at the National Conference on Domestic Violence, Williamsburg, VA, 11 Oct. 1992, 53.

77. William Waldron, "Courthouse Security and the Role of the Consultant," *Court Review* 27(3), 1990, 11.

78. *Louisiana Statutory Criminal Law and Procedures* (St. Paul, MN: West Publishing House, 1994), RS 14:56:1, 758.

79. *Louisiana Statutory Criminal Law and Procedures* (St. Paul, MN: West Publishing House, 1994), RS 14:67:13, 770.

80. Maria Roy, *The Abusive Partner: An Analysis of Domestic Battering* (New York: Van Nostrand Reinhold Co., 1982), 280.

81. Ibid.

82. Ibid.

83. Ibid., 281.

84. Ibid., 282.

85. Ibid., 284.

86. Ibid., 288.

87. American Medical Association, *Diagnostic and Treatment Guidelines on Domestic Violence* (Chicago: American Medical Association, 1992), 18.

88. Ibid., 15.

89. Ibid.

90. Ibid., 16.

91. Ibid., 19.

92. Ibid.